MANHATTAN FIREARMS

Waldo E. Nutter

STACKPOLE BOOKS

Published by
STACKPOLE BOOKS
5067 Ritter Road
Mechanicsburg, PA 17055
www.stackpolebooks.com

Printed in the United States of America

10 9 8 7 6 5 4 3 2 1

First edition

Cover design by Wendy A. Reynolds

ISBN-13: 978-0-8117-0469-4
ISBN-10: 0-8117-0469-6

Cataloging-in-Publication Data is on file with the Library of Congress

THE AMERICAN SOCIETY OF ARMS COLLECTORS, through its Reviewing **Staff**, takes pride in sponsoring this book and in recommending it as **a** standard work of reference in the field of Manhattan Firearms history.

HERSCHEL C. LOGAN
President

Reviewing Staff
SAMUEL E. SMITH
THOMAS J. MCHUGH

ACKNOWLEDGMENTS

The author acknowledges with gratitude the cooperation and assistance so freely given to him by the following collectors, individuals and historical sources:

Mrs. Geraldine Briefer, Prentiss D. Cheney, Connecticut State Library, William B. Edwards, William E. Florence, Thomas E. Hall, Paul Janke, Harry C. Knode, R. C. Kuhn, William M. Locke, Herschel C. Logan, National Archives, New York Public Library, John E. Parsons, Edward J. Patten, C. Meade Patterson, J. Fred Sinn, John Stapleton, Henry M. Stewart.

A special recognition of indebtedness is acknowledged to:

Ronald Sanders, graduate student in History at Columbia University when this work was begun, who did the major portion of the research work.

Thomas J. McHugh, whose scholarly editorial assistance was invaluable.

Miles W. Standish, whose interest surpassed the excellence of his photography.

Leon C. Jackson and Sam E. Smith, for their encouragement which enabled a wishful thought to become a reality.

CONTENTS

LIST OF PLATES

LIST OF PLATES, *Continued*

PROLOGUE

THE COMING of the year 1857 was an important event for the arms makers of the United States and was viewed with reactions which ranged from concern to eagerness. For Colt's Patent Firearms Manufacturing Company, 1857 meant the end of the period of protection afforded by Samuel Colt's original patent of 1836, a period of twenty-one years during which the Colt company exercised a virtual monopoly in the field of revolving, multi-chambered handguns. The monopoly had been established and maintained by the soundness of the patent, by the excellence of Colt's products and by the aggressiveness of Samuel Colt in the development and expansion of his business. Colt's aggressiveness was evidenced in his two attempts to have the life of his valuable patent extended. His first effort for an extension, in 1850, was successful and he was granted an extension of seven years. The second application for an extension was made in 1857 and, although unsuccessful, the negation of this effort was not to become clear until 1858. Thus, the approaching termination of his monopolizing position in the arms field must have been regarded with appropriate concern by the master of Armsmear.

1

Any similar feeling must have been conspicuously absent among Colt's competitors and competitors-to-be. For several years, the burgeoning success of Colt had overshadowed their efforts to circumvent his patent and gain a substantial portion of the widening market for firearms. Only one of their number, Massachusetts Arms Company, had dared to challenge the validity of Colt's patent and had received a thorough trouncing in the court. This important patent case came to trial on June 30, 1851, and held the deepest interest of every arms maker in the country. The decision of the court, for Colt, served to restrict completely the activities of any other would-be infringers during the remainder of the life of the patent. Thus, the coming of the year of 1857 was awaited with much eagerness by a group of would-be competitors and, while their entry into significant competition with Colt was to be delayed for almost a year, plans were laid with much enthusiasm. Included in this group of planners was one of the newcomers to the field of arms making, The Manhattan Firearms Manufacturing Company of New York.

Manhattan Firearms Manufacturing Company was not destined to become a really important factor in the production and distribution of hand guns. Although the company was well into production of their .36-caliber revolvers by the time the War Between the States flared into awesome proportions, creating an immediate demand for satisfactory sidearms of almost any type, Manhattan was not the recipient of any sizeable contracts for government small arms. Instead, Manhattan became a supplier of the civilian market, either by choice or by necessity. An expedient and reasonably accurate measure of Manhattan's operations will be seen in this comparison: the total production of arms by Manhattan and its successor firm, American Standard Tool Company, was probably less than one-half of the production of Colt's most popular percussion revolver, the .31-caliber 1849 Pocket Model.

Despite the diminutive stature of the Manhattan Company as a producer of firearms, we believe the story of its beginning, its progress and its struggles to be worthy of the telling, both as a contemporary of Colt, Remington, Whitney, Smith & Wesson, *et al.*, and as a business venture in one of the most interesting periods of American industry.

This work is the story of Manhattan, but we do not represent it to be the complete story because we were unable to hit the information jackpot of the collector-researcher, "the original records." The information presented is as much as we could learn in two years of active research plus the deductions to be drawn from observation and study of the Manhattan arms during several years of collecting. One of the most significant points to be learned from the study of these arms is the quality of orderliness which pervades the entire line. This is a fortunate circumstance for the collector because it has made easier the accumulation of Manhattan's arms into a reasonably well-formed collection. This quality of orderliness has a more profound connotation when viewed in retrospect: banking institutions are noted for this quality, as anyone who has ever overdrawn a checking account well knows. Manhattan Firearms Manufacturing Company, as a business venture, may have been conceived within the ownership of one of New Jersey's largest banking houses of the middle 1850's.

During one phase of our arms-collecting activities, our interest in Manhattan arms was no greater than our interest in the arms manufactured by Colt, Remington, Whitney and other makers. Concurrent with our collecting activities went some study of the standard reference works on percussion firearms. We were impressed, almost immediately, with the wealth of information which was available on the arms of the well-known makers and the dearth of information which was available on Manhattan arms. Typical of some of the information concerning Manhattan which was, and is yet, available in so-called standard reference works are these excerpts:

1. Manhattan Firearms Mfg. Co., 1840-1870. Plant located at Newark, N. J., 1840-1860. Made percussion pistols and pepperboxes. In 1864, opened offices in New York, N. Y., and established a plant at Brooklyn, N. Y. Made percussion revolvers similar to Colt Navy models and were forced to close the business in 1870 by Colt lawsuit for infringement of patents.[1]

2. Manhattan Fire Arms Company, Brooklyn, N. Y. Active 1849-1862. Probably became the American Standard Tool Company. Produced a three-barrel pepperbox which revolved by hand to avoid infringement on Ethan Allen's patents. Probably less than 300 made in 1849. Made "Hero" single-shot pistols also. Made the Manhattan revolver, patent of December 27, 1859. This arm was an exact imitation of the Colt except that the Manhattan possessed a double number of cylinder stops permitting the cylinder to be locked, by the hammer, between the chambers. This was a better safety device than was offered by Colt who brought suit and forced out of business.[2]

The above quotations are not set up here for purposes of later ridicule, although much of the information contained therein is either incomplete or inaccurate. The quotations are intended as exhibits of information which, coupled with the frequently-heard "Colt imitation" or "Colt copy and infringement" plus the lofty intonation (as in the case of .31-caliber Manhattan revolvers) "probably made by Bacon," developed within us a large inferiority complex as we prevailed in our addiction to Manhattan arms. This complex caused us to assume a half-furtive air as we sought the specimens of our choice; we were always glad to conclude a transaction without having public attention focused on our acquisition of substandard and uncultured hardware of questionable ancestry.

As a result of our continuing interest in this uncharted corner of the arms field, we began to accumulate certain models and variations of Manhattan firearms which we could not verify in any of the standard reference works.

Our entry into the field of research on Manhattan was motivated by our desire for more accurate and more complete information. It is our hope that the following pages will constitute a useful contribution to the growing knowledge of American firearms and, more specifically, that the long-neglected subject of Manhattan Firearms Manufacturing Company will be placed in a more deserving perspective for the interest and appreciation of the arms collecting fraternity.

REFERENCE NOTES

PROLOGUE: 1. *American Firearms Makers*, A. Merwyn Carey. New York: T. Y. Crowell Co., 1953, page 74.

2. *American Arms and Arms Makers*, Robert C. Gardner. Columbus, Ohio: College Book Co., 1944, page 93.

CHAPTER I:

~~~~~~~~~~~~~~~~~~~~~~~~~~~~~~
NEW YORK

While our efforts to discover and develop previously unpublished information followed the usual and accepted avenues, including some totally blind alleys, the following sources proved to be the most fruitful:

1. The directories of New York, N. Y. and Newark, N. J. for the period 1840-1870
2. A review of the presently available data, in standard reference works
3. The records of the United States Patent Office in Washington, D. C.

Our search of the directories produced the first tangible information. Several directories of the City of New York were examined for the period 1840-1870 but only one, Trow's New York City Directory, carries any listings for Manhattan. This circumstance of a listing in a single source of reference is explainable by the fact that city directories of that period were private undertakings and a charge was levied for the privilege of being listed in any directory. Beginning with the 1840 edition, we found the first entry for Manhattan in Trow's edition for 1855-56, as follows: "Manhattan Firearms Manufacturing Company,

5

205 Broadway." In the 1856-57 edition, the address is given as "163 Fulton Street." In the 1857-58 edition, the address is given as "17 Maiden Lane." This latter listing terminated the listings for Manhattan in Trow's New York City Directories. However, from another source, The New York State Directory for 1859, under *Gun & Pistol Makers,* we found: "Manhattan Fire Arms Manuf. Co. 50 Cliff." This is a significant address inasmuch as it was also the address of Herman Boker & Co., "Importers of Guns & Pistols." The significance of the common address and the implied connection between Manhattan and Herman Boker & Company will be set forth in a later section.

All of the foregoing addresses cited for Manhattan were located in the then-commercial section of New York and, because the address for each successive year is a different one, it appears that the addresses were those of office locations rather than factory locations. The information in Trow's Directories served one important purpose: it established the beginning-point, historically, of Manhattan's operations. As will be seen, we were able to correlate this beginning-point with other pertinent data. Our review of the data available in standard reference works gave us the lead which was to unlock the door and reveal the details of the early history of Manhattan Firearms Manufacturing Company.

In Ray Riling's *Guns and Shooting*[1] we found the following citation:

MANHATTAN FIREARMS MFG. CO.
Manhattan Fire Arms Manufacturing Company
vs
Thomas K. Bacon
New London County Supreme Court of Errors
October Term, 1859
Docket 1, volume 8
Norwich, Connecticut
J. W. Stedman, 1859

This item held much promise—the promise of the details of a lawsuit which might lead us behind the curtain of obscurity; here, too, was the name of Bacon. Between the promise and the possible fulfillment, however, was the task of finding a copy of this, by now, much-wanted document. After much searching, and the span of several months, a copy was located in the New York Public Library. The Library was most cooperative in granting permission for reproduction of the document. Actually, and as will be seen, the copy contains much more in the way of pertinent data than is comprised by the premises of the lawsuit; some of the data has been substantiated by our search of other sources of information, including the New York Law Library and the New York City Hall of Records. The Stedman document is not arranged in a manner which best suits the requirement of continuity for our story. We have, therefore, taken the liberty of subdividing the Stedman material and will reproduce the several segments in the order which provides for better continuity.

The initial objective of correlating the data from Trow's Directory with the Stedman material would, quite naturally, deal with some reference to the 1855-56 listing. This objective is attained through the reproduction of that segment of the Stedman document which deals with the formation of the Manhattan Firearms Manufacturing Company, as follows:

[A.]

CERTIFICATE OF THE FORMATION OF THE "MANHATTAN FIRE ARMS
MANUFACTURING COMPANY."

We, Montagnie Ward, Jacob F. Wyckoff, and David W. Bailey, all of the city, county and state of New York, and Alfred L. Dennis, Reuben D. Baldwin, Jeptha C. Groshong, James B. Pinneo, Mathias W. Day, Thomas L. Miller, Charles P. Hall, Charles W. Badger, Linn Adams, William McMurty, Alfred Lyon, Charles T. Day, jr., Daniel Dodd, jr., David C. Berry, and Frederick H. Smith, all of Newark, county of Essex, and state of New Jersey, have formed and do hereby form a company for the purpose and object of manufacturing and dealing in fire arms, ammunition and other articles pertaining to fire arms business; also to secure improvements in fire arms and machinery for manufacturing the same. The corporate name of said company is "The Manhattan Fire Arms Manufacturing Company." The capital stock thereof is forty thousand dollars, and consists of four hundred shares of one hundred dollars each. The term of its existence is twenty years. The number of trustees are five, and their names are as follows: Montagnie Ward, Jacob F. Wyckoff, and David W. Bailey, all of the city of New York, in the county and state of New York, Frederick H. Smith, of Newark, in the county of Essex and state of New Jersey, and Reuben D. Baldwin, also of the city of Newark, county of Essex and state of New Jersey, and that said trustees are all citizens of the United States of America, and that the operations of said company are to be carried on in the city, county and state of New York.

Montagnie Ward, fifteen (15) shares.
Jacob F. Wyckoff, ten (10) shares.
D. W. Bailey, ten (10) shares.

State of New York, city and county of New York, ss.

On this twenty-sixth day of May, A. D. 1855, personally came before me, Montagnie Ward, Jacob F. Wyckoff, and David W. Bailey, known to me to be the persons described in, and who executed the foregoing instrument, and severally acknowledged to me that they executed the same for the purposes therein mentioned.

THOMAS A. RICHMOND, *Commissioner of Deeds.*

A. L. Dennis, forty (40) shares.
Reuben D. Baldwin, fifty (50) shares.
Jeptha C. Groshong, twenty (20) shares.
James B. Pinneo, fifty (50) shares.
Matthias W. Day, twenty (20) shares.
T. L. Miller, five (5) shares.
C. P. Hall, twenty (20) shares.
Charles W. Badger, ten (10) shares.
Linn Adams, fifteen (15) shares.
Wm. McMurtry, ten (10) shares.
Alfred Lyon, five (5) shares.
Charles T. Day, jr., ten (10) shares.
Daniel Dodd jr., twenty (20) shares.
David C. Berry, ten (10) shares.
Frederick H. Smith, eighty (80) shares.

State of New Jersey, Essex county, ss.

On this thirtieth day of May, A. D. 1855, personally came before me Alfred L. Dennis, Reuben D. Baldwin, Jeptha C. Groshong, James B. Pinneo, Matthias W. Day, Thomas L. Miller, Charles P. Hall, Charles W. Badger, Linn Adams, William McMurtry, Alfred Lyon, Charles T. Day, jr., Daniel Dodd, jr., David C. Berry and Frederick H. Smith, known to me to be the persons described in and who executed the foregoing instrument, and severally acknowledged to me that they executed the same for the purposes therein mentioned.

JAMES F. BOND, *Commissioner of Deeds.*

State of New Jersey, Essex county, ss.

I, James J. Terhune, clerk of the said county of Essex, and also clerk of the Court of Common Pleas, in and for said county, do hereby certify that James F. Bond, who purports to have made and signed the foregoing certificate of acknowledgment, was, at the time of making and signing the same, a commissioner of deeds in and for said county, and that full faith and credit may and ought to be given to his official acts, and that the signature set to the foot of said certificate is in the proper hand-writing of the said James F. Bond.

In testimony whereof I have hereunto set my hand and official seal this
L. S.   thirty-first day of May, A. D. eighteen hundred and fifty-five.

J. J. TERHUNE, *Clerk.*

Endorsed—Certificate of the formation of The Manhattan Fire Arms Manufacturing Company. Filed 2d June, 1855.

State of New York, city and county of New York, ss.

I, John Clancy, clerk of the said city and county, do certify that I have compared the preceding with the original certificate of incorporation, on file in my office, and that the same is a correct transcript therefrom, and of the whole of such original.

In witness whereof, I have hereunto subscribed my name, and affixed my
L. S.   official seal, this 14th day of February, 1859.

JOHN CLANCY, *County Clerk.*

[C.]

ARTICLES OF ASSOCIATION AND BY-LAWS OF THE MANHATTAN FIRE ARMS MANUFACTURING COMPANY.

ARTICLE I. The association shall be known by the name of "The Manhattan Fire Arms Manufacturing Company," and shall continue in existence for the term of twenty years.

ART. II. The capital stock of said company shall be forty thousand dollars, divided into four hundred shares of one hundred dollars each.

ART. III. The object and purpose of the company is to manufacture and deal in fire arms, ammunition, and other articles pertaining to the fire arms business; also to secure improvements in fire arms and machinery for manufacturing the same.

ART. IV. The office of said company shall be located in the city, county and state of New York.

ART. V. All matters pertaining to the business of this company, not specified in the foregoing articles, shall be conducted in conformity with the by-laws of the company.

BY-LAWS.

SECTION 1. The business of this company shall be managed by a board of five trustees, who shall be chosen annually by ballot, on the third Tuesday in June, at the company's office, in the city of New York, and each share shall entitle the holder thereof to one vote, which may be given in person or by proxy. Two inspectors of election, (stockholders, but not candidates for office,) shall be appointed to preside, who shall declare the five persons having the greatest number of votes to be duly elected for one year, to serve as trustees of the company, and until others shall be elected in their stead.

SEC. 2. No person shall be or remain a trustee, unless he holds at least ten shares of the capital stock of the company.

SEC. 3. The trustees shall, at their first meeting after the annual meeting of the stockholders, choose one of their number president, who shall hold his office for one year, and until another shall be appointed in his stead. They shall also fill vacancies which may occur in their own body. They shall also from time to time elect a secretary, treasurer, and such other agents as they may deem necessary, who shall respectively occupy said positions during the pleasure of the trustees.

SEC. 4. The president shall exercise a general supervision over the affairs of the company, and shall perform all other duties usually devolving upon such officer.

SEC. 5. A stated meeting of the trustees shall be held at the office of the company, on the second Tuesday in every month, at 12 o'clock M., (which meeting may be adjourned at the pleasure of the trustees,) when the following order of business shall be observed:

1st. Reading the minutes of the previous meeting.

2d. Communications from the president and other officers.

3d. Reports of standing and other committees.

4th. Miscellaneous business.

SEC. 6. The president, or a majority of the trustees, may call a special meeting of the trustees, at such time and place as he or they may deem necessary for the interest of the company, by giving a written notice through the post office, or otherwise, to each trustee, previous to the time of meeting.

Sec. 7. At all meetings of the trustees, a majority shall be required to constitute a quorum, and the concurrence of a majority of the whole number of trustees shall be requisite to transact any business.

Sec. 8. The secretary shall furnish satisfactory security for the faithful performance of his duty, in the sum of twenty-five hundred dollars. It shall be his duty to take charge of and keep the common seal of the company; to keep all the records of the company, and also of the trustees, in suitable books provided for such purpose; to keep regular stock books and transfer books, issue certificates of stock, to be signed by the president and secretary, to the holders thereof, to which the seal of the company shall be attached; to attend to the correspondence of the company, and keep a copy of such correspondence; to see that all necessary records are made in the secretary of state's office, and county clerk's office, according to law; to make an annual statement in writing of the situation and standing of the company, so far as he has the means of knowing the same; to keep a regular account with the treasurer and agents; to keep a correct account of all moneys received and paid out; at all suitable times to keep an office open, and at all times during usual business hours, the books of the company shall be subject to the inspection of the stockholders, or other persons authorized to inspect the same; he shall also keep a book for the transfer of the capital stock of the company; and perform all other duties usually devolving upon a secretary.

Sec. 9. The treasurer shall furnish satisfactory security for the faithful performance of his trust, in the sum of five thousand dollars. It shall be his duty to take charge of the funds of the company, give receipts for the same, which shall be filed in the secretary's office; pay out such sums as may be drawn for by the secretary, countersigned by the president; keep an account of receipts and disbursements, and make a report in writing of the state of the treasury, annually, or oftener, if requested by the trustees.

Sec. 10. The transfer book of the company shall be closed the last three week days previous to, and on the day of, the annual meeting of the stockholders.

Sec. 11 The by-laws of the company may be altered or amended at any meeting of the stockholders, by a vote of a majority in interest, of said stockholders.

Sec. 12. The trustees may call a meeting of the stockholders at such time and place as they may deem necessary, by giving a written notice to each of the said stockholders, either personally or by leaving the same at his residence or at the post office, previous to said meeting, and the concurrence of a majority in interest of said stockholders shall be requisite to transact any business.

From the foregoing information, it will be seen that Manhattan Firearms Manufacturing Company was organized on May 26, 1855, in New York City, for an original capitalization of $40,000.00, by a group of businessmen from New York City and Newark, New Jersey. It should be borne in mind that the period with which we are dealing, the middle 1850's, was marked by rapid expansion of business ventures of various types, including banking. For example, this was the period of preparation for the laying of the Atlantic Cable, a formidable undertaking for that time. The field of firearms manufacturing held out considerable promise to an abundant supply of eager investors.

A study of the list of stockholders in the new venture of Manhattan Firearms Manufacturing Company reveals no names of persons known to have been connected with the firearms field, as of 1855. Mr. Frederick H. Smith, the principal stockholder, was to emerge as president of the new company, a rather logical development.

While genealogical studies are not always pertinent to similar subject matter, we have previously made reference to the fact that Manhattan Firearms Manufacturing Company, as a business venture, may have been conceived within the ownership of one of New Jersey's largest banking houses of the middle 1850's. In substantiation of this premise, we will, in a later section, pursue a limited study of some of the individuals included in the list of stockholders.

The next official proceeding of the Manhattan company, of which we were able to secure a record, comes from the files of the *New York Evening Post* for the month of April 1857. The announcement, as it appeared in the *Post*, was as follows:

> Notice is hereby given, that there will be a meeting of the Stockholders of the Manhattan Fire Arms Manufacturing Company on Wednesday, the 29th day of April next, at eleven o'clock in the forenoon that day, at the office of said Company number 163 Fulton street in the City of New York, for the purpose of diminishing the capital stock of said company from forty thousand dollars—the present amount—to twenty thousand dollars, and the amount of the shares from one hundred dollars to fifty dollars each, and that this notice is given pursuant to the 21st section of the general act under which said company is incorporated, and is signed by the subscribers, a majority of the Trustees of said Company.

F. H. Smith   Majority of
Reuben D. Baldwin Trustees
D. W. Bailey   of said Company

It should be noted that the address which appears in the announcement, 163 Fulton Street, is the address listed for Manhattan in the 1856-57 edition of Trow's New York City Directory.

The official record of the action taken by the stockholders at the meeting announced in the *New York Evening Post* is found in a second section of the Stedman document, shown herewith:

[B.]

CERTIFICATE OF REDUCTION OF CAPITAL

Whereas, The Manhattan Fire Arms Manufacturing Company heretofore duly organized and commenced business under and by virtue of the statute in such case made and provided, as appears by the certificate of such organization, filed on second day of June, 1855, in the office of the clerk of the city and county of New York.

And *whereas,* the capital of said company was originally fixed at the sum of forty thousand dollars, divided in four hundred shares of one hundred dollars each.

And *whereas,* it has been proposed, under and by virtue of the provisions of statute, to diminish said capital to twenty thousand dollars, divided in four hundred shares of fifty dollars each.

And *whereas,* the sum of twenty thousand dollars, being fifty dollars on each share of said original capital stock was, within one year from the original incorporation of said company, actually and in good faith paid in in cash.

Now it is hereby certified that the trustees of said company have published a notice signed by a majority of them in a newspaper published in the city, county and state of New York, called the New York Evening Post, for three successive weeks, specifying that a meeting of the stockholders of said company would be held at the office of said Manhattan Fire Arms Manufacturing Company, No. 163 Fulton street, in said city of New York, on the 29th day of April, 1857, at 11 o'clock in the forenoon, for the purpose of diminishing the capital stock of said company from forty thousand dollars to twenty thousand dollars, and the amount of its shares from one hundred dollars to fifty dollars each, and said trustees also deposited a copy of said notice in the post office in the city of New York, addressed to each stockholder at his usual place of residence at least three days previous to said 29th day of April, 1857.

And it is further certified that at the meeting, of which notice was so published, three hundred and thirty-five shares of stock were represented, either in person by parties owning same, or by proxy, and said meeting was organized by choosing Reuben D. Baldwin, one of the trustees of said company, chairman of the meeting, and Albert Beach, the secretary of said company, secretary of said meeting, and upon calling the roll the number of shares represented, as above stated, was found to be 335, and thereupon the following resolution was proposed:

Resolved, That the capital stock of this company be diminished from forty thousand dollars, its present amount, to twenty thousand dollars, and the amount of the shares from one hundred dollars each, their present amount, to fifty dollars each.

Which resolution was unanimously adopted, the following persons owning the number of shares opposite their respective names having voted in person or by proxy in favor thereof.

Reuben D. Baldwin,	fifty-eight,	58,	shares in person.
David C. Berry,	thirty-seven	37,	" " "
Charles T. Day, jr.,	ten,	10,	" " "
Alfred L. Dennis,	forty,	40,	" " "

Wm. McMurtry,	ten,	10,	shares in person.
Jacob F. Reimer,	sixty,	60,	" " "
Frederick H. Smith,	forty,	40,	" " "
Jacob D. Vermilye,	ten,	10,	" " "
		265	
David W. Bailey,	ten,	10,	shares by proxy.
Mathias W. Day,	twenty,	20,	" " "
James B. Pinneo,	forty,	40,	" " "
		335	shares.

And it is hereby further certified that the amount of capital actually paid in is the sum of twenty thousand dollars, that the business of the company is not extended or charged, and that the whole amount of debts and liabilities of the company is the sum of fourteen thousand five hundred and fifty-six dollars and eighteen cents.

In witness whereof, this certificate is signed and verified by the said chairman, counter-signed by the secretary, and acknowledged by the said chairman this twenty-first day of May, 1857.

REUBEN D. BALDWIN, *Chairman.*

ALBERT BEACH, *Secretary.*
Witness—JAMES F. BOND.

State of New Jersey, Essex county, city of Newark.

Reuben D. Baldwin being duly sworn, says he was the chairman of the meeting in the foregoing certificate mentioned, and that the facts stated in the said certificate are correct and true.

REUBEN D. BALDWIN.

Sworn before me this—day of May, 1857.

JAMES F. BOND.

State of New Jersey, Essex county, ss.

I, James F. Bond, a commissioner for the state of New York, residing in the city of Newark, county and state aforesaid, do certify that on the twenty-first day of May, one thousand eight hundred and fifty-seven, the above named Reuben D. Baldwin subscribed the foregoing affidavit in my presence in the city of Newark, county and state aforesaid, and did depose and swear that the matters therein set forth were true.

In witness whereof, I have hereunto set my hand and affixed my official [L. S.] seal this twenty-first day of May, in the year one thousand eight hundred and fifty-seven, in the city of Newark, county and state aforesaid.

JAMES F. BOND,
A Commissioner for the state of New York in New Jersey.
Endorsed—Filed 23d May, 1857.

State of New York, city and county of New York, ss.

I, Richard B. Connolly, clerk of said city and county of New York, do hereby certify that I have compared the preceding with the original of a "certificate of diminution of capital," on file in my office, and that the same is a correct transcript therefrom and of the whole of said original.

In witness whereof, I have hereunto set my hand and affixed my official seal [L. S.] this 27th day of July, 1857.

RICHARD B. CONNOLLY, *Clerk.*

Several items of informative interest are included in the Certificate of Reduction of Capital. It is to be noted that $20,000.00, one half of the original amount of capital to be subscribed, was actually paid in by the stockholders by June 2, 1856. Likewise, that the total amount of debts and liabilities of Manhattan was $14,556.18 as of May 21, 1857. The existence of debts and liabilities would certainly indicate that Manhattan had, indeed, been engaged in the manufacturing of firearms during the period between June 2, 1855, and May 21, 1857. The scope of operations during this period must have been, of necessity, quite limited. Further, the element of conservative guidance in the affairs of the company is exemplified by the decision to reduce the capital account from $40,000.00, as originally contemplated, to $20,000.00.

It may be interesting to compare the names on the list of original stockholders with the names on the list set forth in the Certificate of Reduction of Capital. Several of the names do not appear on both lists, indicating that some of the original stockholders had either sold out or were not represented. Three new names appear on the stockholders' list as of May 21, 1857, and we will deal with the personal history of one of them: Jacob D. Vermilye. We will also concern ourselves with the personal history of James B. Pinneo who was, together with Alfred L. Dennis, one of the incorporators of Manhattan. Messrs. Pinneo and Dennis, in company with Daniel Dodd, also were incorporators of the Howard Savings Institution, of Newark, N. J., in 1857.

James B. Pinneo was born in Connecticut in 1806 and worked in New York City for a number of years, advancing from the position of a clerk in a dry-goods establishment to a partnership in the firm. In 1832, Pinneo joined with William B. Kinney to establish the *Newark Daily Advertiser;* Kinney had been librarian of the New York Mercantile Library Association, of which Pinneo had been both a member and a director. Pinneo remained with the newspaper for a period of three years, following which he joined the firm of William Rankin & Company. Pinneo became a partner in William Rankin & Company in 1839; he retired from the firm in 1852, with a fortune, at the age of 46. In 1852, Pinneo was made a director of the National Newark Banking Company, the oldest banking institution in New Jersey, and became president of the bank in 1854, the position he held when Manhattan Firearms Manufacturing Company was chartered.

A further connection between the National Newark Banking Company and the founding of Manhattan is indicated by the fact that two other directors of the bank were stockholders in the Manhattan company. These directors were Alfred L. Dennis, who was one of the incorporators of Manhattan and a large shareholder, and Jacob D. Vermilye. Vermilye was the third cashier in the history of the National Newark Banking Company, having been the successor to his brother William in that position in 1843. Jacob Vermilye resigned as cashier of National Newark in 1858 to become cashier of the Merchant's Bank of New York. He was promptly named a director of National Newark and continued in the capacity of advisor to the New Jersey bank for more than twenty years. In 1881, by which time Jacob Vermilye had become president of Merchant's National Bank of New York, National Newark Banking Company drew up a special statement of thanks to Vermilye for his services in guiding the New Jersey bank's investments.

Thus, it would seem that Manhattan Firearms Manufacturing Company may have been an official investment of the National Newark Banking Company; if such was the case, it is quite likely that the Manhattan investment was made at the instigation of Jacob D. Vermilye.

REFERENCE NOTE

CHAPTER I: 1. *Guns and Shooting*
Ray Riling
New York: Greenberg 1952, page 100, cit. 721

CHAPTER II:

~~~~~~~~~~~~~~~~~~~~~~~~~~~~~~~~

NORWICH

W E HAVE followed, thus far, the progress of
Manhattan Fire Arms Manufacturing Company from its beginning point in
May 1855, through the processes of incorporation and reduction of capital
and have probed into the probable circumstances of the formation of the
Company. However, we have not as yet established the area of the early manufacturing operations of Manhattan. As indicated in the preceding chapter, each
of the several addresses listed for Manhattan in Trow's Directory were located
in the commercial or business districts of New York City. The fact that each
of three successive years found Manhattan conducting some phases of its growing affairs in a different location lends support to the opinion that Manhattan
was engaged in annual moving operations involving office furniture rather than
arms-making machinery.

In order to establish the area of the early manufacturing operations of the
Company, and to develop other important facets of the story of Manhattan, it
is necessary for us to introduce the third segment of the Stedman document.
This section, which deals directly with the first case on the docket of the October

155212A

NEW LONDON COUNTY

SUPREME COURT OF ERRORS

OCTOBER TERM, A. D. 1859.

DOCKET.

NORWICH.
JOHN W. STEDMAN, PRINTER, WATER STREET.
1859.

1859 term of the New London County, Connecticut, Supreme Court of Errors under the title "Manhattan Fire Arms Manufacturing Co. vs. Thomas K. Bacon," is the only portion of Mr. Stedman's remarkable document which contains any dramatic values. Perhaps no one, other than a fellow-collector of antique firearms, will agree that this hundred-year-old lawsuit could contain anything in the usually rarified atmosphere of dramatic values. However, we are sure that the exposition of the relationship between Manhattan and Thomas K. Bacon, as well as the details of the lawsuit, contains the elements of real drama. A review of the names of the original shareholders in the Manhattan venture reveals the name of no one known to have been associated with the field of firearms manufacturing of that period. In the forthcoming section of the Stedman document we find a name which was very well known as a maker of firearms, Thomas K. Bacon. We are to find fully authenticated information of the details of the early Manhattan arms, a rather rare discovery at this late date and a tidbit of high flavor for the collector-researcher. The information relating to the prices paid for some components of these early arms is of equal interest. In addition, certain seemingly obscure details which bear upon later aspects of our story are set forth in this segment, beginning with the cover page of the Stedman document. Mr. John W. Stedman had more than a printer's interest in the legal proceedings between Manhattan and Thomas K. Bacon, as will be seen in a later section.

THE MANHATTAN FIRE ARMS MANUFACTURING COMPANY

vs.

THOMAS K. BACON

To the Honorable Superior Court to be holden at Norwich, within and for the county of New London, on the third Tuesday of November, A. D. 1858.

The petition of "The Manhattan Fire Arms Manufacturing Company," a joint stock corporation, duly and legally formed and organized under the laws of the state of New York, having an office in the city, county and state of New York, and having also their manufactory and doing business at Norwich aforesaid, respectfully represents, that the business of said company is the manufacture and sale of fire arms, and that they have full power and authority as such corporation to transact said business and all other powers incidental thereto, and to make all contracts proper and convenient thereto; that on the 1st day of September, 1857, and for some time prior thereto, they had been engaged in the manufacture of fire arms of various kinds, particularly pistols, at said Norwich; that prior to said first day of September, 1857, one Thomas K. Bacon, of said Norwich, had been making arrangements to engage in the same line of business, and had contracted sundry liabilities in relation thereto, and that, wishing to extricate himself from said liabilities, and to engage in business in the employ of the petitioners, on said first day of September, 1857, he entered into an agreement with the petitioners, which agreement was in writing, and as follows, to wit:

"Norwich, Sept. 1st, 1857.

"In consideration of payment to me by the Manhattan Fire Arms Manufacturing Company of fifty dollars, the receipt where of is hereby acknowledged, with which fifty dollars I am to pay Charles A. Converse, to obtain a release from further payment to him for rent of part of his factory, which I had hired, and also in consideration of said company agreeing to pay, and thereby releasing me from all responsibility for bills which I had contracted with the following, namely:

John G. Huntington, ...	$ 2 56
Backus & Barstow, ...	3 04
J. M. Huntington & Co.	9 26
John Breed & Co.	23 46
C. N. Farnam, ...	24 36
Phenix Foundery,	
George H. Brown,	
Charles A. Converse, ...	39 44
Wood, Light & Co.	
Union Machine Co.	

1 hereby covenant and agree to and with said company, that I will not engage, or be in any way concerned, in the manufacture or sale, or in any other way connected with dealing in fire arms of any kind whatever, during twenty years from this date, provided said company allows me, as another consideration, to make for them, at the prices annexed, all that they use of the following parts of pistols:

Barrels for	2 inch single pistols,			5 cents	each.
do.	3 do.	do.	do.	6 1-2	do.
do.	4 do.	do.	do.	8 1-2	do.
do.	5 do.	do.	do.	10 1-2	do.
do.	6 do.	do.	do.	12 1-2	do.
do.	3 barrel revolvers			17	do.
do.	5 do.	do.	do.	23	do.
do.	3 inch 6 barrel do.			25	do.
Barrels for	4 inch 6 barrel revolvers			30	do.
do.	5 inch 6 do.	do.		40	do.

If at any time I relinquish the making of the parts of pistols at the prices annexed, as heretofore mentioned, then the Manhattan Fire Arms Manufacturing Company may employ any others to make such parts without being liable to me in any damages therefor, but in such case I shall then and thereafter be prohibited, as herefore mentioned, from engaging in making or selling fire arms. It is understood that if the company can not supply me with work sufficient to employ my time and that of three boys, in making the kinds of barrels mentioned, then I shall have the preference, over any one else, at same price, in making barrels or cylinders for any other kinds of pistols the company may then require.

It is understood that the foregoing obligations are binding upon T. K. Bacon only so long as the Manhattan Fire Arms Manufacturing Company, or its successor, remains in business.

(Signed)   T. K. BACON.

The petitioners further represent, that in consideration of the agreement aforesaid, they paid to said Bacon said sum of fifty dollars, with which to obtain a release from said Converse, and that they also paid to said several persons all bills which said Bacon had contracted with them for the purposes aforesaid, and that said Bacon was thereby released from all liability for the same, and that they have, from said 1st day of September until the time hereafter mentioned, when said Bacon voluntarily quitted their employ, and refused to make for them any more of the parts of pistols hereinbefore specified, allowed said Bacon to make for them, at the prices before named in said agreement, all that they use or have used of said parts of pistols, and have paid him, from time to time, for the same, and have in all respects executed, performed and fulfilled all the considerations upon which said agreement was made, and have been at all times willing and desirous of allowing him to continue to make for them all that they use of said parts of pistols, at said prices, according to said agreement, but that said Bacon, on or about the 11th day of September, 1858, voluntarily quitted said manufacture, and informed the petitioners that he should no longer continue the same.

The petitioners further represent, that after thus ceasing to manufacture said parts of pistols for the petitioners, the said Bacon, in violation of said agreement, has threatened to engage in the manufacture and sale of fire arms, and has been actively engaged in organizing a joint stock corporation under the laws of this state, called the Bacon Manufacturing Company, and that he is a large stockholder in said company, the business of which corporation, as specified in their articles of association, is the manufacture and sale of fire arms, with other powers incident thereto, having their office and place of business at said Norwich.

The petitioners further represent, that said Bacon, as agent for said company, and a stockholder therein, and in other ways, is preparing to, and threatens that he will engage in the manufacture and sale of fire arms, particularly pistols, in violation of his agreement with the petitioners.

And the petitioners aver, that said violation of said agreement by said Bacon, is contrary to equity and good conscience, and tends to their great and irreparable loss and damage, and that they are without adequate remedy at law, and must lose their just rights in the premises unless relieved by this Court, as a Court of equity.

The petitioners therefore pray this Court to inquire into the truth of the foregoing allegations, and to order and enjoin the said Thomas K. Bacon, under a suitable penalty, not to engage, or be in any way concerned in the manufacture or sale, or in any way connected with dealing in fire arms, during the remainder of said term of twenty years, in violation of said agreement, or in some other or different way to grant the petitioners relief in the premises, and they, as in duty bound, will ever pray.

Dated at Norwich this 4th day of November, A. D. 1858.

The Manhattan Fire Arms Manufacturing Company,
By J. HALSEY, *their Attorney.*

To the sheriff of the county of New London, his deputy, or either constable of the town of Norwich, in said county, GREETING:

By authority of the state of Connecticut, you are hereby commanded to summon Thomas K. Bacon, of said Norwich, to appear before the Superior Court to be holden at Norwich, within and for the county of New London, on the third Tuesday of November, A. D. 1858, then and there to show reasons, if any he has, why the prayer of the foregoing petition should not be granted. Hereof fail not, and make due and legal service and return. Nathan C. Chapell recognized $50 for prosecution.

Dated at Norwich, the 4th day of November, A. D. 1858.

Certified and signed by

JEREMIAH HALSEY, *Justice of the Peace.*

New London county, ss.

NORWICH, November 4, 1858.

Then and there, by virtue hereof, I made service of this petition and citation by placing in the hands of Thomas K. Bacon a true and attested copy of the same.

Attest,	N. C. CHAPELL, *Sheriff's Deputy.*
FEES—Travel	$ 25
Copy	2 50
Service	12
2 indorsements	24
	$3 11

The respondent denies the truth and sufficiency of the allegations in the petition contained.

By EDMUND PERKINS and H. H. STARKWEATHER,
his Attorneys.

Perhaps the most interesting part of the preceding section of the Stedman document, from the collector's viewpoint, is the tabulation showing the range of barrel types and lengths manufactured by Bacon for Manhattan and the surprisingly low prices that he received for his work. When we received the copy of the Stedman document from the New York Public Library, we were under the impression that our collection contained an example of each of the various pepperboxes and single-shot pistols manufactured by Manhattan. The tabulation of barrel types and lengths, as listed in the Bacon contract, quickly showed us that one imporant item was not in the collection, viz: the single-shot pistol with 6″ barrel. Since we had observed no such specimen in several years of searching, our chances of acquiring one in a narrowing market seemed to be considerably less than good. Nearly a year later, through a fortunate set of circumstances (for us) and the cooperation of a fellow collector, the acquisition of this valued specimen was made.

While this experience was not duplicated in acquiring an example of each of the ten types of early Manhattan arms, it is representative of the difficulties, and good fortune, we encountered in accumulating this group. In checking the records of our personal collection of these arms we find that, in the process of assembling the collection and in attempting to improve the quality of the several pieces, we have owned a total of fourteen specimens. In four of the ten different classifications, we have owned two specimens in each classification. In the remaining six categories, we have owned only one specimen per category and in most cases the specimen represents the only one of its type that we have seen. Although we confined our collecting interests to Manhattan arms during a period when there was little or no interest exhibited in them by other collectors, the foregoing analysis indicates the relative scarcity of these specimens. Admittedly, the continuing constriction of the antique arms market, brought about by the entry of thousands of new collectors into the field, may have contributed to the scarcity of the early Manhattan arms. Another factor which probably contributed to the scarcity is the fact that these arms were, originally, relatively low in cost and received no special care or preservation with a resultant survival rate somewhat below average. For these reasons, plus the limitations of the total numbers produced, the early Manhattan arms were never in plentiful supply.

Therefore, we are pleased that we can present the photographs showing a specimen of each item listed in the tabulation of barrel types and lengths in the Manhattan-Bacon contract. The arms shown in the several plates contained in this work are from the author's collection, except where otherwise noted.

The pepperbox displayed as Figure 3 in Plate 4 (see page 32) is from the collection of Miles W. Standish. This specimen is noteworthy in that the barrel-group is approximately ¼″ shorter than the standard length of 3″. The specimen is in excellent condition and appears to be entirely original. Perhaps the barrel-group of this specimen was the handiwork of one of Mr. Bacon's "three boys," as mentioned in the Manhattan-Bacon contract.

It is entirely reasonable to assume that Manhattan manufactured and sold a small quantity of pepperboxes and single-shot pistols prior to the disputed agreement of September 1, 1857, as evidenced by the allusion that "on the 1st day of September, 1857, and for some time prior thereto, they (Manhattan) had been engaged in the manufacture of fire arms of various kinds, particularly pistols, at said Norwich." Because of the minimum number of specimens

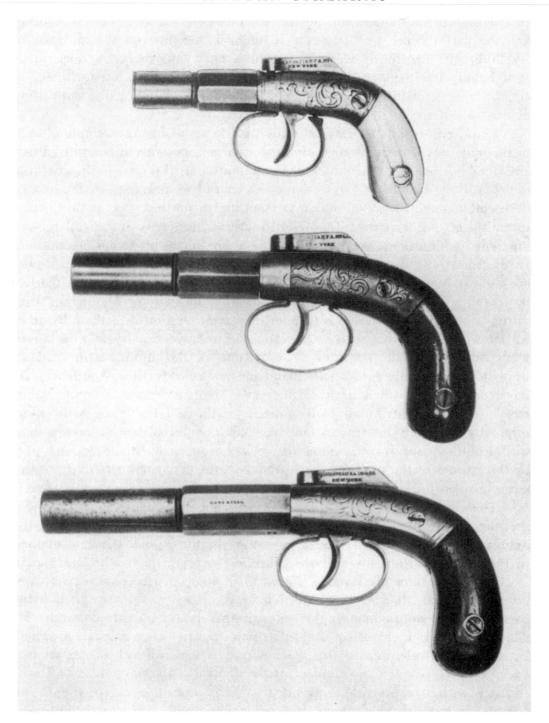

PLATE 1. EARLY MANHATTAN ARMS: BAR-HAMMER SINGLE-SHOT PISTOLS.

Figure 1. Two-Inch Round and Octagon Barrel, Caliber .31, Number 454.

Figure 2. Three-Inch Round and Octagon Barrel, Caliber .34, Number 301.

Figure 3. Four-Inch Round and Octagon Barrel, Caliber .36, Number 64.

The Bar-Hammer Single-Shot Pistols are representative of the earliest arms manufactured by Manhattan in Norwich, Connecticut, where the manufactory was located at No. 6 Central Wharf Street. Production of the early arms was begun in the first months of 1856. The double-action single pistol was a popular arm of the 1850's and 1860's. It is probable that not more than 1500 of the bar-hammer pistols were made by Manhattan.

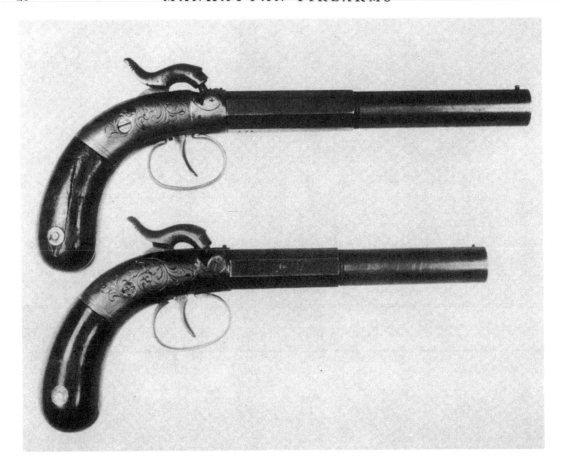

PLATE 2. EARLY MANHATTAN ARMS: SHOTGUN-HAMMER SINGLE-SHOT PISTOLS.

Figure 1. Six-Inch Round and Octagon Barrel, Caliber .36, Number 171.

Figure 2. Five-Inch Round and Octagon Barrel, Caliber .36, Number 232.

A versatile weapon which could be used for target shooting as well as for self defense, the shotgun-hammer single pistol is one of the rarest of Manhattan arms. Single-action and equipped with front and rear sights. The influence of Thomas K. Bacon may have been present in this model as his first firm, Bacon & Co., produced a similar pistol but with ring trigger.

handled, there appears to be no way to establish that certain specimens were made prior to Bacon's association with Manhattan and that others were made during the period of the association. However, the pepperbox shown as Figure 1 in Plate 3 (see page 28) may have been made prior to the Manhattan-Bacon contract. This specimen bears the serial #2 and the signing "Manhattan F. A. Mfg. Co. New York" is stamped in one of the barrel flutes, instead of on the left side of the hammer which is the usual allocation for such signing. In addition this piece is set off with what we believe to be the crudest form of engraving to be found on the signed product of any recognized maker of American firearms. We have in our collection an unmarked, single-shot, percussion pistol which we believe to be of Manhattan origin. This pistol is adorned (the word is used with reservations) with the same pattern of crudely executed engraving and the internal operating mechanism is quite different from other and marked Manhattan pistols. This specimen is serial #26 and is of smooth bore, whereas all other Manhattan single-shot pistols we have handled were rifled; this item may have been of pre-Bacon origin. The pepperbox shown as Figure 3 in Plate 3 (see page 28) may be worthy of comment inasmuch as the trigger-guard, which seems to be original, is a casting instead of the forged iron strap ordinarily used to form the trigger-guard. Once again, we are dealing with a low serial number (#22) and the cast guard may have been an early development or an indication of lack of standardization.

It is generally acknowledged by collectors that Manhattan pepperboxes and single-shot pistols are comparative rarities. A review of the serial numbers listed for Plates 1 through 4 (see pages 24, 26, 28, 32) will lend considerable support to this premise. Like most collectors, we are possessed with a strong desire to know: "How many were produced?" We will express our conjectures in this connection, meanwhile attempting to keep our neck well down in the shell.

As will have been observed, none of the specimens pictured bear serial numbers above #869; this represents the highest serial number of any example of the early Manhattan arms that we have handled. We have no way of knowing whether Manhattan used the lot-number method of serial numbering, as was evidently used by Allen, or whether some other method was used. We do have one very slim lead: the serial number of Figure 1 in Plate 4 (see page 32) is #33, and the specimen is representative of the 6-shot, 5″ barrel-group. More than a year ago, we handled a specimen with a 4″ barrel-group, likewise 6-shot, which also bore the serial #33. While this circumstance proves nothing, it does set out the possibility that each barrel length in the 6-shot model of the pepperboxes may have been given a separate series of serial numbers, beginning with serial #1; further, that the same procedure may have been followed in numbering the 3-shot and 5-shot models of pepperboxes as well as the bar-hammer and shotgun-hammer models of the single-shot pistols. Following this

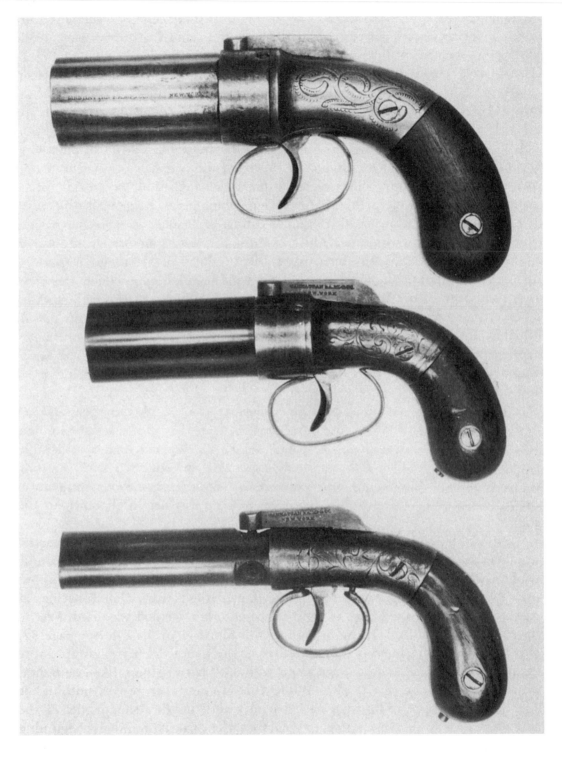

PLATE 3. EARLY MANHATTAN ARMS: PEPPERBOXES.

Figure 1. Six-Shot Barrel Group, Three-Inch Barrel, Caliber 31,
Number 2 (signing on barrel between flutes).

Figure 2. Five-Shot Barrel Group, Three-Inch Barrel, Caliber .31,
Number 296.

Figure 3. Three-Shot Barrel Group, Three-Inch Barrel, Caliber
.31, Number 22 (barrel group turned by hand).

The first examples of the six-shot Manhattan pepperboxes were signed on the barrels, between the flutes, dating their manufacture in 1856; the signing was soon transferred to the left side of the hammer. The five-shot and three-shot models were made in the 3″ barrel length, only. The three-shot pepperbox is regarded as a rarity and, although double-action, required the barrel group to be turned by hand—a warm task for the user in getting off the second and third shots.

possibility through to the point of round numbers, it may be indicated that a total of 3000 pepperboxes and 2000 single-shot pistols were produced by Manhattan, including all models and barrel lengths. It should be pointed out that the foregoing theory hangs by a very thin thread. If an error by one of Manhattan's workmen resulted in the duplication of a serial number and we chanced to examine the gun with the duplicate serial number, our hypothesis would be erroneous. However, it is our opinion that the production figures given in the above estimate are on the liberal side.

Returning to the more factual information contained in the third section of the Stedman document, two points are set out as being of primary interest: (1) the ultimate disposition of the lawsuit between Manhattan Firearms Mfg. Company and Thomas K. Bacon and (2) some further exploration of Bacon's relationship with Manhattan and, because of his position in the field of firearms manufacturing, to follow Bacon's progress after the termination of his connection with Manhattan.

In summing up the details of the lawsuit, it will have been seen that Manhattan's petition, as the plaintiff, was drawn for presentation during the November 1858 term of the Supreme Court of Errors to be held at Norwich, Connecticut. Further, that the petition bears the date of November 4, 1858, and that service of the petition and the summons was made on Bacon on November 4, 1858, and that Bacon through his attorneys, Edmund Perkins and H. H. Starkweather, denied the "truth and sufficiency of the allegations in the petition contained." Presumably, the petition was heard and Bacon's denial was entered on the third Tuesday of November 1858, which would have been the 16th of November, 1858. As will be seen on page 9 of the Stedman document, the court recorded the details of the suit under the date of the January 1859 term of the court. Judge Waldo, before whom the case was tried, reserved the decree "for the advice of the Supreme Court of Errors, to be holden at New London, within and for the County of New London, on the second Tuesday of March, 1859." This is further confirmed by the statement of William L. Brewer, clerk of the court, as shown on page 29 of Stedman's record. Pages 8, 9, 10 and 29 of the Stedman document are reproduced herewith.

New London county, ss.

SUPERIOR COURT, January term, 1859.

THE MANHATTAN FIRE ARMS CO.
            vs.   } Petition for Injunction.
THOMAS K. BACON

Upon the trial of this case upon the issue formed by the pleadings as on file, the following facts are found by the Court:

The petitioners are a joint stock corporation, organized under the laws of the state of New York. The rights, powers and duties of said corporation are contained in the original certificate of the formation of "The Manhattan Fire Arms Manufacturing Company," a copy of which is hereto annexed, marked A; the certificate of the reduction of the capital stock of said corporation, a copy of which is hereto annexed, marked B; the articles of association and by-laws of said corporation, a copy of which is hereto annexed, marked C; and a certain statute law of the state of New York, entitled "An act to authorize the formation of corporations for manufacturing, mining, mechanical and chemical purposes," passed February 17, 1848, which said statute is made a part of this finding for the purpose of reference.

Said corporation was organized in May, 1855, and commenced business in New York city, and continued their business operations in said city five or six months. They then removed to Norwich, in said county of New London, and commenced the manufacture of pistols in said Norwich about the first of January, 1856, and have ever since continued said manufacture in said Norwich; have rented rooms, employed workmen, and have purchased and constructed machinery and materials for said manufacture. But said corporation has had, and still has, an office in the city of New York, where the business meetings of said corporation are held, and where many of their manufactured articles are sold.

Albert Beach, the secretary of said corporation, has acted as its general agent since its organization, has taken the general charge and management of its business at said Norwich, and made all the necessary contracts therefor, but there is no vote of said corporation or of its trustees, appointing said Beach general agent, nor any vote authorizing him to act in that capacity. But he has so acted with the knowledge and consent of said corporation and its trustees, to whom he has annually, and oftener when required, rendered an account of his said transactions.

On the first day of September, 1857, the respondent, Thomas K. Bacon, was, and for some time previous had been, making arrangements to engage in the business of manufacturing and selling fire arms, in said Norwich, and had contracted certain liabilities for the rent of a building in which to carry on said business, and for certain machinery and material to be used in said business. On said day the said Beach, acting for the said Manhattan Fire Arms Manufacturing Company, and the said Thomas K. Bacon, made an agreement respecting the said liabilities of said Bacon, and his giving up his said contemplated business, which was reduced to writing, and is correctly recited in said petition, except so far as the same may be modified by the following facts, to wit: It was understood and agreed that the said agreement between said Beach and Bacon should be reduced to writing in duplicates to be signed by both parties, one of which duplicates was to be kept by one of the parties and the other duplicate by the other party; and thereupon an agreement, a copy of which is set out in said petition, was made by the said Beach, and a duplicate thereof, except the prices affixed to the articles named therein, which said Bacon was to make for said corporation; and the said Bacon signed said agreement, which said Beach took, but said Beach refused to sign said duplicate, and never did sign the same, though requested so to do by said Bacon.

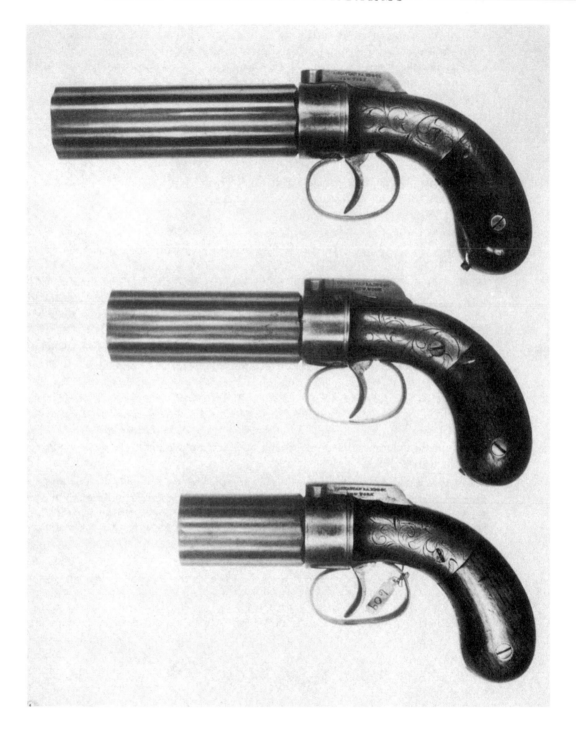

PLATE 4. EARLY MANHATTAN ARMS: PEPPERBOXES.

Figure 1. Six-Shot Barrel Group, Five-Inch Barrel, Caliber .31, Number 33.

Figure 2. Six-Shot Barrel Group, Four-Inch Barrel, Caliber .31, Number 869.

Figure 3. Six-Shot Barrel Group, Three-Inch Barrel, Caliber .31, Number 549.

(From the collection of Miles W. Standish)

Although resembling the Allen pepperboxes in outward appearance, the Manhattan pepperboxes are quite different mechanically and were not infringements of Allen's patents. An external difference is found in the location of the tension screw for the mainspring. Thomas K. Bacon was paid forty cents each for making the five-inch barrels, thirty cents each for making the four-inch barrels and twenty-five cents each for making the three-inch barrels. It is believed that the six-shot pepperbox with five-inch barrel is the rarest of the Manhattan pepperboxes.

Upon the execution of said contract, as aforesaid, Bacon relinquished the idea of commencing said business on his own account; and commenced to work for the petitioners under said contract, making the parts of pistols therein mentioned, and continued so to work until the 11th day of September, 1858. The petitioners paid the said Charles A. Converse said sum of fifty dollars for rent, and assumed the other liabilities named in said contract, and paid said Bacon for doing said work the said sums affixed to the different articles, and in various settlements made between said parties for work between said first day of September, 1857, and the 11th day of September, 1858, the said written contract was referred to by both parties as the rule by which said settlement was to be made. There is no vote of said corporation, or of its trustees, authorizing Beach to make any such contract, nor does it appear that he ever consulted them about it before it was made. He informed them of the existence of said contract with the respondent, but they took no action concerning it, and it does not appear that the corporation or its trustees ever approved or disapproved of the contract, except what may be inferred from their said inaction.

The respondent voluntarily left the employment of the petitioners on the 11th day of September, 1858. Since that time he has been instrumental in organizing a joint stock corporation under the laws of the state of Connecticut, under the name of the Bacon Manufacturing Company, for the manufacture and sale of fire arms. The respondent is a stockholder in this corporation, is the agent thereof and its principal manager. This corporation, before the 4th day of November, 1858, commenced the manufacture of the same kind of pistols, in said town of Norwich, that the petitioners were making at the time the respondent was in their employment, and continue to manufacture and sell said pistols. The respondent has not been, and is not in any other way concerned in the manufacture and sale of fire arms than as a member and agent of said corporation.

The said Manhattan Fire Arms Manufacturing Company are about to remove their said business to the state of New Jersey.

Upon the foregoing facts the question as to what decree shall be rendered is reserved for the advice of the Supreme Court of Errors, to be holden at New London, within and for the county of New London, on the second Tuesday of March, 1859.

By WALDO, *Judge.*

At a Superior Court held at New London, within and for the county of New London, on the 3d Tuesday of January, A. D. 1859.

Present, Hon. LOREN P. WALDO, *Judge.*
WM. L. BREWER, *Clerk*
N. P. PAYNE, *Sheriff.*

The Manhattan Fire Arms Manufacturing Company, a joint stock corporation, duly and legally formed and organized under the laws of the state of New York, having an office in the city, county and state of New York, and having also their manufactory, and doing business at Norwich, in New London county, petitioners, *vs.* Thomas K. Bacon, of said town of Norwich, respondent.

This was a bill in equity, bearing date the 4th day of November, A. D. 1858, and praying that the said respondent be restrained under a suitable penalty from manufacturing or sale of fire arms, &c., as stated in said petition.

The case came to the November term of this Court, A. D. 1858, when the parties appeared, and thence, by continuance, to the present term, when the parties appeared, and were heard.

After such hearing and due consideration, the Court finds the facts as on file, and reserves the questions of law arising thereon for the advice of the Supreme Court of Errors, at its term next to be holden at New London, within and for the county of New London, on the second Tuesday of March, A. D. 1859.

A true copy of record.

Attest.   WM. L. BREWER, *Clerk*.

A continuance of the case from the March 1859 term of the Supreme Court of Errors to have been held in New London, to the October 1859 term to be held in Norwich, is indicated by page 1 of the Stedman document; three cases of the docket are set forth, the first of which is the case of Manhattan vs. Bacon. This concludes the information as given by Mr. Stedman, except for several pages of the document which were not included in any of the foregoing sections. This material deals with certain statutory requirements for New York corporations and makes for dreadfully dull reading, even by attorneys. However, in order that the record may be complete, the deleted material is shown in an appendix.

The only daily paper printed in Norwich during the period with which we are dealing was the Norwich *Morning Bulletin*. A search of the October 1859 issues of the Norwich *Morning Bulletin* reveals the following, as recorded in the copy for Thursday, October 27, (1859): "The Supreme Court was in session on Tuesday. The case of Manhattan Fire Arms Company versus Thomas K. Bacon being the first on the docket, on motion of Mr. Halsey, was continued to the March term." As shown on page 6 of the Stedman document, Mr. J. Halsey was the attorney for Manhattan. For the benefit of our friends who may have spotted the name of Jeremiah Halsey, Justice of the Peace, on page 7 of the same source, may we say that according to the Norwich directory of the period, Mr. J. Halsey, Attorney, and Jeremiah Halsey, Justice of the Peace, were one and the same gentleman.

We again picked up our search for the final disposition of the lawsuit, a bit wearily this time, in the Tuesday, March 13, 1860, issue of the Norwich *Morning Bulletin,* in which an announcement appeared to the effect that the court was to begin its March session on that day, in New London. In the issues for the next two days, five cases were named and described; three on Wednesday, March 14, and two on Thursday, March 15. In none of these cases, or other

PLATE 5. EXPERIMENTAL MODEL .31-CALIBER MANHATTAN REVOLVER (LEFT SIDE).

Five-Shot; Six-Inch Barrel; No Serial Number.

(From the collection of Miles W. Standish)

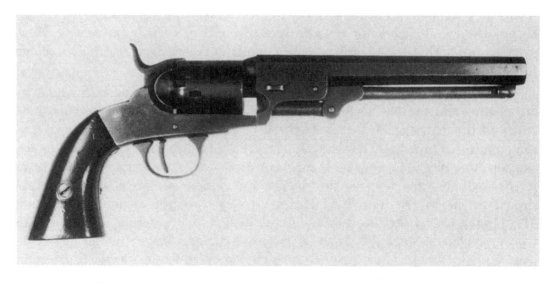

PLATE 6. EXPERIMENTAL MODEL .31-CALIBER MANHATTAN REVOLVER (RIGHT SIDE).

The only example of a prototype of Manhattan's first model of revolver known to the author. Manufactured in Norwich, probably in 1858, and possesses several unusual features. May have been the very first application of Manhattan's design of stagecoach holdup scene.

references to the proceedings of the court, was any mention made of the Manhattan vs. Bacon lawsuit. The last sentence of the March 15, 1860, item. "The court adjourned *sine die.*"

Since we have earnestly and studiously followed a matter of no great consequence squarely into the cross-roads of nowhere, we feel privileged to make a rather profound observation: The Manhattan Fire Arms Manufacturing Company withdrew its suit in equity against Thomas K. Bacon.

The reasons for the withdrawal of the suit may have been these: (1) the tenuous position which Manhattan held from the outset, due to the fact that Beach had failed to sign Bacon's copy of the agreement, and (2) the diminution of the importance of Bacon's services to Manhattan, as time went on, due to the emergence of another significant personality within the Manhattan organization, one Augustus Rebetey. However, it seems likely that Bacon's decision to sever his connection with Manhattan must have caused quite a tumult in Manhattan's operations, along with some sleepless nights for Albert Beach. In fact, Manhattan may have felt that its operations would be seriously damaged when "said Bacon, on or about the 11th day of September, 1858, voluntarily quitted said manufacture, and informed the petitioners that he should no longer contin[u]e the same." Based upon the information revealed thus far, Bacon was the only person affiliated with the Manhattan organization who knew the first thing about the arms business and the loss of his services, if not readily replaceable, might have been little short of calamitous. On the other hand, the loss of Bacon's services may have been less serious than his knowledge of Manhattan's plans for the immediate future, which plans must have included the production of revolvers. The Stedman document makes two references which may or may not bear on this point. The first is on page 6, paragraph 2, wherein Bacon "is preparing to, and threatens that he will engage in the manufacture and sale of fire arms, *particularly pistols;*" (author's italics). The second reference is on page 10, the first complete paragraph, wherein "This corporation (Bacon Manufacturing Company), before the 4th day of November, 1858, commenced the manufacture of *the same kind of pistols.*" (author's italics). In the usage of that period, the word "pistol" could have meant a single-shot pistol or it could have meant a revolver. (We note, in the Manhattan-Bacon agreement, that arms which we identify as pepperboxes are called "revolvers.") In the light of subsequent events, we believe that Manhattan, in filing the lawsuit against Bacon, was motivated by concern over Bacon's knowledge of the company's plans for the manufacture of revolvers, rather than the loss of Bacon's services to the firm. Certainly, there was no one in the Manhattan organization, other than Bacon, who could have had the keen insight into the profit possibilities in the arms field, now that Colt's patent had expired. There was little to keep Bacon from leaving Manhattan, once he began to look for greener pastures.

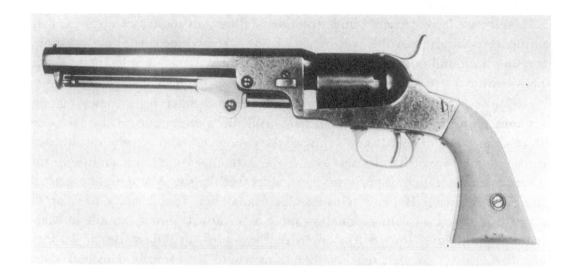

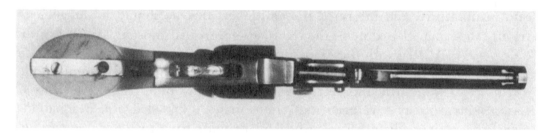

PLATES 7 AND 8. DEVELOPMENT MODEL .31-CALIBER MANHATTAN REVOLVER
WITH ENLARGED GRIPS.

Five-Shot; Six-Inch Barrel; Number 7.

Manhattan .31 caliber revolvers were made with three different sizes of
grips. The above example shows the largest size which became a standard feature in the Series II revolvers beginning with serial numbers between 900 and
1000. Method of attaching extension to butt is shown in Plate 8. This gun was
fully engraved and bears the mark of Joseph Gruler, co-inventor of the company's best patent.

His unsigned (by Beach) agreement with Manhattan was an insignificant obstacle to his ambitions.

The evidence taken into account by the court, as indicated by Judge Waldo's notes, appears to absolve Albert Beach from the part of the villain in this piece. In fact, it is our opinion that there was no villain, neither Bacon nor Beach. If we may read between the lines, Beach was given the job of getting Manhattan into the firearms business. With the assistance of his fellow officials, perhaps, Beach selected Norwich as a base of operations and this was probably a good selection. Both Allen & Thurber and Bacon & Company had been in business in Norwich, thus providing a source of experienced arms workmen. In Norwich, Beach found Bacon and vice versa. Bacon was on his last legs and almost out of business by reason of his not-too-successful venture as a maker of single-shot pistols and pepperboxes. Beach needed competent help in the Manhattan enterprise. Bacon and Beach entered into an agreement which Bacon signed and which Beach did not sign, probably because he lacked the authority to sign it. There are, probably, thousands of Albert Beaches in American industry today. These present-day Albert Beaches have almost unlimited authority to say "No" but the authority to say "Yes" on matters of importance seldom, if ever, devolves into their hands. In Beach's case, the boys with the beards and the beaver hats (back in New York and Newark) didn't say "Yes" and they didn't say "No"; they just sat tight and let Beach work his way out of his difficulties. For more than a year, Bacon and Beach got along very well. Then events began to take shape which neither Bacon nor Beach could control. Bacon elected to go his separate way and Manhattan was planning to move its operations to Newark, N. J. Followed then a little action in the New London Supreme Court of Errors, which ultimately came to nothing. We are somewhat relieved by this development; by this time, we are getting a little tired of The Great Lawsuit.

*   *   *   *

In a previous paragraph, we mentioned that further exploration of Bacon's relationship with Manhattan was a point of primary interest. Page 3 of the Stedman document establishes the relationship as follows, "that prior to said first day of September, 1857, one Thomas K. Bacon, of said Norwich, had been making arrangements to engage in the same line of business, and had contracted sundry liabilities in relation thereto, and that, wishing to extricate himself from said liabilities, and to engage in business *in the employ of the petitioners,* on said first day of September, 1857, he entered into an agreement with the petitioners,". This statement appears to place Bacon in the status of an employee of Manhattan although the agreement appears to place him in the position of a subcontractor for Manhattan, in the manufacture of barrels for single

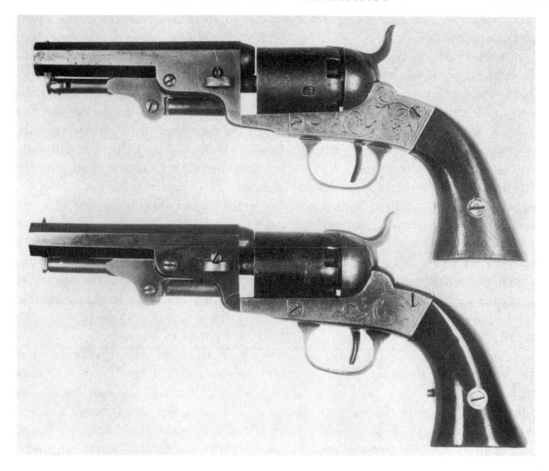

PLATE 9. COMPARISON OF MANHATTAN AND BACON .31-CALIBER REVOLVERS.

Figure 1. Manhattan: Five-Shot, Four-Inch Barrel, Number 44.

Figure 2. Bacon: Five-Shot, Four-Inch Barrel, Number 178.

Illustrating the close resemblance of the copy made by Bacon Manufacturing Company to the original by Manhattan, including the style of engraving on the frames. The pattern of engraving on Manhattan revolvers usually more ornate than applied to Bacon revolvers. As superintendent of the Manhattan manufactory during 1857 and 1858, Bacon played an important part in developing Manhattan's .31 caliber revolver.

pistols and revolvers (pepperboxes). Clarification of the relationship is found in two listings in Boyd's Norwich, Connecticut, Directory for 1857: (1) "Manhattan Fire Arms Manufacturing Company, 6 Central Wharf" and, (2) "Thomas K. Bacon, Superintendent, 6 Central Wharf."

Thus it appears, without question, that Bacon was superintendent of Manhattan's manufactory during the period of their association. The dual relationship of superintendent and contractor indicates that Bacon operated under the "inside contract" arrangement which was prevalent during that period. Samuel Colt is known to have had several "inside contractors"[1] and Benjamin Tyler Henry worked under the "inside contract system" when he was superintendent of Winchester Arms Company, *circa* 1861.

Since Bacon has walked onto our stage (and of his own volition, resolutely and abruptly stalked off stage), let us take a brief look at Thomas K. Bacon, the man, and at his operations prior to and following his association with Manhattan.

Thomas K. Bacon was a scion of one of the oldest and most prominent families of Norwich, Connecticut, and was probably one of Norwich's leading citizens of the period 1850-1870. He was one of the early manufacturers of firearms during the percussion period and is reputed to have established his first firm, in Norwich, in 1852.[2] This firm manufactured percussion single pistols and pepperboxes (notably, with the under-hammer action) which were marked "BACON & CO. NORWICH C-T." Thus, the style of his first firm was Bacon & Company and an advertisement featuring their under-hammer pepperbox is to be found in an early Connecticut directory.[3] It is evident that this first venture of Bacon was not marked with success or long tenure, as he must have been in straightened circumstances when certain of his debts were paid by Manhattan as a condition of the contract between them.

As will have been seen, Bacon severed his connection with Manhattan to form his second firm, the Bacon Manufacturing Company. According to the Stedman document, Bacon held a very prominent position in the new firm, since he was listed as a stockholder as well as the agent and principal manager of the corporation. We were able to find more than one reference to the founding of Bacon Manufacturing Company, including references in the Norwich town records. The announcement of incorporation first appeared in the Norwich *Evening Courier* on Thursday, November 11, 1858, as follows:

BACON MANUFACTURING COMPANY

Pursuant to the provisions of Chapter XIV, Title III, of the Revised Statutes of the State of Connecticut, entitled "An Act Concerning Communities and Corporations," and the Acts in addition to and alteration thereof, the sub-

PLATE 10. DEVELOPMENT MODELS .31-CALIBER MANHATTAN REVOLVER.

Figure 1. Five-Shot, Four-Inch Barrel, Number 37 (plain cylinder); ten stops.

Figure 2. Five-Shot, Four-Inch Barrel, Number 117 (cylinder: five panels of engraving, five stops; ball type loading lever latch).

Manhattan made liberal use of engraving and ivory grips in ornamenting the early examples in their line of .31 caliber revolvers. Despite the higher serial number, the gun shown as Figure 2 may have been made up before No. 37 and, due to its connection with Bacon, is considered to be an extreme rarity.

scribers do hereby associate and become a body corporate and politic, under the name of the

BACON MANUFACTURING COMPANY

The business of said corporation shall be the manufacture and sale of Fire Arms, and the purchase and sale of such materials as are required for the manufacture of said Fire Arms, to purchase and hold such personal and real estate and erect such buildings as may be required in said business.

The Corporate Stock of said Corporation shall be Twenty Thousand Dollars, and consist of Eight Hundred Shares of Twenty-five Dollars each; and the subscribers do hereby agree to pay for the number of shares of stock to their names respectively annexed. The principal office and place of business of said corporation shall be in the town of Norwich.

Dated at Norwich, this 9th day of November, A. D. 1858.

T. K. Bacon	Eighty Shares
W. Huntington	Eighty Shares
A. R. Bingham	Eighty Shares
John C. Luce	Eighty Shares
S. H. Grosvenor	Eighty Shares
John W. Stedman	Eighty Shares
Denison P. Coon	Eighty Shares
W. M. Converse	Forty Shares
T. P. Norton	Forty Shares
Wm. Peckham	Eighty Shares
Wm. H. Hyde	Eighty Shares

The reader will recall our earlier observation that Mr. John W. Stedman had more than a printer's interest in compiling and printing the document relating to the Manhattan *vs.* Bacon lawsuit. Mr. Stedman's interest and motivation are revealed, quite clearly, in the list of stockholders of the Bacon Manufacuring Company. Without inquiring further into Mr. Stedman's interests and motivations, we pause at this point to express our grateful thanks to the memory of this industrious Connecticut Yankee. His interest in the Manhattan *vs.* Bacon lawsuit, and the preservation of the details thereof, has provided the important structure of the Norwich phase of the story of Manhattan.

The details of announcement of the incorporation of Bacon's second venture indicate that Bacon cancelled his arrangement with Manhattan for what appears to be very limited interest in the ownership of the newly formed company. As we search into the story of Thomas K. Bacon, we get the impression that he was a man of great enthusiasm, strong convictions, considerable ability as an arms maker and possessed of a strong tendency to seek the answers to some of his problems in litigation.

Although there is evidence that the Bacon Manufacturing Company enjoyed more than average success for a few years, Bacon failed to find any real success or satisfaction in this second venture. By 1864, according to the town records, Bacon was no longer a shareholder in the company bearing his name. Charles A. Converse appears as a major stockholder, (he was one of Bacon's creditors when Manhattan paid off Bacon's indebtedness), as well as serving in the capacities of Treasurer and General Agent of the company. During this period (1858-1864), John W. Stedman became president of the company.

Bacon Manufacturing Company produced at least three types of percussion revolvers plus several types of cartridge revolvers and single-shot pistols. One of the percussion revolvers, it was probably the first type to be produced, was a close copy of Manhattan's .31-caliber revolver and differed in only one detail. The details of the Bacon copy of the Manhattan revolver will be discussed in a subsequent section.

In 1864, Thomas K. Bacon, by now excluded from the Bacon Manufacturing Company, founded another company: The Bacon Arms Company. This company represented Bacon's third venture in the arms manufacturing field and was probably his final venture. The capital of the company was $20,000.00, according to the town records. According to the Norwich Directory (now published by John W. Stedman), the capital was $30,000.00. The president of The Bacon Arms Company was H. H. Starkweather, one of Bacon's attorneys in the Manhattan lawsuit. In the 1865 directory, the capital of The Bacon Arms Company is given as $40,000.00. By 1868, Bacon Manufacturing Company has disappeared from the directories while The Bacon Arms Company continues to be listed.

Thomas K. Bacon was engaged in litigation on two occasions of which we have a record. The first was with Manhattan in 1858-1859. The second lawsuit was with Charles A. Converse in 1866, in which Bacon was again the defendant. The latter case was docketed for the January 1866 term of the Superior Court of New London, Connecticut; we were unable to ascertain the details and final disposition of the suit. It would seem that Charles A. Converse was some kind of nemesis in Bacon's business life, beginning as a creditor in 1857, later as a major stockholder in Bacon Manufacturing Company (from which company Bacon was excluded by 1864) and finally as a litigant with Bacon in 1866.

While this part of our tale is by no means a comprehensive study of his life, it would appear that Bacon never quite reached the top rung of success in the field of firearms manufacturing. The Bacon Arms Company was to continue in business until 1888, a span of twenty-four years, but there is reason to believe that Thomas K. Bacon was no longer on the scene, as of that date. In the Norwich Directory for 1881, we found the following listing: "Bacon, Thomas K., Mrs. bds, 92 Main St." We have been informed that the abbreviation "bds," as used in the directories of that period, meant "boards" or "rents a room."

Thus, if Mrs. Bacon was boarding or renting a room under her own name, Thomas K. Bacon was probably deceased.

It is our considered opinion that Thomas K. Bacon rendered valuable services to Manhattan during a period when the company sorely needed the technical contributions he could furnish. One can speculate, albeit idly so, on the possible futures of both Manhattan and Bacon if Albert Beach had signed Bacon's copy of their agreement of September 1, 1857.

REFERENCE NOTES

CHAPTER II.   1. *Colt Percussion Pistols*
                  James E. Serven
                  Dallas, Texas. Carl Metzger, 1947, page 9-11.
               2. *American Gun Makers*
                  Arcadi Gluckman & L. D. Satterlee
                  Harrisburg, Pa.: The Stackpole Co., 1953, page 10.
               3. *Pepperbox Firearms*
                  Lewis Winant
                  New York: Greenberg, 1952, page 55.

CHAPTER III

~~~~~~~~~~~~~~~~~~~~~~~~~~~~~~~~

THE MANHATTAN
PATENTS

IN OUR discussion of the schism between Manhattan and Bacon, we made reference to the fact that a new character, in the person of Augustus Rebetey, was standing in the wings, ready to move on stage in the Manhattan story. It is our opinion that Augustus Rebetey made the major contribution to the aspect of Manhattan's operations in which the collector is most interested: the design and production of the Manhattan revolvers.

Unfortunately, we know very little about Rebetey, the man. We learn, from the information in the files relating to the Manhattan patents, that Rebetey was a native of the Republic of Switzerland; that he had been a resident of the United States for a period of more than a year prior to March 1859 and that he had "taken the oath prescribed by law for becoming naturalized in this country." Rebetey was the inventor of two relatively unknown patents which were assigned to Manhattan and, in collaboration with Joseph Gruler, was the inventor of a third patent, also assigned to Manhattan; the latter became the best known and most valuable of the four Manhattan patents. Because of his obvious mechanical abilities, it is our opinion that Rebetey may have become superintendent

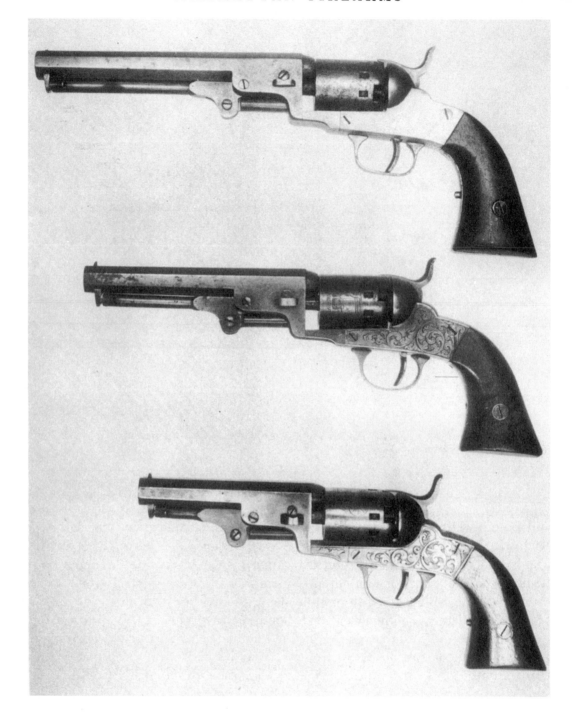

PLATE 11. SERIES I .31-CALIBER MANHATTAN REVOLVERS.

Figure 1. Five-Shot, Six-Inch Barrel, Number 50.

Figure 2. Five-Shot, Five-Inch Barrel, Number 23.

Figure 3. Five-Shot, Four-Inch Barrel, Number 411.

The first of three models of revolvers manufactured by the company, approximately 900 to 1000 Series I .31 caliber revolvers were produced during 1858-59. The gun shown as Figure 1 is an example of one of several variations in this series; frame, back-strap and trigger-guard lack the usual ornamentation of engraving and grips were enlarged by means of an extension attached to the butt. The enlarged grip became a standard feature of the Series II .31 caliber revolvers.

of Manhattan's manufactory following the departure of Bacon. Our information on Joseph Gruler is slightly more vague than on Augustus Rebetey. It is indicated, from the information contained in the patent files, that he was either a native of the Republic of Switzerland or of the Kingdom of Wittenberg, a city in the then Prussian state of Saxony.

The three patents referred to above, and in which Rebetey and Gruler were concerned, were filed within a period of twelve days, March 12, 1859, through March 24, 1859. The issuance of the third patent did not coincide with the relative filing and issue dates of the first two patents, as the third patent (filed March 24, 1859) required an additional five months for processing. As will be seen, there were good and sufficient reasons for this differential in time. Because of the hunger for details usually exhibited by collectors, much of the interesting data contained in the patent files will be reproduced.

The first patent was cleared for issuance on April 26, 1859. However, before clearance was effected, the following correspondence was passed between the Patent Office and the interested parties:

I

Norwich, Conn. March 9, 1859.

To the Commissioner of Patents

I send herewith, a model and papers for a Patent on a Frame etc. Please send the official documents to me directed here.

Respectfully
Albert Beach, Sec'y
The Manhattan Fire Arms Manuf. Co.

I have deposited $40 with the Assistant Treasurer of N. Y. and enclose receipt for the same.

A. B.

————————————

II

Newark NJ March 10, 1859.

To the Commissioner of Patents

I directed a model and documents to be sent today from NY. Also sent $40 to Assistant Treasurer to send receipt for that amount, but he retained only $30. If there are any extra charges, please inform me below.

Albert Beach, Secy
Manhattan Fire Arms Manuf. Co. NY
(address Norwich Conn.)

————————————

III

New York March 11, 1859.

Commissioner of Patents
     Patent Office
          Washington, DC

Sir

I have received the accompanying model & papers from Norwich Conn. which I forward to you by direction of "The Manhattan Fire Arms Manufacturing Company" on which you will please take action.

I have obtained duplicate receipts for the same from the Assistant Treasurer of the United States, on payment of Thirty Dollars ($30) & will forward you one (receipt) by mail & remain

Respectfully
S. H. Harrington
Agent
     for The M. F. A. Mafg. Co.

IV

Norwich Conn. March 15, 1859

To the Commissioner of Patents

A few days since I sent papers and model etc. for a Patent on a Frame to hold Side Plate of Pistol, assigned by Augustus Rebetey.

Please return the papers, retaining the model and money, that I may correct an error.

Respectfully
Albert Beach, Secy
Manhattan Fire Arms Manuf. Co.

V

(Washington, D. C.) April 1, 1859

A. Rebetey
     Care S. H. Harrington
          New York

The specification and drawing of your Improvement on Making pistols are herewith returned. The letters of reference on the drawing are found not to correspond. A statement of what you regard as your invention should be inserted in the specification previous to the reference to the drawings.

Foreman

(Note: E. Foreman was the Patent Examiner in this case).

VI

Newark NJ April 9, 1859

To the Commissioner of Patents

The drawing herewith, that was returned to me with specification etc. enclosed, belongs to another specification sent about the same time.

Respectfully

A Rebetey

per A Beach

For A Rebetey

J Gruler

or Manhattan Fire Arms Manuf. Co

hereafter please address at Newark NJ

———————————

VII

(Washington, DC) April 15, 1859

Augustus Rebetey

care S. H. Harrington New York

Your application for Improvement in Making Pistols being under examination, it is perceived that the claim is somewhat more general in its form than is admissable, as it is common to use a frame or pattern for tracing or cutting out corresponding figures. A slight alteration is therefore suggested, restricting the claim to the precise invention made by you. The specification is returned for the necessary amendment, which should be made on a separate sheet of paper.

Foreman

———————————

VIII

Newark N. J. April 22, 1859

To the Commissioner of Patents

I desire that the claim for improvements on Tools for the manufacture of Pistols (consisting of the use of a Frame to hold the side plate of a pistol, etc) may be amended so as to read thus—as below

Respectfully

Augustus Rebetey

A

(Amended Claim, etc)

What I claim as my invention and desire to secure by letters patent is:

The use of a Frame, constructed as herein described, having a profile in one plate of it, to shape and finish a corresponding recess in the side plate of a Pistol, by means of a revolving cutter, governed by the outlines of such profile.

Augustus Rebetey

Witnesses: Joseph Gruler

Albert Beach

———————————

IX

Newark N J April 22, 1859

To the Commissioner of Patents

Not knowing whether the enclosed amended claim is proper in form, etc, I will be obliged if you will deliver all the papers to some competent person, and request him for me to write out just what is proper to be signed, and inform me as to the amount of his fee, which I will remit on signing, and so of either of the other papers from A. Rebetey or J. Gruler assigned to the Manhattan Co.

I suppose that a compliance with the above request is not inconsistent with your duties to the public, and will be the least troublesome course.

Respectfully
Augustus Rebetey

———————

Rebetey's concern over the issuance of his first patent, indicated in IX, above, was groundless; the patent was cleared for issuance immediately upon receipt of the amended claim. This letter was in Beach's handwriting, although signed by Rebetey, and this procedure appears to have been followed in all of Rebetey's direct correspondence with the Patent Office.

Another point of interest is developed in VI, above, which is dated April 9, 1859. The last line reads: "hereafter please address at Newark, N. J." The reader will recall that Manhattan was planning to move to Newark during the latter part of 1858, according to the information contained in the details of the Manhattan *vs.* Bacon lawsuit. Apparently, the removal of the Manhattan plant from Norwich to Newark had been effected prior to April 9, 1859. We will be able to pinpoint the exact date in a subsequent exhibit from the correspondence relating to the third patent.

The details of the drawing and specifications of the first patent, No. 23,990, are shown on the following page.

The issuance of the second patent, covering the use of a tool for cutting the eccentric area in the slot of a barrel lug and bearing serial No. 23,994, was much more uneventful than was the case of the first patent. At least, issuance of the second patent was secured with a minimum of nervous correspondence on the part of Beach and Rebetey.

However, the preamble of the application for the second patent contained an unusual request. The application was drawn up on the 14th of March, 1859, in what appears to be the handwriting of Albert Beach, and was notarized by Levi H. Goddard. The request is made in the last sentence of the preamble: "and he (Augustus Rebetey) requests that Letters Patent may be dated March 14th, 1859." This was a needless statement because, if a patent was to be forth-

A. REBETEY.

Tools for Manufacturing Pistols.

No. 23,990. Patented May 10, 1859.

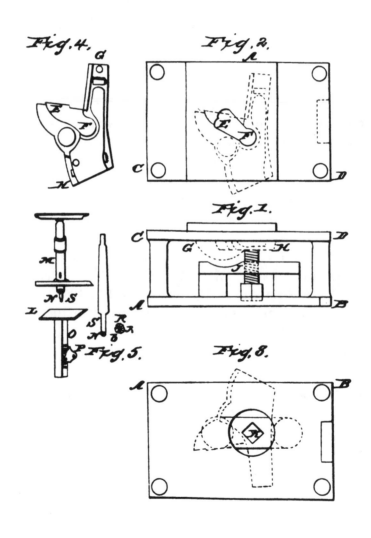

UNITED STATES PATENT OFFICE.

AUGUSTUS REBETEY, OF NORWICH, CONNECTICUT, ASSIGNOR TO MANHATTAN FIRE ARMS MANUF'G CO., OF NEW YORK, N. Y.

TOOL FOR MANUFACTURING PISTOLS

Specification of Letters Patent No. 23,936, dated May 10, 1859.

To all whom it may concern:

Be it known that I, AUGUSTUS REBETEY, of the city of Norwich, in the county of New London and State of Connecticut, have
5 invented certain new and useful Improvements in Tools for the Manufacture of Fire arms; and I do hereby declare that the following is a full and exact description thereof, reference being had to the accompanying
10 drawings, and to the letters of reference thereon.

In the manufacture of a certain kind of pistol, it is desirable, to have a recess, in the side plate thereof, finished smooth, on all its
15 surfaces, and of uniform figure, so that the side plate of one pistol, will answer for any other, of same description. This result cannot be well accomplished by hand tools, and the nature of my invention, consists in the
20 use of a frame, in which, any successive number of side plates, may be regularly adjusted, and a uniform recess cut in each, by means of a revolving cutter, guided by the outlines of a figure or profile in one
25 plate of such frame.

To enable others to comprehend and use my invention, I describe its operation.

A B C D Figure 1, represents, an elevation, and C D Fig. 2, a view of upper plate,
30 and A B Fig. 3, of bottom plate of a frame, to hold the side plate of a cylinder pistol, for the purpose of finishing a recess therein.

The upper plate C D, of frame Fig. 2 has an opening E F in it, shaped like the recess
35 to be finished in the side plate.

The side plate G H Fig. 4, of pistol has a rough recess E F cast in it, which may be finished smooth, by fastening such side plate G H as seen in Fig. 4, by means of the screw I, so that the rough recess, will coincide with the profile E F, in the upper plate C D of frame Fig. 2.

K Fig. 2 represents the head of screw I, Fig. 4, which is operated by a wrench in-
45 troduced through the circular opening in bottom plate of frame.

If the frame Fig. 1, containing the side plate G H, be placed on the bed L of a drill press, and the spindle M, carrying the cutter
50 N (two views of the cutter being shown in Figs. 5 and 6) be revolved rapidly, and the bed L of drill press be elevated, by the rack O and pinion P, so that the flat face R of cutter N, will press against the flat surface
55 of recess E F in side plate, G H, and the frame, A B C D, be moved about, on the bed L of drill press, governed by the shank S of cutter N, bearing against the outlines of profile E F, in upper plate of frame the
60 rough edges of recess in side plate, will be smoothed by the teeth on periphery of cutter N and the flat surface of recess, will be smoothed by the teeth on that face of cutter, in a uniform and expeditious manner.

What I claim as my invention and de-
65 sire to secure by Letters Patent is—

The use of a frame, constructed as herein described, having a profile in one plate of it, to shape and finish a corresponding recess in the side plate of a pistol, by means
70 of a revolving cutter, governed by the outlines of such profile.

AUGUSTUS REBETEY.

Witnesses:
JOSEPH GRULER,
ALBERT BEACH.

coming, the period of protection would have included the date of notarization of the application as a matter of usual procedure.

Apparently, Beach recognized the impropriety of the request within a few days. Under date of March 24, 1859, he addressed a letter from Norwich to the Commissioner of Patents which states in part, "If the petition and assignment of March 14th contained a request to ante date, ... then I request . . . . . . that such request may not exist."

It should be pointed out that while the specification of the second patent does not contain the reference to an assignment of the patent to Manhattan by Rebetey, the assignment was contained in the preamble of the original application. The omission of the assignment was an apparent oversight by the Patent Examiner, Mr. E. Foreman.

We wish to call attention to the last four words of the final sentence of the specification for the foregoing patent: "For the purpose of cutting an eccentric shaped slot in the barrel of a *pistol, or any thing else.*" This wordage implies considerably more latitude than is usually granted by the Patent Office. If the practical application of the patent had not been rather narrowly restricted, a large potential for profit would have existed. "Any thing else" covers a very large field, indeed.

The events contributing to the issuance of the third patent, No. 26,641, were the most interesting of any of the Manhattan patents. In fact, some of the events were quite turbulent. The turbulence was developed by Manhattan's strong convictions with regard to the claim relating to the side-plate type of construction of their .31-caliber revolvers. Although this claim was to be ultimately denied by the Patent Office, the denial was confirmed following a full review of the facts by the Commissioner of Patents and the other members of the Board and represented an unusual amount of consideration.

It should be noted that the original application covered two principal areas of claims: (1) relating to the side-plate type of construction for revolvers and (2) the use of intermediate cylinder stops for purposes of safety (in the case of 5-shot cylinders, for purposes of loading the cylinder, also). The application was originally drawn on the 14th of March, 1859; the papers were received by the Patent Office on March 25th, 1859, along with one part of the model (a second part of the model was received on March 28th); the patent was cleared for issuance on November 16th, 1859, and was finally issued on December 27th, 1859.

Certain parts of the correspondence which preceded issuance of the patent, together with deductive comments, are considered important to a full understanding of this phase of the Manhattan story. Manhattan must have had more than one important struggle during the fifteen years of its tenure in the firearms

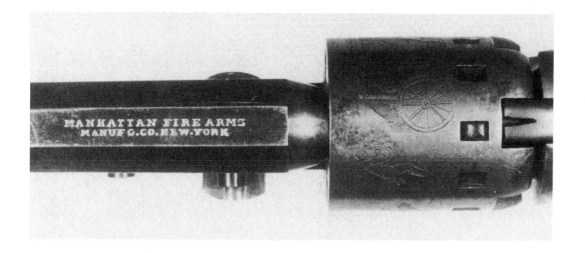

PLATE 12. BARREL SIGNING FOR .31-CALIBER REVOLVERS, SERIES I.

The mode of the barrel signing is one of the distinguishing features of the revolvers in this series. The signing is unlike any other used in identifying Manhattan's arms and is the rarest to be found in the revolver categories.

A. REBETEY.

Manufacture of Fire Arms.

No. 23,944. Patented May 10, 1859.

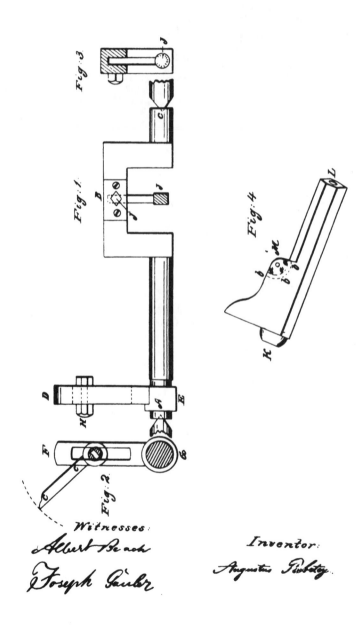

Witnesses
Albert Beach
Joseph Gauler

Inventor:
Augustus Rebetey.

UNITED STATES PATENT OFFICE.

AUGUSTUS REBETEY, OF NORWICH, CONNECTICUT.

TOOL FOR MANUFACTURE OF FIREARMS.

Specification of Letters Patent No. 23.944. dated May 10, 1859.

To all whom it may concern:

Be it known that I. AUGUSTUS REBETEY, of the city of Norwich. in the county of New London and State of Connecticut. have in-
5 vented certain new and useful Improve-ments in Tools for the Manufacture of Fire-arms; and I do hereby declare that the fol-lowing is a full and exact description there-of, reference being had to the accompanying
10 drawings and to the letters of reference thereon.

A B C, Figure 1. represents a crank shaft suspended in an engine lathe at centers A, C.
15 D E. Fig. 1, represents an arm attached to the crank shaft. and F G. Fig. 2, a similar arm, to be attached to the counter shaft of lathe. The arm F G. is shorter than that of D E, so that a revolution of F G. will
20 produce only a partial revolution or a vibra-tion of D E. The arm D E, receives motion from that of F, G. by means of a rod. c. c. attached to the bolt H. on arm D E and a similar bolt on arm F. G. Each arm has
25 a slot, within which the bolt is secured by a nut so that the length of throw of the crank shaft may be varied.

I, Figs. 1 and 3. represents a cutter. se-cured to crank shaft by screw J.
30 K L, Fig. 4. represents a barrel of a cylin-der pistol. The barrel Fig. 4 has a slot cut in it by a circular cutter, as shown by the dotted lines, a, a, a. The shape of this slot is a part of a circle, having its center at M.

But it is essential that the circular or bottom 35 surface of such slot, Fig. 4. be deepened. so that it will become eccentric to the point M. and this cannot be effected by an ordi-nary revolving. circular cutter. To accom-plish this the barrel Fig. 4 is secured to the 40 tool rest of a lathe. in a position similar to that shown in Fig. 4. and the counter shaft of lathe. being caused to revolve. will cause the crank shaft. A B C, carrying the cutter I. to vibrate. If the barrel Fig. 4 be moved 45 by the screw attached to the tool rest of lathe. toward the cutter I. the slot a a a in barrel will thereby be deepened to an eccentric shape. similar to the dotted line b b b. as shown in Fig. 4 in a quick and complete 50 manner. The shape and position of the slot may be varied by raising or lowering the tool rest. by means of the ordinary screw for that purpose. at the outer end of tool rest.

What I claim as my invention. and de- 55 sire to secure by Letters Patent is:—

The use of a crank shaft A. B. C. to carry a cutter I. such crank shaft. suspended at the centers of an engine lathe. or any similar machine. and receiving its motion from the 60 counter shaft. of such lathe or similar ma-chine. For the purpose of cutting an ec-centric shaped slot in the barrel of a pistol. or any thing else.

AUGUSTUS REBETEY.

Witnesses:
ALBERT BEACH,
L. H. GODDARD.

field. The prosecution of this particular patent case furnishes the evidence of one such struggle. One of the most interesting facets of the case is contained in the narrative of the patent application.

I

(Norwich, Conn. March 14, 1859)

Be it known that we Joseph Gruler and Augustus Rebetey of the City of Norwich, in the County of New London and State of Connecticut have invented certain new and useful improvements in the revolving or repeating firearm: and we do hereby describe and ascertain the same, referring to the accompanying drawings, in which Fig. 1, is a side-elevation of the pistol, with the side plate and portion of the recoil plate affixed thereto, detached and shown below, in perspective at a. Fig. 2, a revolving chamber, cylinder detached. Fig. 3, spring *i*, detached.

These improvements are for the purpose of remedying certain difficulties and defects in the construction and practical operation of the well known "Revolver," as made by Samuel Colt (*sic.*), by which its construction is simplified and cheapened, and the machinery therefor reduced.

The first is an improvement upon the present form of constructing the recoil and lock plates in one piece, which involves several difficulties, among which are the forming of the small recess or chamber in which the pawl or dog *b* works, and against the rear side of which the spring *c* of said dog bears and slides: —and, further, the great difficulty of fitting the works into the pistol, out of the sight of the operative. In such a pistol, there is a recess for the parts of the lock, open at top and bottom, requiring to be covered by separate pieces. The recess above named had to be worked out by special tools made for the purpose, and was carried clear down through. Besides, in such a pistol, the small spring for governing the stop and trigger must be secured· by a screw to the lock-frame. In consequence of the inability of the workman to see the parts of this pistol, after they are put in place, owing to the construction of the lock-plate, they cannot, with any certainty, be altered, if made inexact; —and, consequently, an expensive outlay for machinery and tools is required to manufacture advantageously on such a plan. The lock-frame, being open at bottom, requires a bottom plate to be screwed on to cover it, which is dispensed with in the improvement about to be described.—

The piece forming the lock-plate and recoil plate is divided into two parts, so as to remove one portion of the lock-plate and recoil plate from one side, and thus open up the whole interior of the lock. In this portion of the lock-plate removed, is found the recess *a*, in which the dog *b*, and spring *c*, play. It will be perceived that this recess can be cast into the plate by a simple casting, without using a core therefor, or any expensive chasing out of the recess, as heretofor practiced. This cheapens the manufacture, and renders the arm easy to repair and clean by a common workman with ordinary tools. The other portion is also a simple casting, including the recess for the lock, and that for the stop *d*, under the cylinder. The pin *g* for the hammer to turn on, and the pin *f* for the trigger, can be cast into the recess in the stationary part of the lock-frame, or otherwise fastened therein, and the spring *i*, that acts upon the stop *d*, is put into the recess at *h*, and the spring is shown at Fig. 3. This requires no screw to hold it, that is liable to work loose. All the parts of the lock can be put into place and worked, —and their operation inspected while exposed to view, and any part thereof removed or adjusted by ordinary tools: —the parts to which the working pieces of the lock are affixed, being stationary and permanent, and the side plate simply removable.

(Note: the drawing depicting the parts to which the alphabetical letters of reference applied, as set forth in this portion of the narrative, was apparently the original drawing, subsequently modified, and is not available in the file for this patent.)

The other important change, is the addition of recesses, around the revolving chamber at *rr*, between those lettered *ss*, that stop the chamber at the proper point for discharging. These additional recesses *rr*, serve to hold the chamber in the just position to have the hammer fall between the nipple (s) or cones. By this construction, the device for holding the cylinder by the hammer is dispensed with, and the intermediate stop is self-acting, rendering it much easier of application than the hammer-stop, and involving no expense except that of forming the recesses *r*.

To effect this desirable object, the cylinder is not chambered clear down to the recesses at the britch (*sic.*), but the recesses are made in the solid part of the cylinder, otherwise they would cut through or so weaken the cylinder at the chamber so as to be dangerous, or spoil the arm. The recesses *rr*, hold the pistol at the proper point for loading, and at this time the hammer falls between the cones, instead of falling upon them. The construction of the working parts of the lock is such that the stop *d*, is held back until the recess *r* revolves past it, if the pistol be cocked: but if the stop be merely detached by drawing back the hammer a short distance, the cylinder can be turned until the stop catches. This action can be performed with the pistol out of sight, with one hand, if desired, which is not the case when the hammer is used for the center stop.

Having thus fully set forth our improvements, what we claim as new, and for which we desire Letters Patent, is, First, the employment of the removable plate *a*, having a recess formed therein, constructed and arranged in the manner and for the purposes set forth. We also claim the additional series of stops *rr*, in the revolving chamber as, and for the purposes, described.

Joseph Gruler
Augustus Rebetey

In the presence of
Levi H. Goddard
Albert Beach

(Note: A comparison of the details of the above portion of the narrative with the patent drawing, as issued, further indicate that there was an original drawing which differed widely from the issued drawing.)

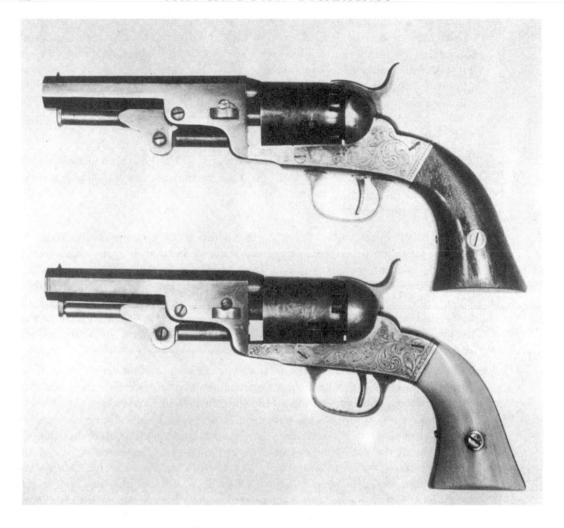

PLATE 13. BACON COPIES OF MANHATTAN .31-CALIBER REVOLVERS.

Figure 1. Five-Shot, Four-Inch Barrel, Number 169.

Figure 2. Five-Shot, Four-Inch Barrel, Number 311.

Believed to be the first model of revolver produced by Bacon Mfg. Company, the above examples are close copies of Manhattan's Series I .31 caliber revolvers. Dissimilar features of the Bacon are ball-type loading lever latch and design of engraving on cylinder and on frame. It is probable that fewer than 1000 of this model were manufactured; gun shown as Figure 2 is unusual due to additional engraving and ivory grips.

Evidence of the exact date of the removal of Manhattan's manufactory from Norwich, Conn. to Newark, N. J., is contained in a letter to the Commissioner of Patents written by Albert Beach from Norwich on March 24th, 1859, which was concluded, as follows:

Please address any letters *after* Tuesday, March 29th (1859) to either Joseph Gruler, Augustus Rebetey or Manhattan Fire Arms Manuf. Co. to Newark, N. J.
Respectfully
for Augustus Rebetey
Joseph Gruler
and Manhattan Fire Arms Manuf. Co
(s) Albert Beach.

It has been established that the third patent was applied for by Joseph Gruler and Augustus Rebetey, jointly, as assignors to Manhattan, and that the claims covered two general areas. We believe it will prove interesting to speculate as to which one of the claims may have been originated by Gruler and vice versa. Some evidence as to the orgin of the claims is found in two letters written to the Commissioner of Patents by Albert Beach:

Norwich, Conn. March 19, 1859.
To the Commissioner of Patents
I enclose $11 with specifications, etc. and model for Patent on invention by Joseph Gruler, and Augustus Rebetey.
$20 was sent by Joseph Gruler in Oct. last which was intended for this application and a partial caveat was then filed.
Albert Beach, Sec'y
Manhattan Fire Arms Manuf. Co.

————————

Newark N. J. April 6, 1859.
To the Commissioner of Patents
I enclose $20 to pay balance of fee on application for Patent of Joseph Gruler and Augustus Rebetey.
Sometime in Oct. last (I think) $20 was sent as caveat fee of Joseph Gruler, and the frame of pistol with it.
This was for the same affair, and if not improper I would like to have that $20 applied and this $20 returned.
I think I did not state in the papers that the applicants were natives of the Republic of Switzerland. If such is the case, I would like to have the papers returned but not otherwise.
Please address for either of us at this place instead of Norwich, Conn.
Respectfully
A. Beach, Sec'y
Manhattan Fire Arms Manuf. Co.

I sent $11 with the model
$10 was for balance
$1 was for recording assignment.

Thus, it may be deduced that Joseph Gruler was the originator of the claim relating to the side-plate type of revolver design and that Augustus Rebetey was the originator of the claim relating to the use of intermediate stops on the cylinder.

Further, we believe that the filing of a caveat fee in October 1858 may have been connected with the separation of Bacon from Manhattan's employ in September 1858.

The record of the first action of the Patent Office on the application for the third patent is contained in the following letter:

U.S. Patent Office
Washington, April 30th/59.

Sir:

Your specification is herewith returned to you, in consequence of informality in the oath. See 14th Article of the accompanying Rules and Directions.

Respectfully
(unsigned)

Messrs. Joe. Gruler & A. Rebetey,
Care of Manhattan Fire Arms Comp'y
Newark, N. J.

The deficiency in the original oath was corrected by a revised oath, drawn up in Newark and dated May 9, 1859.

(Note: the revised oath stated that Joseph Gruler was a native of the Kingdom of Wittenberg.)

Followed then, a letter from the Patent Office which set off a bitter battle with Manhattan that was to endure for six months. While the engagement was to end in a draw, the outcome undoubtedly operated to the disadvantage of Manhattan and, in all likelihood, was a determining factor in Manhattan's future policies and plans.

U. S. Patent Office
Washington, May 21st, 1859.

Gents:

Your claims to letters patent for Improvements in Firearms, have been examined, and rejected, for want of novelty in the device.

For the subject matter of the first claim, see Ethan Allen's Patent of Dec. 15th, 1857.

For that of the 2nd claim, see James Warner's Patent of July 15th, 1851; and E. K. Root's Patent of Dec. 25th, 1855.

Respectfully,

Jos. Gruler & Augustus Rebetey
Care of Manhattan Fire Arms Manuf. Co.
Newark, N. J.

(Note: the above letter (or copy) was unsigned; it was probably written by the examiner in this case).

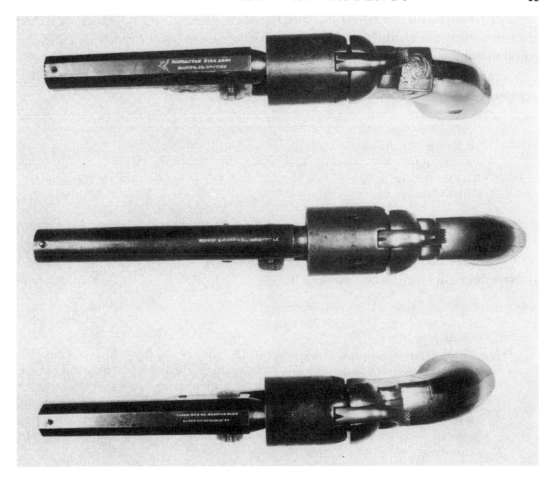

PLATE 14. CASE OF THE WANDERING ENGRAVING DIE.

Figure 1. Manhattan: Five-Shot, Four-Inch Barrel, Number 117.

Figure 2. Hopkins & Allen: Five-Shot, Five-Inch Barrel, Number 796.

(From the collection of Sam. E. Smith)

Figure 3. Bacon: Five-Shot, Four-Inch Barrel, Number 178.

Depicting a rare circumstance, this plate shows application of the same engraving die to the cylinders of revolvers produced by three different arms makers. Progressive usage appears to have been: (1) Manhattan Fire Arms Mfg. Co., (2) Bacon Mfg. Co. and (3) Hopkins & Allen Mfg. Co. Signing on the barrel of the Bacon revelover "Bacon Mfg. Co. Norwich, Conn.—Depot 297 Broadway NY," may be quite rare. Usual signing for this model is "Bacon Mfg. Co.—Norwich, Conn.," in two lines.

On August 4th, 1859, Gruler and Rebetey drew up an amended specification of claims which did not, however, differ very much in context from the original claims.

Accompanying the amended specification of claims was the following certification from Beach:

New York August 5, 1859

The Manhattan Fire Arms Manufacturing Company, of NY, hereby authorise J. James Greenough to act in their behalf, in procuring a Patent on a Pistol,—application having been made by Augustus Rebetey—and Joseph Gruler—for such Patent they having assigned it to the said Manhattan Fire Arms Manuf. Co.

Albert Beach, Secy
Manhattan Fire Arms Manuf. Co.

The second rejection by the Patent Office was sent out after what appears to have been an appropriate lapse of time:

(Washington, D. C.)
Sept. 30, 1859

Gentlemen:

Your application for Improvement in Fire Arms has been re-examined with reference to your amended claims filed Sept. 3rd. The Office can however perceive no essential novelty in either point presented, in view of the references formerly given. As regards the purpose of the recess in the removable side-plate, this is a mere question of use—which does not affect the novelty, or absence of novelty in the device itself. Your application must accordingly be a second time rejected.

Respectfully
(unsigned)

J. Gruler & A. Rebetey
Care of J. J. Greenough
N. York

——————————

Mr. J. James Greenough, a terse and outspoken individual, now moves in to fully enjoin the issue:

(New York)
Oct. 5th, 1859

Commissioner of Patents
Sir:

Our application for Patent having been a second time rejected on the original reference we hereby appeal from the examiner's decision for reasons already given after the first rejection. We do not consider the reference pertinent. The devices for stopping the cylinder intermediate, to which reference is made, are complex and inefficient and involve more expense than ours, while there is more difficulty in setting the cylinder in that position than by our device. The recess that we chase into our movable plate is not to be found in the reference but instead thereof there is an accidental recess or hollow made to tighten the casting simply. We say accidental because it would not have been made but for the fact that the casting is curved on the outside. It was intended for no such purpose as ours nor could it be used for the same purpose as is apparent from the most casual observation. We therefore submit that in view of these references all our claims should be allowed.

Respectfully,
Gruler & Rebetey
per J. J. Greenough

(Note: J. J. Greenough was an attorney and a very competent one on fire-arms patents as shown in footnote.[1] The contents of his letter referred to the Allen, Warner and Root patents which formed the basis for rejection of Manhattan's claims by the Patent Office.)

Greengough's letter was responsible for the following report, apparently prepared within the Patent Office for review by the Commissioner of Patents and the Board:

Application of *Joseph Gruler*)
& *Augustus Rebetey,* for a   )
patent for an improved   )
Fire-arm.   )

Patent Office
Nov. 3rd, 1859

Sir:

The applicants claim first, "the use of a removable side plate having a recess therein, constructed specifically to receive a dog and guide it by means of a spring attached thereto so that the cylinder will be revolved when the pistol is being cocked—such spring pressing against the rear edge of such recess and so variously guiding the dog in the act of cocking and firing the pistol, in combination with the use of such dog, as and for the purpose described."

Referring to the specification we find that the object of this combination

---

[1] J. J. Greenough was a prominent witness in the Colt vs Mass. Arms Co. patent suit of 1851. The following excerpts, concerning himself, are from his testimony as given during the trial:

I am a mechanical engineer—have been engaged for some years as a Solicitor of Patents. Was engaged as counsel for Mr. Wesson (Edwin) in obtaining his letters-patent (Wesson & Leavitt revolver). My residence is in Washington. I was retained by Messrs. Wesson & Leavitt to oppose the extension of Colt's patent (in 1849). I was in the Patent Office for some years, four or five or six years, I do not recall exactly—was an assistant examiner part of the time and also was principal examiner a short time.

Ref.: *The Trial of Samuel Colt;* Rywell, pages 173-199.
    GUN COLLECTOR, issue #41, page 738.

and arrangement of these devices is to permit all the parts of the lock to be put into place and worked while the side plate is displaced so that the operation can be inspected and any part of the lock removed or adjusted by ordinary tools;—the parts to which the working pieces of the lock are affixed being stationary and permanent, and the side plate simply removable. But this object is not fully attained by the applicants, for, while the side plate is removed the pawl is without guide or stay, and the shock of the hammer on the nipple when the pistol is snapped, throws it and its spring from their position unless firmly held and guided by the workman. This, however, is not a defect incident to Allen's arm patents (of) Dec. 15, 1857; for, while like Gruler & Rebetey's, that has a side plate with a recess therein on the removal of which all the working parts of the lock are exposed to view, such removal of the side plate does not remove also the hold and guide of the pawl and spring. But the attorney for the assignees of the applicants denies the main fact:—he says, "the recess that we chase into our movable plate is not to be found in the reference, but instead thereof there is an accidental recess or hollow made to tighten the casting simply. We say accidental, because it would not have been made but for the fact that the casting is curved on the outside. It was intended for no such purpose as ours, nor could it be used for the same purpose, as is apparent from the most casual observation."

Now, passing the apparent contradiction in the first part of the first paragraph, it is as clear as anything can be that Allen's removable plate is not "curved on the outside" at that point opposite to which the recess occurs; and it is no less clear that this recess is not "accidental" because if it were omitted the plate could not be screwed upon its seat:—the surface of the pawl extending up above the plane of said seat.

As to the *intention* of an inventor in the production of a particular device we need not, in any case, particularly inquire. The question is:—"Is the thing shown?" If it be shown its existence cannot be ignored whether it owe its being to accident or to design. But we have said enough above to make it plain that this recess in the removable plate of Allen's revolver was, in the words of the applicant's claim *designed* "specifically to receive a dog." (or pawl); and it requires no minute examination to make it apparent that "it could be used" as a guide for the said dog through the instrumentality of the spring "pressing against the rear edge of the said recess" if it should be preferred to adopt a plan under which the spring would be inoperative on the removal of the plate.

Finally, touching this claim, we fully agree with the Examiner when he says that the *"purpose* of the recess in the removable side plate is a mere question of *use* which does not affect the novelty or absence of novelty in the device itself."

The applicants claim, second, "the use of the immediate recesses rr in combination with the stop d actuated by the hammer in pistols where the cylinder is rotated in the act of cocking the pistol as described, thereby effecting a self acting lock of the cylinder or otherwise between any two cones." (Note: the foregoing quotation is from Gruler and Rebetey's amended claim of August 4, 1859.)

PLATE 15. NEPPERHAN COPY OF MANHATTAN .31-CALIBER REVOLVER.

Five-Shot, Four-and-a-Quarter-Inch Barrel, Number 4356.

Produced in Yonkers, N. Y., the Nepperhan revolver featured side-plate construction and a lock mechanism similar to·Manhattan's .31 caliber revolver. Dissimilar features are non-integral trigger-guard of brass, bearing wheel on hammer and location of rear side-plate screw.

We need not particularly describe the elements embraced in this claim, nor the manner in which in conjunction they operate to effect the desired result. It is sufficient to observe that we have carefully examined Warner's patent of July 15, 1851, and Root's patent of Dec. 25, 1855—the references in this connection—and notice, with respect to the former, that it has the precise evil it is the applicants' design and object to cure. Warner holds his cylinder in intermediate positions by means of the hammer which is not described as working automatically, while by the applicants' construction the device for holding the cylinder by the "hammer is dispensed with, and the intermediate stop is self acting." As regards the latter (Root's patent) it has both the spring and the loading stops, but the cylinder is not revolved nor locked by the operation of the hammer but by the trigger, and under such an arrangement of subordinate devices as leads to a complication of manipulation which, we should think, would not conduce materially to coolness in the field nor to rapidity of firing.

It has however suggested itself to our minds that these intermediate recesses are but duplications of the ordinary recesses in revolvers, but reflection finds a sufficient answer to this in the fact that the claim does not rest solely upon the intermediate recesses; it involves also the stop *d* and such a disposition of the mechanism as enables the stop *d* to serve the purpose of locking the cylinder in both positions. If the Examiner had produced a pistol in which the stop was actuated by the hammer as in the applicants case and the applicants had done nothing more than add the intermediate recesses the result might have been different. As it is we think there is a sufficient distinction between *Gruler & Rebetey's* implement and those patented to Warner & Root to justify the allowance of this claim.

We accordingly recommend that the first claim in this application be finally rejected, and such claim being erased and the specification being amended to correspond therewith, that a patent be ordered to issue on the second claim alone.

> Respectfully submitted
> A. B. Little
> Rufus R. Rhodes
> DeWitt C. Lawrence"

Hon. W. D. Bishop)
Com'r of Patents   )

(Note: the hand-written report appears to have been written by Mr. A. B. Little).

The report carries the following appendage, in what appears to be the hand-writing of Mr. W. D. Bishop:

> The foregoing report is confirmed and patent allowed on the 2nd claim, the first claim being first erased and the amendments made as suggested by the Board.
>
> Wm. D. Bishop
> Com'r.

Nov. 5th, 1859

The official notice of the action taken by the Commissioner of Patents was contained in the following letter:

U. S. Patent Office
Washington, Nov. 7th/59

Gents:

Your application for letters patent, for Improvements in Fire Arms, has been examined on appeal; and the "patent allowed on the 2nd claim; the first claim being first erased, & the amendments made, as suggested by the Board"; for reasons on file.

Respectfully
(unsigned)

J. Gruler & A. Rebetey
Care of J. J. Greenough, Esq.
New York City

Thus, the efforts of J. J. Greenough in filing an appeal from the Examiner's second rejection were partially successful. While Albert Beach was commendably persistent in pursuing the objectives of the patent application, it may be reasonably assumed that he was totally inexperienced and inept in such matters. Beach could have made no better move than to retain Greenough, or someone like him, to direct Manhattan's prosecution of the case.

There was some additional correspondence between the Patent Office and Greenough, dealing with the amendments required by the Board, before the patent was finally cleared for issuance on November 16, 1859. The patent, assigned serial No. 26,641, was issued on December 27, 1859.

A study of the drawing for this patent reveals at least two discrepancies between the specification and the drawing. The first discrepancy is evident in the side elevation of the cylinder, in which the intermediate recesses in the cylinder are not delineated. The drawing indicates only one recess per chamber instead of two recesses per chamber as required to meet the description of the specification. In view of the events surrounding the procurement of the patent, it seems little short of ludicrous that this important detail should have been omitted. The omission may have been an oversight; on the other hand, the element of a possible attempt towards deception of would-be competitors may have been present. The latter procedure of deception is not unknown in patent matters and may have been practiced in this case. In any event, the specification and the drawing are certainly not in accord on this important detail.

The second discrepancy between the specification and the drawing is indicated in the end view of the cylinder. The last sentence of the third paragraph of the specification refers to the use of the intermediate recesses for purposes of loading, as follows: "The recesses *rr* hold the pistol at the proper point for loading, and at this time the hammer falls between the two cones, instead of

J. GRULER & A. REBETEY.
REVOLVING FIRE ARM.

No 26,641.   Patented Dec. 27, 1859.

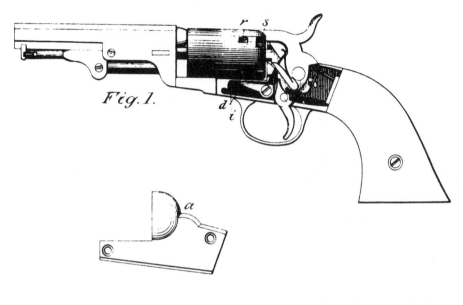

Fig.1.

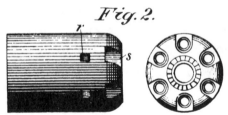

Fig.2.

Fig.3.

Witnesses.   *Inventor.*

UNITED STATES PATENT OFFICE.

JOS. GRULER AND AUGUSTUS REBETEY, OF NORWICH, CONNECTICUT, AS-
SIGNORS TO THE MANHATTAN FIRE-ARMS MANUFACTURING COMPANY,
OF NEW YORK, N. Y.

IMPROVEMENT IN REVOLVING FIRE-ARMS.

Specification forming part of Letters Patent No. **26,641,** dated December 27, 1859.

To all whom it may concern:

Be it known that we, JOSEPH GRULER and AUGUSTUS REBETEY, of the city of Norwich, in the county of New London and State of Connecticut, have invented certain new and useful Improvements in Revolving or Repeating Fire-Arms; and we do hereby describe and ascertain the same, referring to the accompanying drawings, in which—

Figure 1 is a side elevation of the pistol, with the side plate and portion of the recoil-plate affixed thereto detached and shown below in perspective at *a;* Fig. 2, a revolving chamber-cylinder detached; Fig. 3, spring *i* detached.

The important change is the addition of recesses around the revolving chamber at *r r,* between those lettered *s s,* that stop the chamber at the proper point for discharging, in combination with the stop actuated by the hammer. These additional recesses *r r* serve to hold the chamber in the just position to have the hammer fall between the nipples or cones. By this construction the device for holding the cylinder by the hammer is dispensed with, and the intermediate stop is self-acting, rendering it much easier of application than the hammer-stop and involving no expense, except that of forming the recesses *r.* To effect this desirable object the cylinder is not chambered clear down to the recesses at the breech, but the re-cesses are made in the solid part of the cylinder; otherwise they would cut through or so weaken the cylinder at the chamber as to be dangerous or spoil the arm. The recesses *r r* hold the pistol at the proper point for loading, and at this time the hammer falls between the cones, instead of falling upon them.

The construction of the working parts of the lock is such that the stop *d* is held back until the recess *r* revolves past it, if the pistol be cocked; but if the stop be merely detached by drawing back the hammer a short distance the cylinder can be turned until the stop catches. This action can be performed with the pistol out of sight, with one hand, if desired, which is not the case when the hammer is used for the center-stop.

We claim—

The use of the intermediate recesses, *r r,* in combination with the stop *d,* actuated by the hammer, in pistols where the cylinder is revolved in the act of cocking the pistol, as herein described, thereby effecting a self-acting lock of the cylinder, midway or otherwise between any two cones.

JOSEPH GRULER.
AUGUSTUS REBETEY.

In presence of—
LEVI H. GODDARD,
ALBERT BEACH.

falling upon them." The end view of the cylinder is that of a six-shot cylinder. According to our analysis of this point, the intermediate recesses would be used to hold the cylinder in a "safe" position and for the purposes of loading the several chambers only in the case of a five-shot cylinder. In loading a six-shot cylinder, the hammer would be resting on the cone of the chamber directly opposite the chamber being loaded and the intermediate recesses would not be involved in the process of loading a six-shot cylinder, in any way. The sole purpose of the intermediate recesses in a cylinder with six chambers would be to hold the loaded cylinder in a "safe" position, while being handled or carried as a part of a revolver. Further, the application and use of six-shot cylinders in Manhattan's .31-caliber revolvers could scarcely have been effected by December 27, 1859, according to our information and analysis regarding this detail. However, there is a possibility that the drawing may have been looking to the future in the matter of five-shot *vs.* six-shot cylinders.

There is a further omission on the drawing, although the omission is not of any real significance: the signatures of Joseph Gruler and Augustus Rebetey, as inventors, and of Levi H. Goddard and Albert Beach, as witnesses, are not shown. In our opinion, the drawing for Patent No. 26,641, the most important of the Manhattan patents, is a thoroughly confused situation. It is regrettable that we were unable to find the original patent drawing, as it would have been more informative than the issued drawing.

There was to be a fourth Manhattan patent, No. 41,848, issued on March 8th, 1864. This patent is not involved with the immediate chronology of the Manhattan story and because the invention found its application on Manhattan's .36-caliber revolvers, the patent will be reviewed under an appropriate part of a later section which deals with these arms.

Before proceeding to our discussion of the Manhattan .31-caliber revolvers, we refer again to Patent No. 26,641—a subject which we are reluctant to leave without further comment. It is apparent, from the information developed thus far, that Manhattan held considerable hopes for the future of that portion of the claims related to the removable side-plate. These hopes are indicated in certain of Manhattan's actions and reactions. An example of one of the company's reactions is seen in the filing of a caveat on the side-plate, by Joseph Gruler, in October of 1858. This event took place about thirty days after Bacon's separation from his erstwhile employer and is suggestive that Manhattan was fearful that Bacon would copy their model of revolver. Subsequent developments proved the fears to be well founded when Bacon produced a copy of the model in his new venture, the Bacon Manufacturing Company. Bacon's model of the side-plate revolver did not include the use of the intermediate recesses in the cylinder and did not, therefore, constitute an' infringement of the Manhattan model within the definition of the eventual patent. However, this does not alter the fact that Bacon must have had knowledge of the side-plate type of construction and that Bacon Manufacturing Company was flying in the face of a patent suit in producing their model. At least one other arms maker copied Manhattan's side-plate revolver, this maker being Nepperhan; in fact, Nepperhan may have produced more of the side-plate revolvers than were produced by Manhattan.

Further evidence of Manhattan's regard for the side-plate revolver is seen in the fact that all three of the patents, No. 23,990, No. 23,994 and No. 26,641, related to the removable side-plate. Manhattan's objectives in the design of the side-plate revolver were very commendable: lower costs, less machinery, ease of assembly and repair of the lock parts, plus a lowered requirement of skill on the latter operations. In our opinion, there was considerable merit in the side-plate revolver and there is little doubt that it was better than a number of the odd-ball products of the period. At this late date, it is not revealed to us whether Manhattan was disappointed in its failure to secure a patent on the side-plate revolver to an extent that production of the model was discontinued, whether the model proved to be less satisfactory or less saleable than was expected or whether the company became convinced of greater potentials in the .36-caliber and .22-caliber models. One fact is clearly evident: Manhattan turned to the production of other models while the fate of Patent No. 26,641 was indeterminate, awaiting the final decision of the Patent Office.

The claims awarded to Manhattan under Patent No. 26,641 provided a much-needed safety feature for hand guns of that period. The hand guns of the percussion period were fraught with several safety hazards, including the occasional but always startling discharge of all loaded chambers at one and the same time, and the lack of safety was an inherent characteristic of the product. The objective sought by every maker of firearms was to provide safety for the user while the arm was being handled or carried. The obvious approach was to devise a means of securing the hammer in a "safe" position, midway between any two cones of the cylinder. Colt's patent of September 10, 1850, covered two areas, one of which was a safety feature consisting of the use of small pins fastened to the rear of the cylinder, one for each chamber, in conjunction with a recess in the hammer to receive a pin. Subsequent to 1850, this device was used by Colt for as long as the company produced percussion revolvers. Remington, Whitney and Metropolitan, to name a few, used the principle of milled recesses between the cones, located circumferentially around the rear of the cylinder, into which the hammer was set to provide "safe" positions. Examinations of existing specimens of each of the foregoing makers will furnish ample evidence that the devices employed, to provide reasonable safety in their products, were not completely satisfactory.

It is our opinion that Manhattan's safety feature was the only effective means to lock the cylinder, with the hammer midway between the nipples, that came into use during the percussion period. The means employed by

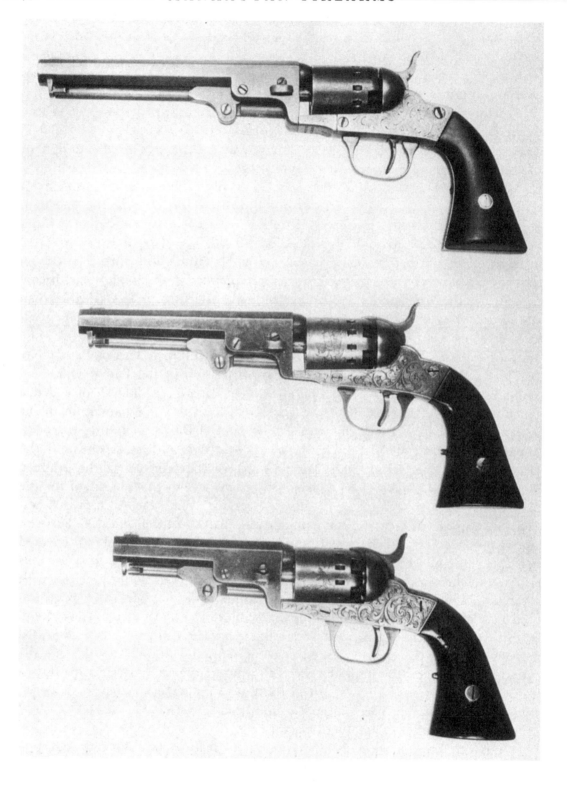

PLATE 16. SERIES II .31-CALIBER MANHATTAN REVOLVERS.

Figure 1. Six-Shot, Six-Inch Barrel, Number 1824.

Figure 2. Six-Shot, Five-Inch Barrel, Number 1175.

Figure 3. Six-Shot, Four-Inch Barrel, Number 3808.

The Series II .31 caliber revolvers were unquestionably the most graceful arms manufactured by Manhattan. The model incorporated the sum total of the company's contribution to the field of arms invention. Identified with this series are the six-shot cylinder, larger grips and blade-type front sight; this type of sight became a standard feature of Manhattan revolvers.

Remington, Whitney, Metropolitan and others were variations of Colt's pin-and-slot device and were much inferior. Continued use of the safety let-down on the Colt arms, and the arms of the other makers, was conducive to breakage of the locking bolt as the forked end of the locking bolt was under continual strain. Manhattan's safety feature reduced this undesirable characteristic to the point of negligible importance.

There were at least three instances of use, or infringement, of Manhattan's safety feature by other makers. One instance was the use of the feature by Rigdon & Ansley, makers of Confederate revolvers. A second instance was the use of the feature by Colt's Patent Firearms Mfg. Company on its Richards conversion model of 1871; at the time of this usage, Manhattan had been succeeded by American Standard Tool Company. However, the most significant usage of the feature was on the Starr percussion revolvers. Starr probably manufactured more percussion revolvers than were manufactured by Manhattan. The safety feature used on the Starr revolvers is very similar to Manhattan's device and leads to the opinion that usage of the feature by Starr was either an out-and-out infringement or was had under license from Manhattan. We are inclined towards the latter view; Manhattan was a small company but its management was not lacking in courage nor inexperienced in the use of legal means to sustain its convictions.

We conclude the discussion of the first three of the four Manhattan Patents with the feeling that as regards the aspects of infringement, imitation and copying, Manhattan was considerably more sinned against than sinning.

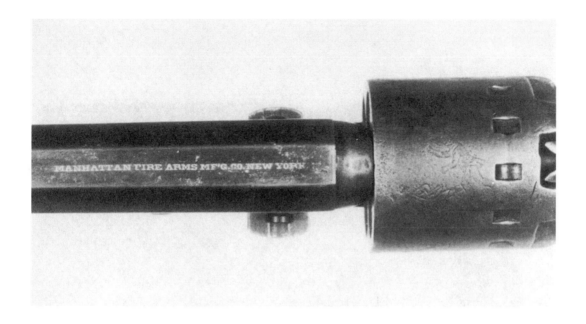

PLATE 17. BARREL SIGNING FOR .31-CALIBER REVOLVERS, SERIES II.

The one-line New York signing appeared on 3600 to 3800 .31 caliber revolvers in Series II and may have set the pattern for a similar signing used on the Series I and Series II .36 caliber revolvers.

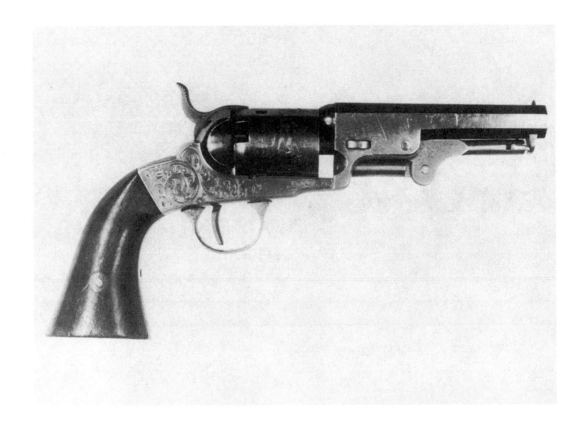

PLATE 18. ODD VARIATION OF .31-CALIBER MANHATTAN REVOLVER.

Five-Shot, Four-Inch Barrel, Number 231 (intermediate-size grip).

The above example has a five-shot cylinder and brass post-type front sight, features associated with Series I. It also bears the 1859 patent stamping on the bottom of the frame, forward of trigger-guard, a characteristic of Series II .31 caliber revolvers. Size of grips and heavier trigger-guard are other unusual points.

CHAPTER IV

NEWARK: 31-CALIBER MANHATTAN REVOLVERS

ALTHOUGH Manhattan did not file for the patents relating to their removable side-plate revolver (this type of construction was to be limited to the .31-caliber model) until March of 1859, it is clearly evident that development of this model was started no later than 1858 and possibly during the latter months of 1857. Some reference to a possible starting of the work during the latter part of 1857 is seen in the Manhattan-Bacon contract, which was dated September 1, 1857, as follows: "then I (Bacon) shall have the preference, over any one else, at the same price, in making *barrels or cylinders for any other kinds of pistols* (author's italics) the company may then require." Certainly, this language may be construed to mean that Manhattan and Bacon were looking forward to the manufacture of pistols with cylinders as early as September 1, 1857.

The absence of definitive information necessitates the use of surmise and conjecture in estimating when the development of the .31-caliber revolver was started. In view of the available facts, we estimate that the development work was begun in the early part of 1858; further, that development of the new

PLATE 19. BARREL SIGNING FOR LONDON PISTOL COMPANY REVOLVERS.

The barrel identification for a few hundred revolvers manufactured by Manhattan and possessing all of the usual characteristics of the company's .31 caliber guns. Absence of an address indicates that the signing was devised as a trade name.

revolver was well advanced by September 11, 1858, when Bacon disavowed his agreement with Manhattan. Ready substantiation of this fact is to be found in the details of the lawsuit, on page 10 of the Stedman document, as follows: "This corporation (Bacon Manufacturing Company), before the 4th day of November, 1858, commenced the manufacture of the same kind of pistols, in said town of Norwich, that the petitioners (Manhattan Firearms Mfg. Company) were making at the time the respondent (Bacon) was in their employment, and continue to manufacture and sell such pistols." As far as we have been able to ascertain, Bacon Manufacturing Company did not make any pepperboxes or single-shot pistols. We are positive that Bacon Manufacturing Company did make a .31-caliber revolver with removable side-plate which resembles closely the .31-caliber Manhattan revolver. Therefore, the reference to "the same kind of pistols" must have meant Manhattan's .31-caliber revolvers and the manufacturing processes must have been well under way when Bacon took his leave on September 11, 1858.

It should be borne in mind that the number of workmen employed by Manhattan during the years of 1856-1858 must have been quite small. If the work involved in the manufacture of the barrels for the company's pepperboxes and single-shot pistols amounted to one-fourth or even one-third of the total work required for completed products and if fabrication of the barrels was carried out by Bacon and three boys, as has been indicated, it is reasonable to deduce that the company employed twelve to sixteen "hands" during the period of 1856-1858. While the development of the new revolver was probably begun during the early part of 1858, it is more than probable that Manhattan continued to manufacture pepperboxes and single-shot pistols during 1858 because of the practical requirements of the business for continuity of sales, production and income in this period of transition and development.

The information introduced thus far indicates that the credit for the development of Manhattan's .31-caliber revolver must be divided between Thomas K. Bacon, Joseph Gruler and Augustus Rebetey. While the existing records do not credit Bacon with any part in this development, consideration must be given to the fact that Bacon was associated with the company during the period of development and he was too competent in the making of arms to have failed in contributing to the new revolver, even though the extent of his contribution must remain a matter of conjecture. Gruler's contribution is given some measure through the filing of the caveat for the removable side-plate in October, 1858. Rebetey's contribution is definitely measurable in the development of tools for the new revolver plus his indicated invention of the principle of the intermediate cylinder stops. Thus we may assume that at some time or other during 1858, Bacon, Gruler, and Rebetey were working on the development of Manhattan's .31-caliber revolver, although not necessarily on a team basis. There is some evidence which indicates that Bacon's ideas for certain details

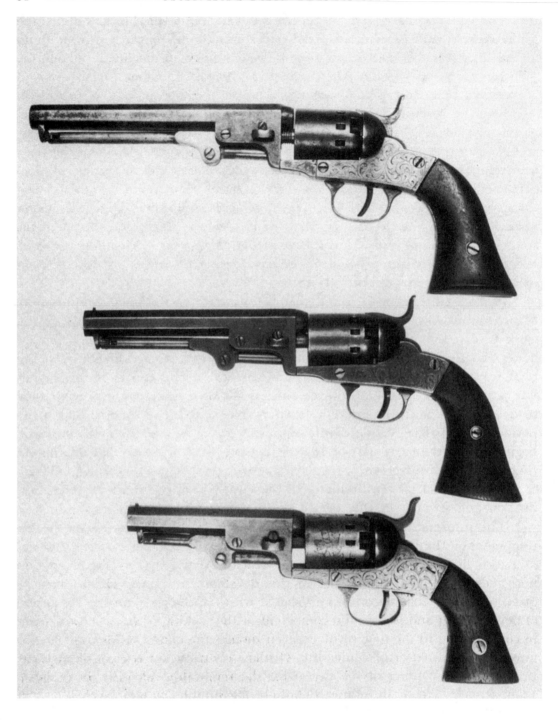

PLATE 20. LONDON PISTOL COMPANY .31-CALIBER REVOLVERS.

Figure 1. Five-Shot, Six-Inch Barrel, Number 40.

Figure 2. Five-Shot, Five-Inch Barrel, Number 180.

Figure 3. Five-Shot, Four-Inch Barrel, Number 190.

As illustrated by the serial numbers listed above, the majority of the London Pistol Company guns observed have numbers below 1000, indicating a period of manufacture concurrent with the Series I Manhattan .31 caliber revolvers. It is believed that the London Pistol Company products were regarded as second quality and, for this reason, were marketed under a trade name to avoid any connection with the company.

of the revolver may have differed from Gruler's and Rebetey's; at least, there is evidence of two separate lines of thought in these details.

A specimen representing an early stage in the development of Manhattan's .31-caliber revolver is displayed in Plates 5 and 6. (See page 36.) This example is from the fine collection of arms owned by Miles W. Standish and has been in his collection for more than twenty years. The gun is definitely of Manhattan manufacture and, in our opinion, was made in 1858 and prior to Bacon's separation from Manhattan. The revolver possesses several attributes which indicate that it was: (1) an experimental model, as it is not serially marked; (2) that it was not intended for shooting, as it was made without a front sight and (3) that it was not manufactured for sales purposes as it was partially unfinished, including the absence of the barrel signing. Therefore, we consider this specimen to have been an early prototype, manufactured for the specific purposes of development and possible changes in design and mechanical details. The cylinder of the prototype revolver has one important attribute which was to be adopted as a permanent characteristic of the .31-caliber Manhattan model: the stagecoach holdup scene. There is some evidence, to be introduced later, that Manhattan considered an alternative type of cylinder engraving which was ultimately used by Bacon on the cylinders of his copies of the Manhattan .31-caliber revolver.

The specimen depicted on Plates 5 and 6 may be described generally as an experimental .31-caliber revolver with a five-shot cylinder and a six-inch barrel. The cylinder retains a considerable amount of the original blued finish and is engraved with the Manhattan stagecoach holdup scene. The barrel, frame, and other metal parts retain a medium brown finish and may have been of blued finish, originally. The frame and grip straps are notable for the absence of engraving. The barrel is unsigned and was made without a front sight. There are no serial numbers on any parts of the gun; the number 962 and a proof mark, which resembles a lower-case letter "g" laid on its side, are stamped on the left side of the grip frame, underneath the left half of the walnut grips. The number 962 has no apparent significance and could scarcely be considered as a serial number; if the proof mark definitely represented a lower-case letter "g," there might be a possible connection with Gruler.

The prototype has several interesting characteristics which were not used in the later production models or were subjected to change. These characteristics are:

1. Cylinder: Has a notch filed into the rounded surface, at the rear. The notch is of the same size and shape as the notch filed in the top of the hammer, to form the usual rear sight. The notch on the cylinder is located directly in line with the front wheel of the stagecoach. When the notch in the cylinder is aligned with the notch in the hammer, the alignment

serves to center the stagecoach scene for viewing and this was the obvious purpose of the two notches. The cylinder of the prototype merits further consideration in the matter of development, having been made with only five stops. The absence of the additional or intermediate stops would indicate that this specimen was made prior to the introduction of Rebetey's safety feature. Further, the stops are of a size different from that which was ultimately adopted, being longer and more narrow than the stops found in the cylinders of the production models.

2. Cylinder bolt:

(a) The spring used to actuate the bolt is a single-prong spring, instead of the V-shaped spring used in the later production models and as shown on the drawing for Patent No. 26,641.

(b) The screw which holds the bolt in place extends through the right side of the frame and is visible in Plate 6. In the majority of the later production models, this screw does not extend through the right side of the frame and the change may have been effected by a change on the inside of the casting in the form of a lug or projection into which the screw was threaded.

3. Barrel lug: Only one pin was inset into the base of the barrel lug, for the purpose of connecting the lug to the frame, instead of two pins as used in the production models.

4. Barrel catch: The barrel catch for the latch of the loading lever is much heavier than the type used on production models and is shaped so as to round off the junction of the barrel catch and the end of the loading lever.

5. Loading lever assembly: The loading lever assembly has an additional part not used in production models. The added part is a link, inserted between and connecting the lever and the plunger, which made for smoother operation of the loading-lever assembly. The outline of the link is visible in Plates 5 and 6.

6. Grip screw: The grip screw of this specimen enters from the right, instead of from the left, as on the production models.

All of the features just described for the experimental .31-caliber Manhattan contribute, along with the excellent condition of the piece, to make it one of the most interesting guns in the Manhattan category that we have ever examined.

Although we have not been fortunate enough to locate the .31-caliber Manhattan revolver bearing serial #1, we were able to get reasonably close to this point. The example shown in Plates 7 and 8 (See page 38) bears serial #7 and merits consideration in tracing the development of the arms in this classification. The specimen is not an experimental piece but it does have several interesting features, including one such feature in the field of development. The point of development lies in the enlargement of the grip-

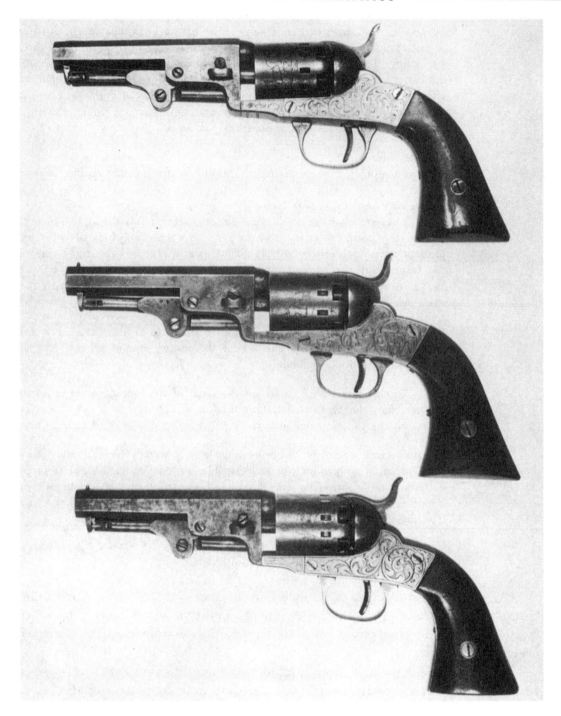

PLATE 21. LONDON PISTOL COMPANY .31-CALIBER REVOLVERS.

Figure 1. Six-Shot, Four-Inch Barrel, Number 1721.

Figure 2. Five-Shot, Four-Inch Barrel, Number 440.

Figure 3. Six-Shot, Four-Inch Barrel, Number 883 (brass trigger guard).

An occasional example of the London Pistol Company marking will be found on a revolver with the features of Manhattan's Series II revolvers, as represented by Figure 1. Figure 2 shows an unusually good example with flared grips. Figure 3 exemplifies the transition from Series I to Series II in Manhattan's .31 caliber revolvers of which the brass trigger-guard was an interesting detail.

frame through the attachment of an extension, ¼″ in depth, to the bottom or butt portion of a grip-frame identical in size to the grip frame of the experimental model. The attachment of the extension to the grip-frame was effected by the use of two screws extending upwards through the extension into the butt portion of the grip-frame, as shown in Plate 8. (See page 38.) As will be seen in the photograph, neither of the two screws is exactly in the centerline of the extension and this leads us to believe that this specimen was not made for resale but was probably used for purposes of display and as an example of the enlarged and improved size of the grip. An examination of the grip-frame, with the grips removed, provides another bit of interesting information: the left side of the grip-frame is stamped with a large 7 and a small letter G; the right side of the grip-frame is stamped with a small D-shaped proof mark, the area within the outline of the D being cross-hatched. Another specimen with identical markings is shown as Fig. 3 on Plate 11. (See page 49.) It requires no great amount of imagination to conjure up a connection between the G stamping and Gruler who, as we have mentioned, must have had an active part in the development of the early Manhattan revolvers. This specimen has three other features which are significant: (1) the barrel is signed with the two-line New York address which became a standard feature of the first series of the .31-caliber Manhattan revolvers; (2) the five-shot cylinder is engraved with the stagecoach-holdup scene which was to become a standard feature of this model and (3) the frame, trigger-guard, back-strap and barrel are engraved with the pattern and style of engraving which was likewise to become a standard feature of the .31-caliber revolvers. It would seem that Manhattan's efforts, probably in the person of Joseph Gruler, were extended to the utmost in the production of this specimen, with its embellishments of engraving and ivory grips of the enlarged and improved type.

It is understandable that examples of deviations from the eventual or usual types will exist in the development of any product. It has been said, and truly so, "Nothing was ever invented and perfected at one and the same time." This condition appears to have existed in the production of the first two hundred of the .31-caliber Manhattan revolvers. Following this approximate point of production, however, the condition of orderliness, to which an earlier reference has been made, becomes evident and continues with but minor variations throughout the entire line of Manhattan revolvers. An example of deviation from what was to become the usual type of .31-caliber Manhattan revolver is illustrated in the specimen displayed as Fig. 1 in Plate 9. (See page 40.) This specimen also illustrates, in some of its details, the divergent line of thought to which earlier reference has been made; we believe that the divergent details represent the influence and, perhaps, the handiwork of Thomas K. Bacon. These details are represented in four items:

(a) The cylinder is not engraved and has only one stop per chamber, instead of two stops per chamber.

(b) The serial number of the loading lever is located on the top side of the lever, instead of the usual location on the right side of the lever and adjacent to the screw-hole.

(c) The engraving on the frame is quite similar to the engraving on the frame of the Bacon revolver shown as Fig. 2 in Plate 9. (See page 40.) (This similarity in type of engraving has not been found in any other .31-caliber revolver we have examined.)

(d) The absence of any of the stampings (initials or proofmarks) usually found on the grip-frames of other specimens in this category. The only stamping on the grip-frame of this specimen is the serial number.

In all other details, this specimen conforms to the features usually identified with the first series of the .31-caliber Manhattan revolvers including the location of the serial number on the cylinder. The location of this number is at the rear of the cylinder, on the face of the area between two of the nipples or cones.

A fourth specimen considered to be in the development category is displayed as Fig. 1 in Plate 10. (See page 42.) This revolver is equipped with ivory grips and the frame, grip straps, and barrel are engraved with the pattern and style of engraving which was to be adopted as a standard feature of the model. The other and usual characteristics of the model are to be found in this example, with two exceptions:

(a) The five-shot cylinder, while it has the intermediate cylinder stops, is plain and without any engraving (very few specimens of this model are to be found with plain, unengraved cylinders), and

(b) The loading lever is stamped with a small six-pointed star on the top side of the lever. The significance of the star stamping is, of course, unknown. However, the presence of the stamping plus the ornamentation of ivory and engraving might indicate that this revolver was made for the purposes of exhibition and sales promotion.

The fifth specimen considered to be in the development category is shown as Fig. 2 in Plate 10. (See page 42.) Except for the experimental model previously discussed, and displayed in Plates 5 and 6. (See page 36), we consider this revolver to be the most interesting of the several specimens under discussion. The revolver is of extraordinary interest due to its unusual features which are, in turn, conducive to a combination of conjecture and factual deduction. These features are to be found in the serial number, the loading lever and the cylinder and give further evidence of the divergent details discussd under the third example in the development category (serial #44).

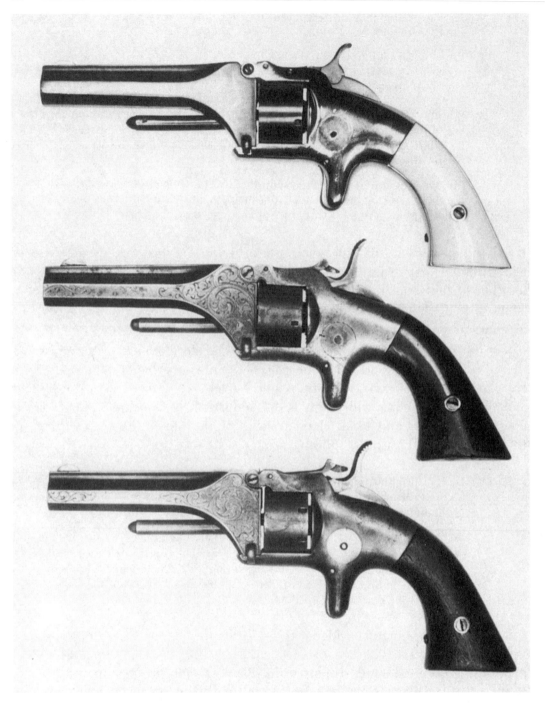

PLATE 22. MANHATTAN FIRST MODEL .22-CALIBER REVOLVERS.

Figure 1. Smith & Wesson (fifth variation) Number 5750.
(From the Collection of Dr. John E. Byrne.)

Figure 2. Manhattan (first variation) Number 1551.

Figure 3. Manhattan (second variation) Number 2835.

This study shows a general comparison of Smith & Wesson's First Model First Issue revolver with two copies by Manhattan. It is believed that Manhattan's .22 caliber model stemmed from the sixth variation of the Smith & Wesson, although the vertical hammer-spur was a characteristic of the latter's very early revolvers. Manhattan used a one-piece hammer in conjunction with an ingenious cylinder release which also served as the rear sight.

(a) The gun bears two serial numbers: the barrel, wedge and grip-frame are stamped with serial #7; the loading lever and cylinder are stamped with serial #117.

(b) The loading lever is equipped with the rounded, ball-type latch which is found on some models of Whitney percussion revolvers and, more specifically, on the Bacon copy of the Manhattan .31-caliber revolver.

(c) The five-shot cylinder has only one cylinder stop per chamber and is engraved with five panels of the pattern and style of engraving usually found on the cylinders of the Bacon copies of Manhattan's .31-caliber revolvers.

We are certain that the arms dealer from whom we acquired this gun considered it to be a "battlefield assembly" (due to the mixed serials and the presence of the Bacon-type cylinder), as this was indicated by his price tag. For several years, until study and comparisons led us to feel otherwise, we shared the dealer's opinion. However, there is credible evidence that this specimen is a rare example of the development phase of the model. Since we have previously discussed a revolver with serial #7 on all parts, it is quite obvious that the #7 serial on the subject example is a duplication—a circumstance likely to occur with more than one individual engaged in the development work. It would appear that the duplication of serial numbers was discovered and remedied by the reassignment of serial #117 which was then stamped on the loading lever assembly and on the cylinder. It is to be noted that the location of the serial number on the loading lever of this gun is on the top side of the lever, the same as on #44, previously discussed; further, that the stamping on the grip-frame of #117 is the same as the stamping on the grip-frame of #44. Certainly, the loading-lever latch is the same as the type used on the Bacon revolver. Likewise, the engraving on the cylinder is readily identifiable as the same type of engraving found on the cylinder of the Bacon revolver. However, the cylinder of the subject revolver does not resemble a Bacon cylinder in two details: (1) the manner in which the serial number is stamped on the rear of the cylinder and (2) the absence of the milled recesses usually found on Bacon cylinders, into which the hammer is set to provide a "safety" rest. The cylinders of Bacon revolvers (similar to the .31-caliber Manhattan revolvers) which we have examined were made with the milled recesses just mentioned and the serial number was stamped into the recesses, *one digit to a single recess*. The cylinder of gun #117 has the serial number stamped at the rear of the cylinder, on the face of the area between two of the nipples or cones; the cylinder of gun #44 is stamped in the identical manner and this feature conforms with the procedure followed in stamping the serial numbers on the cylinders of all Manhattan percussion revolvers. It is to be noted that the cylinders of both revolvers were made without the milled recesses which served as "safety" rests for the hammer. It is our opinion that the subject specimen (#117) was produced by, or under the supervision of, Thomas K. Bacon. The ball-type loading-lever latch and the engraved panels on the cylinder may have represented Bacon's ideas on these features and the gun may have been made up to incorporate these details for presentation to Manhattan's management. In his capacity as superintendent of Manhattan's manufactory, Bacon was probably responsible for procuring the engraving dies used for cylinder decoration. The die which produced the stagecoach-holdup scene was accepted by Manhattan; the type of engraving on the subject specimen may have received consideration but was rejected, after comparison with the first and accepted type. Following rejection of the latter die, Bacon may have acquired it or may have owned the die in the first instance. At any rate, the impressions from this five-panel die were ultimately to be found on the cylinders of revolvers marked "Bacon Mfg. Co." In this manner, we have rationlized a gun which we once regarded as a bastard piece into a specimen which we now regard as Bacon's contribution to the development of the .31-caliber Manhattan revolvers. It appears to us that the facts are too evidential to be denied.

The conclusion of the discussion of the development phases of the .31-caliber Manhattan revolver brings us to the consideration of the standard or production models of this category. Examination of the standard models of the .31-caliber Manhattan revolvers reveals that the standard models may be divided into two well-defined groups, by reason of differences in features and other characteristics. We will designate these groups as Series I and Series II.

The standard models in Series I of the .31-caliber Manhattan revolvers are represented by the guns displayed in Plate 11. (See page 48.) The revolvers in Series I were made in 4", 5" and 6" barrel lengths, with the 4" barrel length apparently the most common, the 5" barrel length being scarce and the 6" barrel length being a definite rarity. The cylinders of the revolvers in Series I were engraved with a stagecoach-holdup scene which is quite different from the scene found on the cylinders of Colt's .31-caliber Pocket Model revolvers of 1849 designation. The frame of the revolvers in Series I were hand-engraved with a scroll design similar to that employed by Wolfe (the work may have been done in Wolfe's shop) and the engraving was extended to include the back-strap and the trigger-guard bow. In all cases the barrels and cylinders were of blued finish. In some cases the frames and grip straps of the revolvers in Series I were of blued finish; in other cases these parts were silver plated. Silver plating of these parts eventually became standard practice because the parts were of cast iron and did not satisfactorily retain a durable blue finish. The loading levers and hammers were case hardened in colors. The two-piece wood grips were made of walnut, both plain and burled, and occasionally of rosewood. Serial-number locations on the various parts were as follows: barrel: bottom flat, forward of lug; loading lever: right side, adjacent to screw hole; plunger:

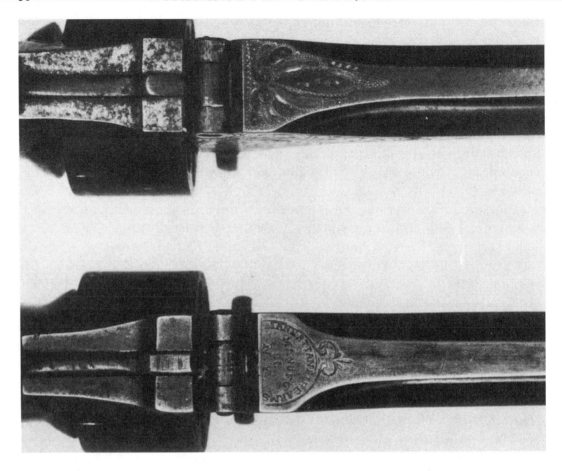

PLATE 23. BARREL SIGNING FOR FIRST MODEL .22-CALIBER REVOLVERS.

Figure 1. Unmarked: Number 1551.

Figure 2. Semicircular Stamping: Number 2835.

Unmarked Manhattan .22 caliber revolvers are uncommon and omission of the stamping on the barrel shown in Figure 1 was probably unintentional. In this case, the barrel engraver applied the ornamentation as a substitute for the usual marking. The usual semi-circular stamping appears on the barrel in Figure 2. The stamping itself was entirely plain and was outlined by the engraver to conform with the barrel (sides) ornamentation.

right side of flat portion; cylinder: at rear, on face of area between two nipples or cones; grip-frame: usually on left side, occasionally on right side, underneath grip; grips: usually right grip, in pencil; wedge: bottom side.

The features which distinguish the .31-caliber Manhattan revolvers in Series I are as follows:

1. Five-shot cylinder, with ten cylinder stops.
2. Brass post-type front sight. Rear sight, a V notch, filed in top of hammer.
3. Small trigger-guard.
4. Small-size grips (same dimensions as grips on the experimental model, plates 5 and 6; see page 36).
5. Two-line New York address (see Plate 12, page 57).
6. No patent date on frame.

Based upon our survey of serial numbers of the .31-caliber revolvers in Series I, we estimate that the quantity produced in Series I ranged between 900 and 1000 guns, beginning with serial #1. Further, that all of the revolvers in Series I were produced prior to January 30, 1860.

Before leaving the subject of the Series I .31-caliber Manhattan revolvers, we wish to comment on two of the specimens displayed on Plate 11. (See page 48.) Fig. 1 of that plate shows an example which could be placed in the development category for two reasons: (1) although the cylinder is engraved with the usual stagecoach holdup scene, the frame, back-strap and trigger-guard are entirely plain (not engraved), as in the case of the experimental model shown on Plates 5 and 6 (see page 36); (2) the grip-frame was enlarged by means of an extension attached to the butt of the original frame, as in the case of the revolver shown on Plates 7 and 8. (See page 38.) The method of attachment of the extension differs in that the screws extend downward through the butt of the original frame into the extension. We do not consider the enlarged grip as a characteristic of the Series I .31-caliber revolvers; however, this is the only specimen we have seen in the 6″ barrel length which has the other characteristics belonging in Series I. Fig. 2 of Plate 11 (see page 48) shows an example which is somewhat of a paradox: despite the relatively low serial number (#23), this specimen has all of the features associated with the standard example of a Series I .31-caliber revolver. A minor variation is represented by the rear corner of the butt which is clipped instead of forming the usual sharp point.

Since we have discussed the Series I .31-caliber Manhattan revolvers, and before proceeding with a similar discussion of the revolvers in Series II of this model, we wish to consider examples of two models of revolvers which were copies of Manhattan's .31-caliber revolvers.

The first such copy is the Bacon revolver, displayed as Fig. 2 in Plate 9, (see page 40), to which we have made previous references. As mentioned previously, the Bacon revolver differed from the Manhattan model in one important detail in that Bacon's model was made without the intermediate cylinder stops and that absence of the stops kept his model from being infringement on Manhattan's eventual patent. There is evidence to indicate that Bacon may have become fearful of the results of possible infringement on Manhattan's pending patent applications, in consequence of which Bacon may have discontinued making this model. This evidence is found in a single specimen of the Bacon copy of Manhattan's .31-caliber model which is in the collection of Sam E. Smith. This specimen bears serial #828 (the highest serial number for this model of which we have knowledge) and, most importantly, the barrel is unsigned. Unsigned specimens of arms are, not infrequently, evidential of some kind of patent complications. In this case, we believe that Bacon may have been advised by Manhattan of its pending patents with the result that Bacon stopped signing the barrels of his revolvers and ultimately discontinued the model altogether. It is to be remembered that Manhattan withdrew its suit in equity against Bacon sometime between October 1859 and January 1860. We do not believe it would constitute drawing an hypothesis from thin air to presume that a condition of the withdrawal of the suit was a requirement that Bacon cease and desist in the manufacture of his copy of the Manhattan .31-caliber revolver. At any rate, it is probable that Bacon manufactured fewer than 1000 revolvers of this model or about the same quantity manufactured by Manhattan in Series I of its .31-caliber model. The Bacon model differed from the Manhattan in two other details. The first of these was the use of the ball-type loading-lever latch, which Bacon eventually discontinued, and the second was the elimination of the link between the hammer and the mainspring; the latter detail reduced the cost of manufacture of his model but probably was not an improvement. Two additional examples of the Bacon revolver are shown in Plate 13. (See page 62.) The specimen displayed as Fig. 2 in this plate is the only example of a Bacon revolver with an unusual amount of ornamentation that we have seen. While it is scarcely in the category of a "fully-engraved" piece, the muzzle and top flats of the barrel, the forward portions of the frame, the trigger-guard and back-strap are artistically touched with engraving and, in combination with the ivory grips, make it a most desirable specimen. Plate 14 (see page 65) is illustrative of what might be called "The Case of the Wandering Engraving Die" since the cylinders of the revolvers depicted thereon, each one from a different maker, were engraved by the same die. (Note: the die produced five oval panels of woodland hunting scenes, featuring a stag and a left-handed gunner; the artistic details were not of a high order and the engraving was quite shallow.) The progressive use or application of the die, as illustrated in Plate 14, appears to have been as follows: on the cylinder of a Series I .31-caliber

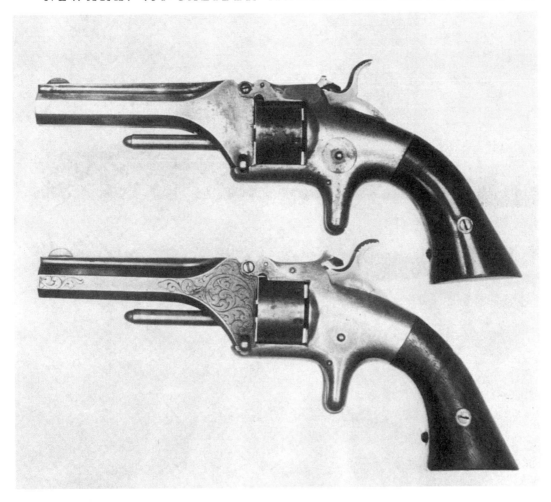

PLATE 24. MANHATTAN FIRST MODEL .22-CALIBER REVOLVERS.

Figure 1. Third Variation (plain barrel): Number 4842.

Figure 2. Third Variation (presentation): Number 6657.

The example shown as Figure I is a departure from the usual Manhattan First Model .22 as it has a silver plated barrel (blued finish was standard) that was not engraved. The frame of the presentation revolver, Figure 2, appears to have an unusually heavy application of silver plating, much of which has been retained.

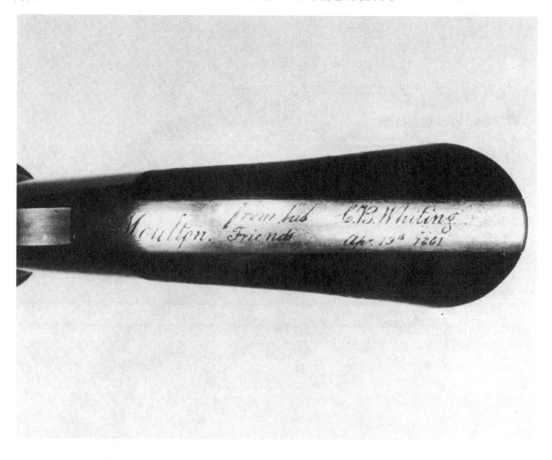

PLATE 25. PRESENTATION INSCRIPTION ON FIRST MODEL .22-CALIBER REVOLVER.

    The above inscription appears on the back-strap of the revolver shown as
Figure 2 in Plate 24. The date of the inscription was close to the terminal
point of production of Manhattan's First Model .22 caliber revolver. A dated
presentation piece occupies a prized place in any arms collection.

Manhattan revolver (Fig. 1); on the cylinder of a Bacon copy of Manhattan's revolver (Fig. 3) and on the cylinder of a Hopkins & Allen percussion revolver. (Fig. 2). The latter model, a scarce gun, featured the removeable side-plate construction in conjunction with a round barrel instead of an octagonal barrel. Thus, the die apparently was transferred from Manhattan's plant to the plant of Bacon Mfg. Company and thence to the plant of Hopkins & Allen, all within the confines of Norwich, Connecticut; while it is probable that fewer than 2000 cylinders bore the impressions from its face, this little die made history with its nomadic existence.

The second copy of Manhattan's .31-caliber revolver, to be considered at this juncture, is the revolver manufactured by Nepperhan and shown in Plate 15. (See page 69.) This specimen is of .31-caliber, with 4¼″ barrel which is marked "NEPPERHAN F. A. CO. YONKERS, N. Y." The iron frame and grip straps are formed by two castings, similar to Manhattan's construction, but are not engraved. The brass trigger-guard is a separate part (not integral with the casting forming the grip straps and the right side of the frame) which slides into two beveled recesses in the right side of the frame and is held in place when the side-plate is joined to the frame by the two screws. The cylinder of the Nepperhan copy is five shot and has only one cylinder stop per chamber; milled recesses at the rear of the cylinder, in the areas between the nipples, provide for "safety" positions for the hammer. The lock parts of the Nepperhan are identical to similar parts of the Manhattan .31-caliber revolver with the exception that Nepperhan eliminated the link between the hammer and the mainspring through the use of a wheel-bearing in the base of the hammer, upon which the spring bears directly. The serial number of the subject specimen is #4356 and indicates that Nepperhan may have manufactured more revolvers in this category than were manufactured by Manhattan. It is probable that the Nepperhan revolvers were made in 1860 and thereafter.

The standard models in Series II of the .31-caliber Manhattan revolvers are represented by the guns shown in Plate 16. (See page 76.) The revolvers in Series II, as in Series I, were made in 4″, 5″ and 6″ barrel lengths, with the 4″ barrel length again being the most common, the 5″ barrel length more scarce and the 6″ barrel length a definite rarity. All of the other details described for Series I, relating to engraving, finish, grips, serial number locations, etc., also apply for Series II except that the frames and grip straps of the majority of the revolvers in Series II were plated.

The features which distinguish the .31-caliber Manhattan revolvers in Series II are as follows:

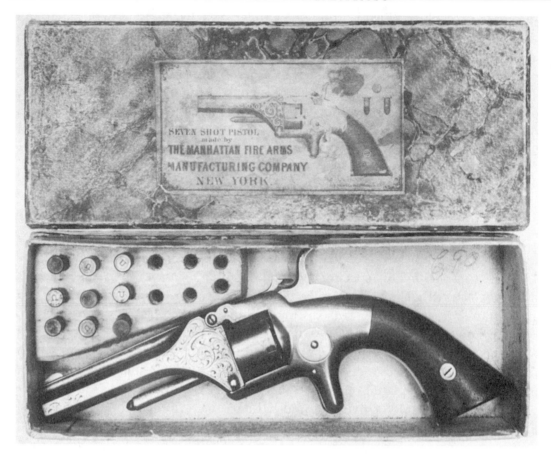

PLATE 26. MANHATTAN FIRST MODEL .22 IN ORIGINAL CARDBOARD BOX.

Fourth Variation: Number 7716.

An extremely interesting example of what is believed to have been the usual method of packaging the revolver of a century ago. The fragile nature of the box places the combination in a category exceeding, considerably, the rarity of wood or hard-rubber casings which are seen on infrequent occasions.

1. Six-shot cylinder, with twelve cylinder stops.

2. Blade-type front sight of German silver (became standard on all Manhattan revolvers except one .36-caliber variation). Rear sight same as Series I.

3. Larger trigger-guard.

4. Larger size grips (same dimensions as grips on the gun displayed in Plates 7 and 8, see page 38).

5. One-line New York address (see Plate 17, page 79).

6. Patent date stamping (December 27, 1859), located on bottom of frame, forward of trigger-guard.

We recall seeing only one revolver which represented a variation from the features set forth above. This specimen, with 5″ barrel and bearing a serial number above 1200, had a brass trigger-guard. The guard appeared to be original and we believe the existence of this specimen, and others like it, represents a development in the transition from the small trigger-guard to the larger trigger-guard.

However, we have a specimen which is typical of those exceptions that upset the best-laid plans of mice and men, including the hypotheses of gun collectors. This revolver is pictured in Plate 18 (see page 80) and combines some of the features of both Series I and Series II. Within the definition of Series I, it has these characteristics: (a) five shot cylinder; (b) two-line New York address; (c) serial #231; (d) brass post-type front sight and (e) a small trigger-guard of much heavier construction than is usually found on the Series I revolvers. Within the definition of Series II, the revolver bears the patent date stamping (December 27, 1859) in the prescribed location on the bottom of the frame. Departing from the definitions of either series, the revolver has a grip of intermediate size which is smaller than the grips described for Series II (Plate 16, see page 76) but larger than the grips described for Series I (Plate 9, Fig.'s 2 and 3; see page 40). Finally, the screw which holds the cylinder bolt in place projects through (but not beyond) the right side of the frame; the end of the screw is engraved to blend with the engraving on the right side of the frame. In our opinion, the revolver is not representative of the development phase discussed earlier; instead, we believe that the gun was incompletely produced rather early in the period of the Series I revolvers and was finished after January 30, 1860. It is an oddity that lends zest to a hypothesis by reason of its lack of conformity.

Based upon our survey of serial numbers of the .31-caliber revolvers in Series II, we estimate that the quantity produced in Series II ranged between 3600 and 3800 guns, with a beginning point between serial numbers 900 and 1000; the terminating serial number should be found between 4500 and 4800.

PLATE 27A. VIEW OF BOX LABEL: MANHATTAN FIRST MODEL .22.

PLATE 27B. CASED MANHATTAN FIRST MODEL .22 CAL. REVOLVER.

(From the collection of M. R. Waddell)

Serial #259; barrel marked with semi-circular stamping; blue cylinder and barrel; silver plated frame. (Not discussed in the text.)

Further, that all of the revolvers in Series II were produced after January of 1860 and production of this model probably ceased not later than 1862.

The following observations appear to be appropriate in concluding our discussion of the .31-caliber Manhattan revolvers: The design and production of this revolver represented the whole of Manhattan's contribution to the field of arms invention. It is true that another patent was to appear in connection with their .36-caliber model but the inventor, Benjamin Kitteredge, was associated with the company as a distributor of their products rather than as an employee. In the design of the .22-caliber rimfire revolvers and the .36-caliber percussion revolvers, Manhattan chose to follow closely the designs of Smith & Wesson and Samuel Colt. Thus, Manhattan's capacity for invention is to be found only in their .31-caliber model.

The design and production of their .31-caliber revolver was a strong and successful effort by Manhattan to enter a very competitive market. It is probable that the model was less expensive than corresponding models offered by Colt, Remington, Whitney, etc., against which Manhattan was forced to compete. Beyond any question or doubt, Manhattan's .31-caliber revolver was a very attractive arm, with the appealing features of hand-engraving, silver plating and grips of fancy woods. It may be assumed that a few revolvers were cased, although we have not seen any of these casings nor have we seen any .31-caliber bullet moulds with Manhattan markings.

It is significant that Manhattan produced such a relatively small quantity of their .31-caliber revolvers. Except for their pepperboxes and single-shot pistols, Manhattan made fewer arms in the .31-caliber model than in any other category. This circumstance may have been the result of fewer sales for this model than was expected or anticipated by the company. A more logical explanation may be found in the assumption that other models, in production at the same time, were much more profitable. As in any well-managed company, the consideration of profit was given preference over pride of invention.

This good and graceful arm served an important purpose in enhancing the company's position in the field of arms making; without it, the story of Manhattan would not have been worth the telling.

Newark N. J. April 6 th 1861

Mr E K Root Hartford Ct,

Sir

The Manhattan
Fire Arms Mafg Co,, Are desireous of procureing Drops
of some kinds, to forge the frames to the Matalic Cartridge pistol
And I have Recomended your Compown Crank Drop to them
of one length of posts,, They have Requested me to write you,
to Assortain if your, or Colts patent Fire Arms Mafg Co,
Will Sill them one for that use, with all your present improvements, (and if any new improvements Contemplated by
you to have them Applied to the machine), Also your
Lowest Cash price for the machine at your place, and the
probable Cost of Setting up the machine by your helps
Also the Shortest time you Could furnish one after you
should Receive an order for one,, Also If you would let
Mr Beach the Agent of the Manhatan Co,, see yours Dr
in operation, as they are new to him, and he desires to see one
in operation,, (We shall Buy them or Build some ourselves
and your Drops being the Best adapted of any at present
in use is the Reason of my Recomending them)

Aere Respectfuly Yours
A R Arnold

My Best Respects to you Mr Lord and the Company for
past favours, and Confidence shown to me, while in your
imploy, Hopeing Ever to Retain the Esteam Bestowed on
me aso for past Assistance I Return you my thanks —
A R A,

PLATE 28. LETTER TO E. K. ROOT FROM A. R. ARNOLD.
(Courtesy Connecticut State Library)

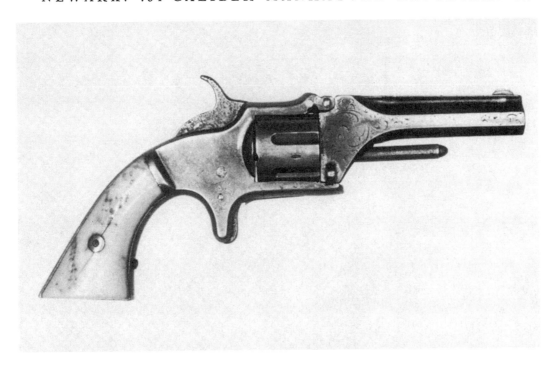

PLATE 29. EXPERIMENTAL MANHATTAN SECOND MODEL .22-CALIBER REVOLVER.

Right Side View. Number 111.

The frame and grips of this revolver are somewhat smaller than similar parts of later examples of Manhattan's Second Model .22. The classification of "experimental model" is given because of unusual cylinder. Cylinder is of brass with six chambers, instead of usual seven, and appears to have been made for .22 caliber *long lipfire* cartridges. Flutes in cylinder and location of cylinder stops are additional features of unusual nature. Cylinder locking-bolt located in bottom of frame.

CHAPTER V

~~~~~~

LONDON PISTOL
COMPANY REVOLVERS

THE opinions generally prevalent among gun collectors concerning the origin of the percussion revolvers bearing the name "LONDON PISTOL COMPANY" have been, in most cases, either erroneous or without objective conclusions. However, we are certain that many discerning collectors have noted that the characteristics of these revolvers are quite similar to the characteristics of Manhattan's .31-caliber revolvers. The essential difference, apart from the barrel signing, is that the Manhattan revolvers have well-defined attributes which permit classification within two series while the London Pistol Company revolvers possess these features in combinations that are sometimes perplexing. Existence of the London Pistol Company revolvers gives rise to the compound question: "For whom, or for what reason, were the London Pistol Company revolvers made?" We have searched diligently for the answer to this question, devoting more effort, perhaps, than is justified by the subject matter or the end result. A completely factual answer is unavailable at this time but, like the chap who was "sometimes in error but never in doubt," we have an opinion for later disclosure.

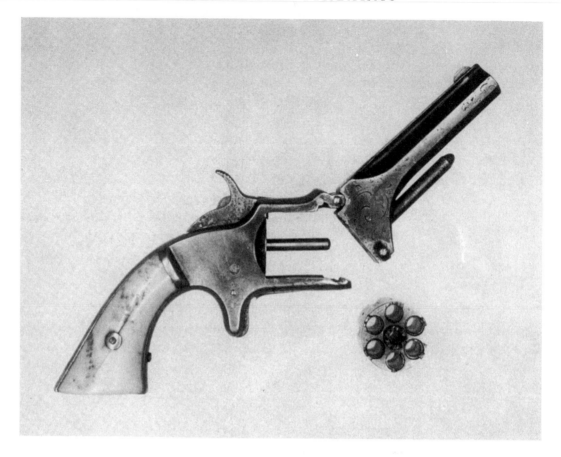

PLATE 30. EXPERIMENTAL MANHATTAN SECOND MODEL .22-CALIBER REVOLVER.

Right Side View, Cylinder Removed. Number 111.

Purpose of this study is to show details of cylinder: the rear portion of each chamber is recessed with a slot extending to the outside edge of the chamber. These details are very similar to the usual procedure of chambering a cylinder for use of lipfire cartridges, as found in larger calibers. Note cylinder pin, one of the innovations of Manhattan's Second Model .22 caliber revolver.

The subject of London Pistol Company revolvers is not a totally unexplored one, as has been the case with Manhattan arms. In carrying out our research on London Pistol Company, we had ready access to an article written the several years ago by Sam E. Smith.[1] Since distribution of the information was somewhat limited, and before presenting the results of our analysis, we consider reproduction of the Smith article to be in order and of prime interest. The material contained therein represents the only information previously published, of which we have knowledge, on any phase of the Manhattan story.

THE AMERICAN LONDON PISTOL COMPANY

For years collectors and dealers alike have assumed that the percussion revolver illustrated above and stamped on the barrel "London Pistol Company" was the product of the London Pistol Company which succeeded Col. Colt's factory in London, England in 1857. In other words, that it was an English-made gun.

As evidence of this assumption, we find that L. D. Satterlee in both his 1927 and 1939 editions of "A Catalog of Firearms for the Collector" describes this revolver and claims for it an English origin. The Nunnemacher Collection Bulletin printed by the Milwaukee Public Museum in 1928 agrees with Satterlee perfectly. Dealers such as The Far West Hobby Shop, Locke, Dexter, Van Rensselaer, etc., have repeated this. And going back even farther, the same thing is found in the old New York auction catalogs of Merwin Sales Co., Walpole, etc.

A couple of years ago the thought came to me that, if these revolvers were the product of the London Pistol Company of England, why did they not have English proof marks on barrel and cylinder in accordance with British law? I decided that the marking on the under side of the frame "Patented Dec. 27, 1859" might give a bit more data, but about that time I received my "Greetings" from the President and immediately had other things to think about.

Upon my return to civilian life last spring, the question was recalled and I wrote to the U. S. Patent Office for a copy of patent number 26,641 of December 27, 1859. The revolver in question is entirely an American product, being patented on this date by Joseph Gruler and Augustus Rebetey of Norwich, Conn. and assigned to the Manhattan Firearms Co. Newark, N. J.

This patent claim is as follows: "The use of the intermediate recesses (rectangular cyclinder slots) in combination with the stop 'd' (a spring activated hand engaging these slots), actuated by the hammer, in pistols where the cylinder is revolved by the act of cocking the pistol, as herein described, thereby effecting a self-acting lock of the cylinder, midway or otherwise, between any two cones."

Collectors will recognize the similarity between this patent description of a cylinder lock and the subsequent ten cylinder slot, five shot, Manhattan Firearms Co. revolver. As will be noted from the illustration, the London Pistol Co. specimen is also a ten cylinder slot, five shot, revolver (although this is not shown in the patent drawing). It is evident that the Manhattan Firearms

Co., assignees of this patent by Gruler and Rebetey, used it as the basic patent on their arms product. Proof of this are the Manhattan revolvers marked "Patented Dec. 27, 1859" on the rear end of the cylinders. It is the same patent date as that of the London Pistol Co. Since the drawing on patent number 26,641 is that of the London Pistol Co. product with the large removable side plate, it is evident that this revolver is the forerunner of the later and more numerous Manhattan models.

Why the name "London Pistol Company" and where were the pistols made? I believe the answer to the first question lies in the address of the patentees which is given as "Joseph Gruler and Augustus Rebetey, of the city of Norwich, in the county of New London, and State of Connecticut." The patentees evidently took for the name of their product the name of their county, quite probably because of the prestige of the name "London." It will be remembered that Sam'l Colt marked his product with a New York City address although the guns were manufactured in Hartford, Conn. As to where the pistols were made, it is probably a subject for future research in this magazine. There were numerous arms makers and factories throughout Connecticut in the early 1860's but it seems more likely that the pistols were manufactured by the Manhattan Firearms Co. in Newark, N. J. under the London Pistol Company trade name. I judge this because the original patent papers show the patent assigned to the Manhattan Firearms Company.

It will probably be impossible to determine exactly how many pistols were manufactured, but the serial number 328 is the highest I have located thus far. It would be safe to say that less than one thousand appeared.

Briefly describing this revolver, it is marked "London Pistol Company" on the top of the barrel reading towards the cylinder. On the frame under the cylinder appears "Patented Dec. 27, 1859." Serial 328 on various parts. Stage coach robbery engraving, which is similar to but not identical to the one appearing on the Colt revolvers, is on the round cylinder. Five shot cylinder with ten cylinder stops or slots. Four inch rifled octagonal barrel of .31 calibre. The engraved frame is customary on all specimens. Large removable side plate on left side as is shown on patent drawing.

Now that we have determined that this London Pistol Company product is the forerunner of the Manhattan Firearms Company and thus is of course American made, the question comes up . . . what type of revolver was made in England by the London Pistol Company which succeeded Colt in 1857? I believe the best answer to that appears in Pollard's book, "A History of Firearms" on page 135. He writes, "Colt's invasion was not a success and the London factory was closed in 1857. The relics were taken over, and a small company appears to have used up the surplus of parts as The London Pistol Company, a name I have seen impressed over an almost obliterated London Colt stamp." I believe we may judge from that that the true English London Pistol Company product is one of left-over Colt parts and that few were manufactured. It is significant that J. N. George's book, "English Pistols and Revolvers," the best book on that subject, makes no mention of the London Pistol Company which succeeded Colt.

With this information, the men who collect American percussion revolvers can add another name to the list of makes they are after. I hope this informa-

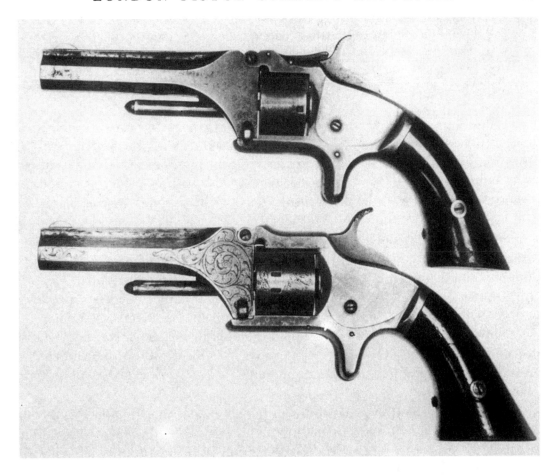

PLATE 31. MANHATTAN SECOND MODEL .22-CALIBER REVOLVER.

Figure 1. Smith & Wesson First Model, Second Issue, Number
30305

Figure 2. Manhattan Second Model, Number 6257.

Two points of superiority possessed by Manhattan's Second Model .22 caliber revolver are shown in this photographic comparison: (1) the safely feature, evidenced by the additional cylinder stops (patented Dec. 27, 1859) and (2) the longer cylinder which was chambered for the .22 caliber *long* cartridge. The Smith & Wesson product had one point of superiority which Manhattan could not overcome: Rollin White's patent of April 3, 1855.

tion will enable our membership in the Gun Collector's Letter to get the jump on the rest of the arms collectors, since it is apparent that there are not enough specimens of the London Pistol Company revolver to go around.

Sam E. Smith
Markesan, Wisconsin

While our research and study of London Pistol Company revolvers has developed facts and opinions which are at variance with certain parts of the foregoing article, we wish to be first in pointing out that our efforts are entirely supplemental to Sam Smith's original study. In this instance, a quotation from another of his excellent writings on firearms is most appropriate: "He who leads the way copies from no one."[2]

Since it has already been established that the .31-caliber Manhattan revolvers in Series I were produced prior to December 27, 1859, and since all of the London Pistol Company revolvers we have examined bear the patent stamping of that date, it would seem a certainty that Manhattan revolvers preceded, rather than followed, the London Pistol Company revolvers. Although this fact appears to be well founded, we hold the opinion that such was not the case. In our opinion, the London Pistol Company revolvers were produced concurrently with the production of the Manhattan .31-caliber revolvers, both Series I and Series II.

We believe that the total answer to the enigma of the London Pistol Company revolvers is to be found in this statement: these revolvers were second quality Manhattan revolvers, the greater number being produced during the period of the Series I .31-caliber Manhattans (with serial numbers below 900). It appears plausible that these second-quality guns were held in stock in a partially completed state of manufacture until sometime after January of 1860, at which time the frames were stamped with the December 27, 1859, patent date, the barrels were stamped with the London Pistol Company name and the remainder of the manufacturing operations were completed. Another possibility is that existence of the London Pistol Company revolvers may have come about by reason of a clearing out of second-quality guns following Manhattan's decision to discontinue their .31-caliber model.

An example of the barrel signing to be found on London Pistol Company revolvers is shown on Plate 19. (See page 82.) We do not believe that such a company existed as a corporate entity. This opinion is based upon the fact that our research in Norwich and New York produced no record of the formation or operation of the company; the lack of an address as a part of the barrel signing (Norwich, New York or Newark) lends further support to the conclusion. It would seem that London Pistol Company was a trade name devised for the purpose of selling the product under a name other than that of Manhattan Firearms Company or it may have been a brand name for the exclusive use of a distributor of Manhattan arms. The selection of the name was probably made for purposes of prestige, although we doubt the possible connection with New London County, Connecticut. At least, the selection was a dignified one and in better taste than the colorful sobriquets for firearms which came into general use during the 1870's.

Examples of the London Pistol Company revolvers are displayed on Plates 20 and 21. (See pages 84 and 88.) As will be seen, specimens are to be found with 4″, 5″ and 6″ barrel lengths and their general details are the same as those described for the Series I .31-caliber Manhattan revolvers, including the details of engraving, finish, etc. The defects which caused the guns to be classified as being of substandard quality fall into several categories. The most common defect appears to have been caused by the cylinder-bolt screw extending through (but not beyond) the right side of the frame. Other defects are to be found in the castings which form the frames, such as sand holes and, occasionally, hard spots which caused the engraver's tool to deviate from the intended pattern. The irregular shape of the grip-frame (see Fig. 2 in Plate 20, page 84) represents a rather unusual defect.

Evidence that the London Pistol Company revolvers were produced concurrently with Manhattan's .31-caliber revolvers is to be found in the serial numbers, and other characteristics, of the guns shown in Plates 20 and 21. (See pages 84 and 88.) Each of the guns shown in Plate 20, plus the gun shown as Fig. 2 in Plate 21, has the characteristics usually associated with the Series I Manhattan .31-caliber revolvers (small trigger-guard, five-shot cylinder and serial numbers below 900) while the gun shown as Fig. 1 in Plate 21 has all of the characteristics of the Series II revolvers, including the blade sight and a serial number above 900. The specimen shown as Fig. 3 in Plate 21 is especially noteworthy as it appears to represent the point of transition between the Series I and Series II Manhattan .31-caliber revolvers. This gun has a brass post-type front sight (Series I), a six-shot cylinder (Series II), bears serial #883 and has a brass trigger-guard which we regard as a transition between the small and large sizes of trigger-guards. Because of the evidence indicating concurrent production of London Pistol Company and Manhattan .31-caliber revolvers, it is our opinion that no separate series of serial numbers was provided for the London Pistol Company revolvers. If this conclusion is logical and accurate, there remains no way to estimate the total number of guns which were stamped with the London Pistol Company marking except the tenuous one of guessing the number of second quality guns Manhattan might have manufactured in their .31-caliber model. The usual method of estimating production of arms through a study of serial numbers does not apply in this case, since the total number of London Pistol Company revolvers must necessarily be included in the total of 4800 guns estimated for both series of Manhattan's .31-caliber model, and a relatively high serial number (above 1700) becomes meaningless. We agree with Sam Smith's original conclusion that less than one thousand revolvers appeared with the London Pistol Company marking, although we have reached this conclusion by means of a more circuitous route than he used; we would qualify the quantity further with an estimate that only a very few hundred were so marked.

Despite the fact that London Pistol Company revolvers may have been considered as second quality arms by the Manhattan company, we do not regard them as less desirable, from the collector's viewpoint, than their alleged first-quality cousins, the Manhattan .31-caliber revolvers. Instead, we consider the London Pistol arms to be more interesting and more desirable because of their rarity.

REFERENCE NOTES

CHAPTER V: 1. *The Gun Collectors Letter*
              Issue #5, December 25, 1946.
           2. *The American Arms Collector*, Vol. 1, No. 2
              Towson, Md.: The Collectors' Press, Inc. 1957.

CHAPTER VI

NEWARK:
.22-CALIBER REVOLVERS

IN THE early months of 1858, a new model of revolver made its appearance in the arms emporiums of New York, Boston, and other eastern cities of the United States. The product met with immediate success and it was destined, with its successor models, to sound the death knell of percussion firearms in America and elsewhere. The new firearm was Smith & Wesson's First Model, First Issue, .22-caliber Single Action Cartridge revolver. Infringers and imitators followed in its wake as a natural consequence and, although probably not the first company to offer a competitive model, Manhattan's copies of Smith & Wesson's First Model revolver were on the market early in 1860. This action placed Manhattan in the company of several arms makers who were ultimately judged to be infringers of Rollin White's patent of April 3, 1855, and assigned to Smith & Wesson on November 17, 1856. Manhattan managed to achieve some distinction within the group of infringers, albeit the achievement may have been a dubious one in the opinion of collectors of Smith & Wesson arms: Manhattan's first model .22-caliber revolver appears to have been the only copy which resembles closely the original by Smith & Wes-

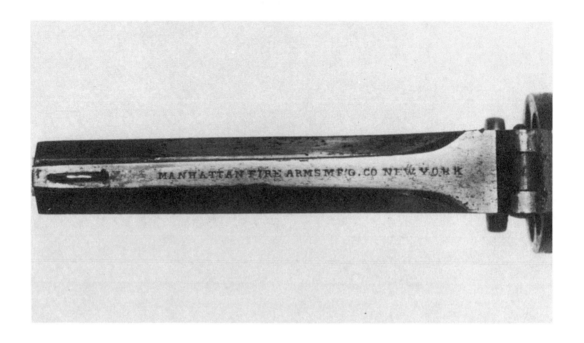

PLATE 32. BARREL SIGNING FOR SECOND MODEL .22-CALIBER REVOLVERS.

Any significant model change appears to have brought about a change in the barrel signing on Manhattan's arms. At least, a change was made on the Series II .31 caliber revolvers and on the Second Model .22, as shown above. The above signing was also similar to the signing used on Series I and Series II .36 caliber revolvers.

son; Manhattan Firearms Company was an *indirect* party in the second of several legal actions brought by Rollin White in seeking enforcement of his patent rights; the copies manufactured by the Manhattan company apparently escaped the ignominy of being restamped "made for Smith & Wesson."

The phenomenal success of Smith & Wesson's First Model revolver undoubtedly governed Manhattan's decision to make a .22-caliber cartridge revolver, although the move was probably guided by two other considerations. The validity of White's patent must have been questionable in the views of Manhattan's legal counsel, as this opinion appears to have been held by a number of makers, and the Manhattan company was on the march to expand its position in the firearms field. Already engaged in the production of their .31-caliber and .36-caliber percussion revolvers, Manhattan was represented in New York City by an aggressive dealer in firearms and related products, Herman Boker & Company. Without question, Boker & Company played an important part in this phase of Manhattan's operations and we suspect that Boker was influential in the initial decision to manufacture the .22-caliber revolvers.

In an earlier section, Chapter I, we made reference to the fact that commencing in 1859, Manhattan shared a common address at #50 Cliff Street, New York City, with Herman Boker & Company. It is probable that Boker & Company became sales agents for Manhattan firearms in 1858, as evidenced by the directory listings. The early models of Manhattan's .31-caliber percussion revolvers, incorporating the features of their up-coming patent of December 27, 1859, may have motivated Boker's interest in the products of the new company. It should be noted that exclusive sales agencies for the products of Colt, Smith & Wesson, Remington, and other leaders in the field were very difficult to obtain. Likewise, the prospective possibilities of a new and sound firearms patent were most attractive to any aggressive agent selling these products. It was of utmost importance to the Manhattan company to establish contact with a distributor who could locate and exploit the market for their arms. In their connection with Herman Boker & Company, Manhattan found a very necessary outlet for the products of their small manufactory.

As noted in Chapter I, Herman Boker & Company were listed in a New York Directory of 1859 as "Importers of Guns and Pistols." Some measure of the eminent position of Boker's firm is indicated by the volume of business transacted between the Ordnance Department, United States Army, and Herman Boker & Company during the years of 1861 through 1865. From August 30, 1861, to and including March 12, 1866, U. S. Army Ordnance purchased firearms and related articles from Herman Boker & Company in the amount of $2,808,740.16.[1] These purchases covered the following items: rifled muskets, with bayonets, of Prussian, Austrian, and English manufacture (the latter being Enfield muskets); sabres and swords for use by infantry, artillery, and

PLATE 33. CYLINDER OF EARLY .36-CALIBER REVOLVER, SERIES I.

Illustrating Cylinder Stops of Trapezoidal Shape.

Cylinder stops of trapezoidal shape are occasionally found on cylinders of .36 caliber Manhattan revolvers of early manufacture. Intended use of the unusual shape is unknown but may have been for the purpose of improved engagement of the stop by the locking bolt. Application of this feature has not been observed on cylinders of guns with serial numbers above 800.

cavalry forces; Sharps carbines; Lefaucheux revolvers and appendages (cartridges, etc.). At least one of these purchases, involving rifled muskets, was anything but advantageous to the Government's interests and Boker was charged with being a "sharper".[2] This incident occurred in 1861 and while it was a serious matter, it appears to have had no effect on Boker's relationship with the Ordnance Department.

Boker is listed as having been a dealer for Smith & Wesson arms during the War years, although purchasing them (when available) through J. W. Storrs, New York agent for Smith & Wesson.[3] Boker's connection with Smith & Wesson's products may have been established earlier than this time (1861-63). If such was the case, he would have been in the best kind of position to have complete knowledge of the success, and scarcity, of the Smith & Wesson .22-caliber revolver. Thus it seems possible that Boker may have turned to Manhattan and importuned the company to manufacture the fast-selling firearms which he could not purchase from Smith & Wesson's agent. Regardless of the circumstances attending their decision to proceed with the program, the undertaking was of major proportions to Manhattan and involved the problems of design, tooling, procurement of machinery and materials plus obvious attempts to improve on the original product. Several months must have passed between the time the program was started, probably during the latter half of 1859, and production of the first acceptable models.

Despite the fact that the First Model of Manhattan's .22-caliber revolver bears a close resemblance to Smith & Wesson's First Model, there is no exact resemblance to any one of the several variations of the original. Duplication of the features of two of the variations are present in the early examples of Manhattan's revolver; these features are associated with the third variation (vertical barrel latch, dating from September of 1858) and with the sixth variation (ratchet on cylinder, dating from June of 1859).[4] Manhattan's copy of the Smith & Wesson probably stemmed from the sixth variation of the original but incorporated enough differences in individual characteristics, and overall appearance, to prove that Manhattan employed original thinking and ingenuity in the design of their revolver. The difference in overall appearance is illustrated by the examples shown in Plate 22 (see page 92); the Smith & Wesson revolver is of the fifth variation while the Manhattan revolvers are of reasonably early vintage. The graceful lines of the Smith & Wesson are contrasted by the compact appearance of the Manhattans. The items of difference referred to above are exemplified in the Manhattan revolver displayed as Fig. 2 in this plate, being composed of the solid or one-piece hammer of vertical inclination and the mechanism of the cylinder-stop release. Thus, it would appear that Manhattan made use of the one-piece hammer prior to its usage by Smith & Wesson although vertical inclination of the hammer spur is to be found in the earliest

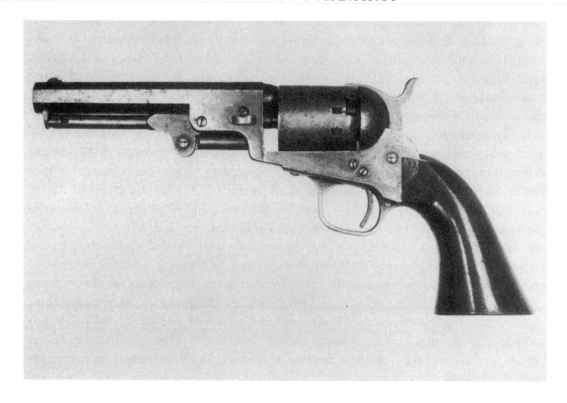

PLATE 34. EARLY .36-CALIBER REVOLVER, SERIES I.

Five-Shot, Five-Inch Barrel, "Fat" Grip, Number 250.

A well-preserved example which incorporates two characteristics associated with the .36 caliber revolvers of early vintage: the fully-rounded or "fat" grip and clyinder stops of unusual shape. The most significant feature represented by this model is the application of caliber .36 to the lighter-than-Navy-size frame. Manhattan may have antedated Colt by more than a year in applying caliber .36 to the lighter frame.

variations of the Smith & Wesson. The cylinder-stop release of the Manhattan, an ingenious device and probably an improvement over the corresponding mechanism of the Smith & Wesson, was well described in an early article on Smith & Wesson revolvers, and similar types, as follows: "The cylinder-stop has a nose which is set at an angle to the nose on the hammer, so that in cocking the latter raises the former, but in firing the two noses pass one another." [5] The foregoing reference does not mention the fact that the top of the cylinder-stop release of the Manhattan revolver also served as the rear sight; this feature may have been insignificant in a firearm of small size but it indicates clearly inventive thinking and careful design.

The specimen under immediate consideration (Fig. 2 in Plate 22, page 92) possesses several features that set it apart from First Model Manhattan .22-caliber revolvers bearing higher serial numbers. These features are: (1) frame plate is iron, instead of brass; (2) absence of tension screw for the main spring, usually located on the inner curve of the grip-strap; (3) bearing on the front of the cylinder is a "headed" pin, instead of a round-head screw; (4) rifling of the barrel consists of six lands and grooves of right hand twist, instead of three lands and grooves and (5) the barrel is unsigned, as shown in Fig. 1 of Plate 23. (See page 96.) The collection of Herschel Logan contains another unsigned example, bearing serial #7, but it is not our opinion that any large quantity of these revolvers were unsigned; we have records of other specimens in the 200 and 300 serial ranges that are signed with the usual semi-circular Manhattan stamping, located on top of the barrel near the hinge. No conclusion should be drawn that Manhattan was attempting to evade identification because of the existence of unsigned arms. All of the evidence points to a contrary conclusion; there is ample indication that the company had a strong desire to be identified with their products in this category.

The Manhattan revolver displayed as Fig. 3 in Plate 22 (see page 92) bears serial #2835, is signed in the usual manner as shown in Fig. 2 of Plate 23, and has several characteristics which differ from those ascribed to gun #1551 mentioned just above. Three of these became standard features of Manhattan's First Model: (1) frame plate is of brass; (2) rifling of the barrel becomes three lands and grooves, of right-hand twist and (3) the bearing on the front of the cylinder is a round-head screw. The fourth difference is represented by a slight change in the contour of the hammer, for the apparent purpose of placing the lug of the hammer in closer relationship to the nose of the cylinder-stop release; the latter change extends through serial #4603, by which time the size of the nose of the cylinder-stop release had been enlarged, but is not found on guns with serial numbers above 4800. Additionally, the back-strap and butt-strap of this revolver are decorated with two copper inlays. The inlay on the back-strap is located up close to the hammer, is a pointed oval in

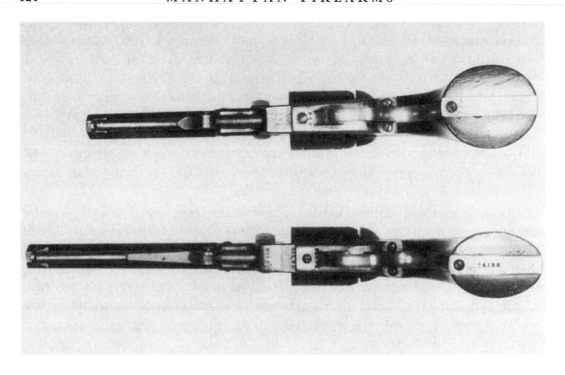

PLATE 35. COMPARISON OF GRIP-BUTTS: .36-CALIBER MANHATTAN REVOLVERS.

Figure 1. Series I, Five-Shot, Five-Inch Barrel, Number 250.

Figure 2. Series IV, Five-Shot, Five-Inch Barrel, Number 56,180.

Illustrating the progression from the fully-rounded grip-butt of an early example in Series I to the "Slim Jim" grip-butt found in the Series IV revolvers. Also shown are the two methods of serially marking the butt-straps; numbers of four digits, or less, were stamped across the shorter dimension of the butt-strap while numbers comprised of five digits were stamped parallel with the long dimension of the butt-strap.

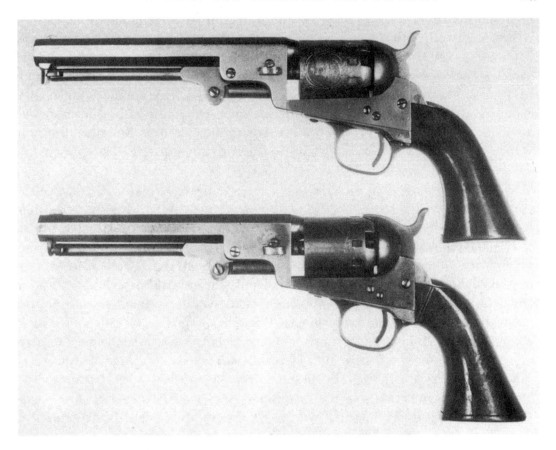

PLATE 36. EARLY .36-CALIBER MANHATTAN REVOLVERS, SERIES I.

Figure 1. Five-Shot, Six-Inch Barrel, Number 876; Extended Barrel Catch.

Figure 2. Five-Shot, Six-Inch Barrel, Number 895; Standard Barrel Catch.

It is believed that .36 caliber revolvers with 6″ barrels occupy a similar position in Manhattan's arms as that attributed to Colt's Navy revolvers with square-back trigger-guards. The 6″ barrel length appears to have been confined to the first 1000 .36 caliber revolvers manufactured, and all observed examples were equipped with the fully-rounded or "fat" grips. It is probable that fewer than 500 guns of the .36 caliber model were made with 6″ barrels.

shape and is engraved; the inlay on the butt-strap is rectangular in shape and is not engraved. This method of decorating the back-straps and butt-straps, with minor variations including knurling on the butt-straps, appears to have been not uncommon on Manhattan's First Model .22-caliber revolvers. Our study of serial numbers for Manhattan's First Model has not been sufficiently exhaustive to establish variations with the same exactness as has been so well done for the Smith & Wesson but we regard the features described for gun #1551 as the first variation and those mentioned for gun #2835 represent the second.

Decorative engraving stands out as one of the distinctive characteristics of Manhattan's First Model .22-caliber revolvers, as it did with their .31-caliber percussion revolvers. The vertical flats of the barrels of the .22-caliber revolvers were hand-engraved with a scroll design similar to the pattern followed in engraving the frames of the .31-caliber percussion revolvers. Barrels were usually finished blue, occasionally were silver plated; the seven-shot cylinders, 5/8" in length, were not engraved, had only one cylinder-stop per chamber with no provision for safety rests and were finished blue; hammers were case-hardened in colors; the iron frames and grip-straps were usually silver plated and the grips of walnut or rosewood were polished and varnished to a high finish. Serial numbers of very small size were stamped on the breech of the barrel, on the rear of the cylinder and on the grip-frame, underneath the grips; the inside surface of one grip was marked with the serial number, usually in pencil but occasionally die-stamped in the higher ranges of serial numbers.

Two examples of the third variation of Manhattan's First Model .22-caliber revolver are depicted on Plate 24. (See page 99.) The modification is a slight one and is found in a more distinct curvature of the hammer spur. The gun shown as Fig. 1 in this plate is representative of the point of change to the third variation as it bears serial #4842 and is worthy of further comment because the barrel was not engraved and was silver plated; the grip-strap and butt-strap have the copper inlays mentioned for gun #2835 and the butt-strap .was knurled. The knurling found on the butt-straps of the Manhattan revolvers was accomplished by means of a die impression; the pattern is a series of regularly curved lines that do not intersect each other. The revolver shown as Fig. 2 in Plate 24 is a presentation piece and, fortunately, bears the date of the presentation. The inscription, shown in Plate 25 (see page 100), reads as follows: "O. Moulton . . . from his friend C. B. Whiting . . . Apr. 19th 1861." As will be seen, the date of the presentation was close to the terminal point of production of Manhattan's First Model .22-caliber revolvers, although the inscribed gun was probably manufactured during the latter part of 1860 or the very early months of 1861.

It should be noted that on each of the Manhattan revolvers discussed thus far (#1551, #2835, #4842 and #6657), the sides of the barrel latch extended over the joint of the barrel and frame in a manner similar to the Smith & Wesson First Model revolvers dating from September of 1858. This feature was covered by patent No. 30,990 issued to Smith & Wesson on December 18, 1860, and one of the purposes of the vertical latch was to prevent lateral motion of the barrel when the latch was engaged.[6] It appears to be more than coincidental that Manhattan altered the mechanism by moving the projections of the latch to a point above the junction of the barrel and frame on the guns in the fourth variation of their First Model. We are inclined to the opinion that the greater number of the Manhattan .22-caliber revolvers with the latch extending down over the joint of the barrel and frame were manufactured during 1860 and that all of their revolvers with the sides of the latch located above the frame and barrel joint were manufactured in 1861. It is a matter of singular contradiction that Manhattan appears to have respected Smith & Wesson's patent of December 18, 1860, but, apparently, had little regard for Rollin White's patent of April 3, 1855.

The fourth variation in the First Model of Manhattan's .22-caliber revolver is illustrated in Plate 26. (See page 102.) On this example, the sides of the barrel latch are located above the frame and barrel joint in the manner previously described; the change was effected by milling a slightly deeper slot into the frame, to take the rounded shape of the latch bar, and this method seems to have served as well as the previous arrangement. In addition, a small pin was eliminated from the top of the frame; as applied on the preceding revolvers, the purpose of the pin had been to limit the amount of upward movement of the arm of the cylinder release. An interesting feature of this specimen is the original cardboard box which has managed to survive for nearly a century. The box was covered with a type of marbleized paper still used for lining the inside covers of ledgers, stock record books, etc. Four of the cartridges displayed in the cartridge board appear to be of the type originally used in the gun as they are very old and bear no head stamps. The label on the box, shown in enlarged form in Plate 27 (see page 104), furnishes the clearest kind of evidence that the Manhattan company did not conceal, or attempt to conceal, its relationship with a revolver similar in appearance to the Smith & Wesson revolver. Existence of the label would indicate that Manhattan had no fear of future misfortune with regard to possible infringement of Rollin White's patent.

Manhattan's First Model .22-caliber revolver was an excellent arm and was by no means inferior to the original from which it was copied; there was an insurmountable "difference" between the original and the copy, however, and that was furnished by White's patent. Based upon a study of serial numbers, it is estimated that Manhattan manufactured 9000 or more of their First Model

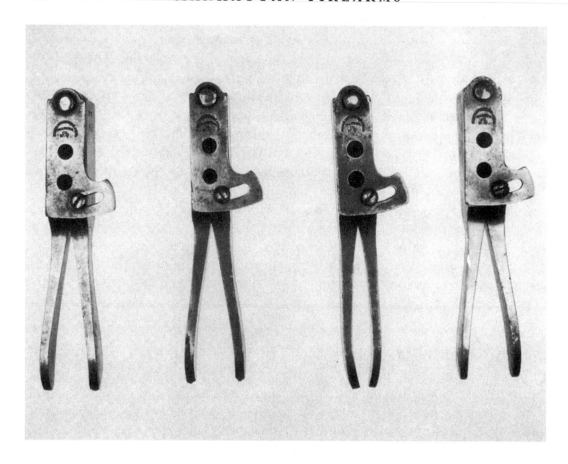

PLATE 37. .36-CALIBER MANHATTAN BULLET MOLDS.

The Manhattan .36 caliber bullet molds have a definite association with the development of the company's .36 caliber revolver. Inasmuch as paper cartridges of proper size were unavailable when the revolver was developed, molds to cast bullets for the revolvers were a required accessory. It is likely that many guns in this category were sold in cardboard boxes which included marked Manhattan molds. The distinctive horse-shoe-shaped stamping may have made its first appearance on the molds although the stamping was also used to mark the barrels of Manhattan First Model .22 caliber revolvers.

.22's, beginning with serial #1, and that the period of production extended from the early part of 1860 until June of 1861.

It would appear that Manhattan began preparations for production of their Second Model .22-caliber revolver not later than March of 1861. This approximation is taken from the letter reproduced on Plate 28. (See page 106.) The letter makes specific inquiries concerning forging machines and because the design of a product and its tooling are prerequisite to procurement of equipment, it is reasonable to presume that design of the new model of revolver was begun prior to the date of the letter. With a few corrections in spelling, the letter reads as follows:

Newark N. J. April 6th 1861

Mr. E. K. Root   Hartford, Ct.
Sir
The Manhattan

Fire Arms Mafg. Co. are desirous of procuring drops of some kind, to forge the frames to the Metallic Cartridge pistols and I have recommended your Compound Crank Drop to them of one length of posts. They have requested me to write you, to ascertain if you, or Colts Patent Fire Arms Mafg. Co., will sell them one for that use, with all your present improvements, (and if any new improvements contemplated by you to have them applied to the machine). Also your *Lowest Cash price* for the machine at your place, and the probable Cost of Setting up the machine by *your help*. Also the shortest time you could furnish one after you should receive an order for one. Also if you would let Mr. Beach the Agent of the Manhattan Co. see your Drop in operation, as they are new to him, and he desires to see one in operation. (We shall buy them or build some ourselves and your drops being the best adapted of any at present in use is the reason of my recommending them).

Very Respectfully yours
A. R. Arnold

My best respects to you, Mr. Lord and the Company for past favors, and confidence shown to me while in your employ. Hoping ever to retain the esteem bestowed on me and for past assistance I return you my thanks—
A. R. A.

It is not known whether the Colt company supplied the forging machines to Manhattan; the answer to this question may yet be revealed when classification of the voluminous Colt files has been completed by the Connecticut State Library. The phrase "of one length of posts" is not clear but it is believed to have been a reference to the size of the machine. The "compound crank drop" was probably similar to a forging press, or punch press, of the present time. Mr. Arnold's connection with Manhattan is not mentioned in his letter but, as will be seen, he was General Superintendent of the company's plant. It is

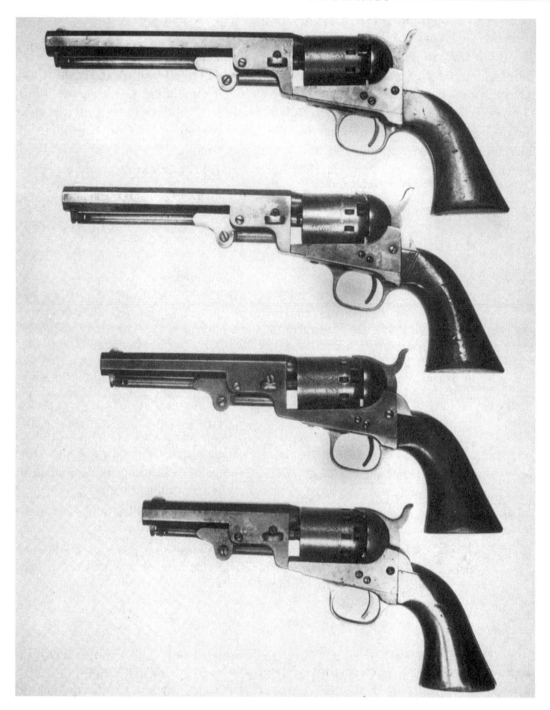

PLATE 38. SERIES I .36-CALIBER MANHATTAN REVOLVERS.

Figure 1. Five-Shot, Six-and-a-Half-Inch Barrel, Number 1932.

Figure 2. Five-Shot, Six-Inch Barrel, Number 895

Figure 3. Five-Shot, Five-Inch Barrel, Number 1183.

Figure 4. Five-Shot, Four-Inch Barrel, Number 3531.

Manufactured prior to January of 1860, the Series I revolvers are the more scarce examples of regular production in the .36 caliber model. Standard features of the model were established early in the period of this series and were maintained, with only minor modifications, until production ceased in 1868. It is estimated that 4200 guns were produced in this series.

interesting to note that Arnold was a former employee of the Colt company; this fact may have been responsible, in part, for the excellence of the Manhattan arms.

The Manhattan Second Model .22-caliber revolver resembled the Smith & Wesson First Model, Second Issue, .22-caliber revolver in a general way and specifically with regard to the larger, removable side plate which provided improved accessability to the parts of the lock. However, Manhattan incorporated several changes in the design of their Second Model .22-caliber revolver which may have made it superior to the corresponding model by Smith & Wesson. The principal design change consisted of the contemplated use of a new and more powerful cartridge: the .22-caliber long. The Smith & Wesson First Model, in all three Issues, was designed to use the .22-caliber short rimfire cartridge. There is some evidence that Manhattan considered the use of, or experimented with, .22-caliber long lipfire cartridges in an early example of their Second Model revolver. It is an indisputable fact that the later and more numerous specimens of this model were made to use the .22-caliber long rimfire cartridge. We do not consider it to be within the scope of this work to delve into a study of the early .22-caliber cartridges or to determine the source of the first .22-caliber cartridges of long size. It is known that Smith & Wesson held the patents on the early rimfire cartridges, that Ethan Allen made lipfire cartridges (we have no information that Allen made lipfire cartridges of .22-caliber) and that patent litigation between the two firms extended over a period of years. We are confident that the source of the first .22-caliber long cartridges will be revealed by some other reference. Until evidence to the contrary is available, it is our opinion that Manhattan's Second Model .22-caliber revolver was the first such revolver to use the long-size cartridge.

An example of an early Manhattan Second Model is shown on Plates 29 and 30. (See pages 107 and 110.) The barrel, grip-frame and grips of this specimen are marked with serial #111. The cylinder is not marked with a serial number, or other marking, but it was obviously made for the gun; this is evidenced by the precision of the ratchet, the hole for the cylinder pin, dimensions of the cylinder slots, etc. The brass cylinder, 15/16" in length, was chambered for six shots instead of the usual seven and the flutes were formed with a rough or "hogging" cut on a milling machine and were not otherwise finished. The most unusual characteristic of the cylinder is shown in Plate 30 (see page 110): the rear of each chamber was recessed, with a slot extending to the outer edge of the cylinder, for the apparent use of lipfire cartridges. Since we have not seen another revolver of this model with a cylinder of similar features, it may be assumed that gun #111 was an experimental piece; we are confident that the workmanship was "factory" in origin and, as has been indicated previously, the Manhattan company was inclined to the use of ivory grips on their de-

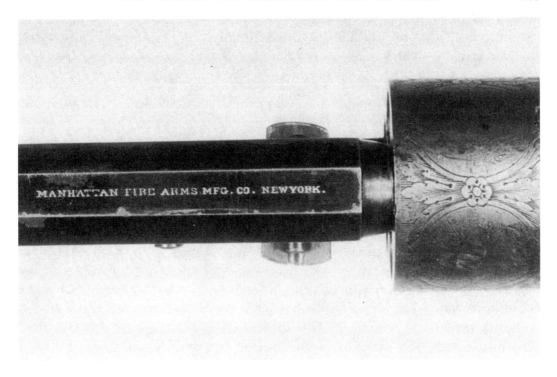

PLATE 39. BARREL SIGNING FOR .36-CALIBER REVOLVERS, SERIES I AND SERIES II.

The one-line New York address appeared on the barrels of slightly more than 14,000 .36 caliber revolvers, being used on both Series I and Series II of this model. The signing is similar to the one used on the barrels of the Series II .31 caliber revolvers although minor differences are present.

velopment or experimental models. It is to be noted that the frame of this specimen is smaller in size than the frames of the later examples of this model; the grip-frame is smaller than the similar part of the First Model revolvers and considerably smaller than the grip-frames of the later guns of the Second Model.

In addition to the long-size cartridge, the other design changes to be found in Manhattan's Second Model were: (1) the adaptation of the safety provisions of their patent of December 27, 1859, to the cylinders of their .22-caliber revolvers; (2) the relocation of the cylinder-stop mechanism from a position on top of the frame to a position within the bottom of the frame, the cylinder-bolt being operated by the action of cocking the hammer and the bolt engaging the stops located near the front end of the cylinder and (3) the addition of a cylinder-pin to the frame assembly, an obvious improvement which provided for better alignment of the cylinder, much more bearing surface for the cylinder and greater rigidity between the frame and the barrel. An evaluation of these improvements plus a visual comparison of specimens of the Smith & Wesson First Model, Second Issue and the Manhattan Second Model, as shown in Plate 31 (see page 113), will furnish ready evidence that the Manhattan may well have been the better arm of the two. Although the Smith & Wesson continues to possess graceful lines, the Manhattan presents a more sturdy appearance and the advantages of the safety feature (the Smith & Wesson had no provision for the hammer to be set in a "safe" position) plus the longer cartridge are very compelling.

The silver-plated revolver displayed as Fig. 2 in Plate 31 (see page 113) is representative of the guns in the higher serial ranges of the Second Model and exemplifies several changes from the features of the First Model; these are in addition to the improvements enumerated in the preceding paragraph. The changed features were: (1) the flat brass frame with larger side plate; (2) the rear sight, a slot filed in the top of the frame; (3) an engraved scene on the cylinder, depicting hand-to-hand combat between Settlers and Indians, in which one of the Settlers is being scalped; (4) a revised barrel signing, as illustrated in Plate 32 (see page 118); (5) the stamping of the 1859 patent date on the bottom flat of the barrel and (6) the slightly enlarged grips. Except for the revised signing, the barrels of the revolvers were not changed as a result of the model change. The other characteristics of engraving the barrels, types of finish of the parts, mode of serially marking the parts, etc., were the same for the Second Model as have been described for the First Model. Serial numbers of the Second Model began with serial #1; it is estimated that more than 8000 Second Model .22-caliber revolvers were produced between June of 1861 and October of 1862.

Production of the Second Model revolvers probably continued without interruption until the early part of 1862 when the storm clouds of a patent

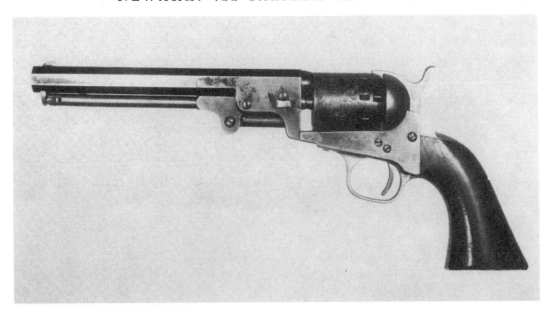

PLATE 40. SERIES II .36-CALIBER REVOLVER OWNED BY EUGENE LITTELL, U.S.N.

Five-Shot, Six-and-a-Half-Inch Barrel, Number 6054.

A fine example of a Manhattan revolver whose owner served in the Union Navy during the War Between the States. The gun is regarded as unusually desirable because of its association with military service, even though it was not of service issue. Guns with historical attachments are entitled to the highest degree of appreciation by collectors and gun enthusiasts.

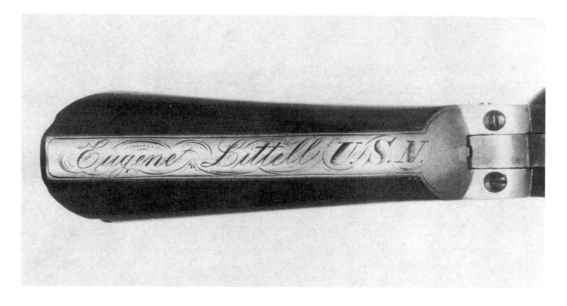

PLATE 41. INSCRIBED BACK-STRAP OF EUGENE LITTELL REVOLVER.

The Littell revolver is believed to have been a presentation piece and has been carefully preserved. Eugene Littell was commissioned in the grade of Assistant Paymaster at New York on July 3, 1863. He served on the following warships: U.S.S. Racer, U.S.S. Dan Smith and U.S.S. Kansas and was discharged on October 17, 1865.

suit, filed against Herman Boker & Company by Rollin White and Smith & Wesson, began to gather. The ensuing storm extended over a period of several months and served to halt production of the Manhattan .22-caliber revolvers and the possible development of other models of cartridge revolvers.

The lawsuit against Herman Boker *et al.* was filed by the attorneys for White and Smith & Wesson in the United States Circuit Court, Southern District of New York, probably during the latter part of November 1861. Upon first examination, it may seem unusual that the suit should have been filed against Herman Boker & Company, previously identified as sales agents for Manhattan, instead of against Manhattan Firearms Manufacturing Company, makers of the arms which formed the basis of the lawsuit. The reason for the action against Boker is found in the basic right provided by a patent such as was held by Rollin White: "The patent grant creates a right to exclude others from making, using or selling any embodiment of the patented invention during the life of the patent." [7] In this case, the plaintiffs elected to proceed against the seller rather than against the maker in the prosecution of their rights under the patent. We have previously cited Boker's eminent position as well as Manhattan's small stature as a manufacturer. There may have been other considerations but it is probable that Boker loomed as a more prosperous target for the legalistic seige guns of Rollin White.

The complete details of the lawsuit are preserved within the National Archives in Washington, D. C. While it is impractical to reproduce any substantial part of these details, since they comprise several hundred pages written in longhand, the Court's records of the suit have been reviewed and summarized by Lt. Col. R. C. Kuhn. Certain parts of Col. Kuhn's summarization are directly related to Manhattan, as well as Boker's relationship with the company, and are reproduced for their informative values.

From the complainants: "Said defendants have wrongfully made and sold, since November 17, 1856, about 12,000 pistols and revolving firearms. All consisted of extended chambers through the rear of the cylinder for the purpose of loading them at the breech from behind, either by hand or by self-acting chargers from a magazine placed in the rear of said cylinder. The defendants' gains and profits are believed to be about the full sum of Sixty Thousand Dollars and the petitioners pray that the defendants may be required to make a disclosure of all such gains and profits. That although requested to desist and pay Smith & Wesson for such arms as they had already made, the defendants refused to do so. The petitioners request that, by a decree of this Court, the defendants be made to account for and pay over to Smith & Wesson all such gains and profits and all (of the defendants) be enjoined by decree from making or causing to be made, in any manner, any Revolving or Repeating Firearms containing the said improvements granted by said letter patent. The petitioners

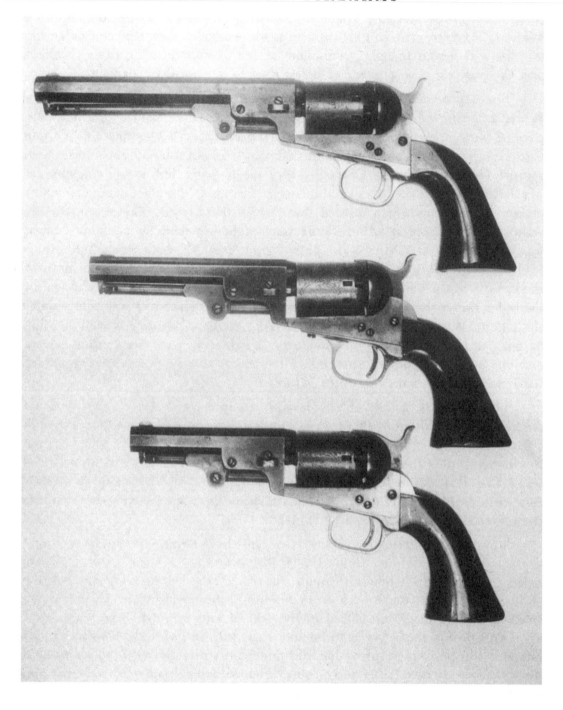

PLATE 42. SERIES II, .36-CALIBER MANHATTAN REVOLVERS.

Figure 1. Five-Shot, Six-and-a-Half-Inch Barrel, Number 11,121.

Figure 2. Five-Shot, Five-Inch Barrel, Number 7795.

Figure 3. Five-Shot, Four-Inch Barrel, Number 7432.

Manhattan's .36 caliber revolvers in Series II differed only slightly from those in Series I. Chief item of difference is the patent date "DEC 27, 1859" which was stamped on the cylinders of the Series II revolvers. Additionally, all of the Series II guns are identified by in-plant inspection markings. Approximately 10,000 guns were produced in Series II (estimated serial numbers 4200 to 14,500) between the approximate dates of January 30, 1860 and September 1, 1861.

also request that all (infringing firearms) be destroyed or delivered to the Court and that the defendants pay any and all court costs. The petitioners ask for a preliminary or provisional injunction until such time as a perpetual injunction is issued."

The date of November 17, 1856, referred to above, was the date on which Rollin White granted an exclusive assignment of his patent No. 12,649 to Smith & Wesson and, while very pertinent to the case, does not indicate the date of the beginning of manufacture of the Manhattan .22-caliber revolvers. The estimated claim by White's attorneys as to the quantity of arms involved (12,000) was probably much closer to the true quantity than they realized. However, the claim for $60,000 in "gains and profits" was a ridiculous one, probably more than twice the true amount if Boker had really sold all of the 12,000 pistols as claimed.

The response of Boker *et al.* to the complaint and petition of White *et al.* was signed by Henry Boker and was dated April 8, 1862. The response included the following: "And the defendants further answering admit they have sold revolving pistols the chambers of the cylinder of which were bored right through to the rear, so that they could be loaded at the rear end by a made cartridge and they aver the truth to be that all the revolving pistols constructed on the plan above described, and which are averred in said bill to be an infringement on the invention of said Rollin White conveyed by him as set out therein, which they have sold were sold by them as Agents for the Manhattan Fire Arms Co., for which sales they received a regular commission.

"And these defendants expressly aver that neither they nor either of them have ever manufactured revolving pistols constructed on the plan above described at any time, nor are they, nor either of them, interested in any way in the said Manhattan Fire Arms Company either as officers or stockholders in said company." The response also stated that the Manhattan revolving pistols were not infringements on White's patent, that Herman Boker & Co. did not sell 12,000 pistols nor make $60,000 in gains and profits and asked that the defendants be dismissed from the suit.

It would seem to be abundantly clear that in making their response to the suit, Boker & Company also made an effort to shift the onus of the action to the Manhattan company. This attempt to gain an easy release was not allowed and the case came to trial about two months later. The defense made a strong effort to prove that White's patent had been antedated by other patents, both foreign and domestic. As will be readily understood, there were many other individuals and companies who had a serious interest in the proceedings and, more particularly, in the welfare of the defendants' case. The names of the witnesses called by the complainants and the defendants included the following: Charles H. Pond, B. F. Hart, William J. Syms, John J. Spies, Joseph Cooper,

Marcellus Hartley, Charles Folsom, George G. Moore, Jacob R. Schuyler, Jubal Harrington, Thomas P. Wheelock, Benjamin Kittredge, James Warner, Thomas K. Bacon (*sic*), William Reed, Christian Sharp and John P. Lower.

Some of the testimony recorded on June 6, 1862, bears directly upon Manhattan and is considered to be very informative:

> *Question:* By whom was this Mr. Arnold employed?
> *Answer:*   By the Manhattan Company who make the pistols that the defendant sells. . . . .
>
> *Question:* What is your name, age and occupation?
> *Answer:*   My name is Andrew R. Arnold. I am 53 years of age. My occupation is General Superintendent of the Manhattan Company's Mechanical business. . . . .

The foregoing statement, "the Manhattan Company's Mechanical business," gives rise to the probability that Manhattan was engaged in operations additional to the manufacturing of firearms. We consider it to be a strong likelihood that the company was engaged in the manufacture of metallic cartridges. The indicated evolvement of the .22-caliber long rimfire cartridge in connection with Manhattan's Second Model revolver, plus the statement of purpose in the company's Articles of Incorporation of May 26, 1855: "for the purpose and object of manufacturing and dealing in firearms, *ammunition* (author's italics) and other articles pertaining to the firearms business" and a similar statement of purpose when Manhattan was rechartered under the laws of New Jersey on September 15, 1863, lend substantial weight to this opinion.

The decision of the Court in the case of White *et al. vs.* Boker *et al.* was rendered by Judge Samuel Nelson on October 25, 1862, to the effect that "The defendants shall make good all gains and profits, submit books, records, etc., and pay up."

The permanent stop order, restraining Herman Boker & Company from infringing on Rollin White's patent, was issued by Chief Justice Roger B. Taney on October 31, 1862. Examination of the Court's records failed to disclose whether Herman Boker & Company complied with the order to "pay up." It is doubtful that any damages were paid by the Manhattan company, since none were later credited to White, by Smith & Wesson, from this source.

A certain consequence of the outcome of the case was that Manhattan ceased the production of their .22-caliber revolvers during the life of Rollin White's patent. There is some evidence that the company manufactured a quantity of unmarked .22-caliber revolvers during the period of transition connecting it with American Standard Tool Company and this point will be discussed in a later chapter.

REFERENCE NOTES

CHAPTER VI: 1. National Archives (Washington, D. C.)
Records of Purchases, U. S. Army Ordnance

2. *Lincoln and the Tools of War*
Robert V. Bruce
New York: The Bobbs-Merrill Co. Inc. 1956, page 51

3. *Smith & Wesson Revolvers*
John E. Parsons
New York: William Morrow & Co. 1957, page 28

4. *Ibid.,* p. 20

5. *The Smith & Wesson Revolvers, First Model, No's 1, 2 & 3*
Fred A. Moats
Akron, Ohio: The Gun Report, Inc.
The Gun Report, Vol. 1, No. 2, Monograph No. 2 1939

6. Parsons, *op. cit.,* p. 17

7. *Encyclopedia Britannica*
Chicago: Encyclopedia Britannica, Inc. 1946, XVII, 372

CHAPTER VII

NEWARK:
.36-CALIBER REVOLVERS

IN CHAPTER III, "The Manhattan Patents," it was established that Manhattan Firearms Manufacturing Company moved its manufactory from Norwich, Connecticut, to Newark, New Jersey on or about March 29, 1859. Further, in Chapter IV, ".31-Caliber Manhattan Revolvers," an estimate was given that 900 to 1000 of these revolvers were produced prior to January 30, 1860. Since production of their .22-caliber revolvers did not begin until early in 1860, the combination of these facts raises the question: how could the Manhattan company have sustained its operations during all of 1859 on the very small production of 900 to 1000 .31-caliber revolvers? The answer to this question is found in the existence of the model that became the mainstay of their arms production, the .36-caliber percussion revolver. This model not only sustained the company's operations during 1859, when approximately 4000 of these arms were manufactured, it likewise became Manhattan's "bread and butter" product and was responsible for maintaining the company's position in the field of firearms manufacturing until the end of 1868. It is estimated that 78,000 of the .36-caliber revolvers were produced during the years

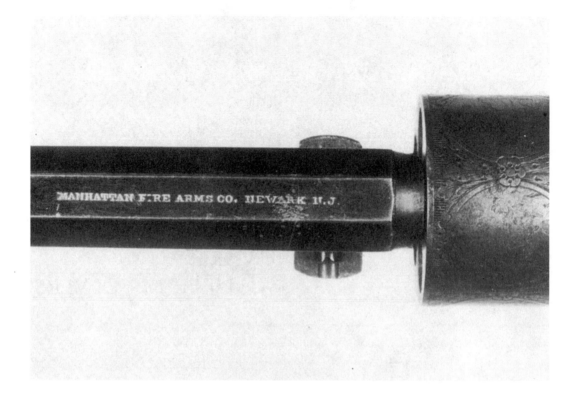

PLATE 43. BARREL SIGNING FOR .36-CALIBER REVOLVERS, SERIES III.

The one-line Newark address accounted for the principal difference between the guns produced in Series II and those of Series III. It is to be noted that the abbreviation for the word "Manufacturing" was discontinued in the one-line Newark address, after having been a part of the company's identification on all of its products until this change was made. The change was, in fact, indicative of the re-chartering of the Manhattan company in New Jersey.

of 1859 through 1868, inclusive, and the model probably accounted for 75% of the company's total output of firearms.

The Manhattan .36-caliber revolver was a copy of the over-all design of two models of Colt revolvers, the 1851 Navy and the 1849 Pocket Models. Although adhering closely to Colt's basic design, Manhattan appears to have been first in adapting caliber .36 to a revolver with a frame lighter than that of the 1851 Navy model. Colt's first similar adaptation is found in the "Pocket Pistol of Navy Caliber," otherwise known as the Model of 1853, which was probably produced not earlier than 1860. Therefore, Manhattan appears to have antedated Colt by at least a year on the model just referred to, and by about three years on the 1862 Police Model, in the application of caliber .36 to the lighter frame. One consequence of this development must have been to create a need for a percussion (paper) cartridge of a size not then available. It is here emphasized that Manhattan's .36-caliber revolver was a copy of Colt's design but it was not, in the least degree, an infringement. We consider it proper, at this point, to correct two erroneous impressions which have prevailed concerning the relationship between Colt and Manhattan. The first of these falsities holds that Colt forced Manhattan out of business through a lawsuit for infringement, or for some other vague reason; the second, that Manhattan operated under a license from Colt. We have found no shred of evidence which would confirm either of these opinions; they were probably founded in the otherwise well-intentioned small talk of gun collectors and were passed along until they took the form of accepted facts, with some part of the misinformation finding its way into printed material.

Development of Manhattan's .36-caliber revolver may have been started while the company was operating in Norwich. We have made an earlier reference, in Chapter III, that the lack of immediate success in obtaining a patent on the side plate construction of their .31-caliber revolver may have influenced some of Manhattan's policies. In view of the early date of development of their .31-caliber revolver (1858) plus the fact that not more than 1000 of this model were produced during 1859, it would seem that a decision must have been made to accelerate the production of the .36-caliber model and to withhold or limit production of the .31-caliber model. Our research and study relating to the development of the .36-caliber revolvers produced no results similar to those set forth in Chapter IV. This fact leads us to the view that there was no period of development of the .36-caliber model which paralleled that of the .31-caliber model. Several years ago, we had an opportunity to examine a .36-caliber Manhattan revolver bearing serial #1. Although in relatively poor condition, this revolver appeared to possess all of the features usually associated with the model and it had none which would set it apart from a similar specimen of later manufacture. Our rather meticulous examination of the gun confirms

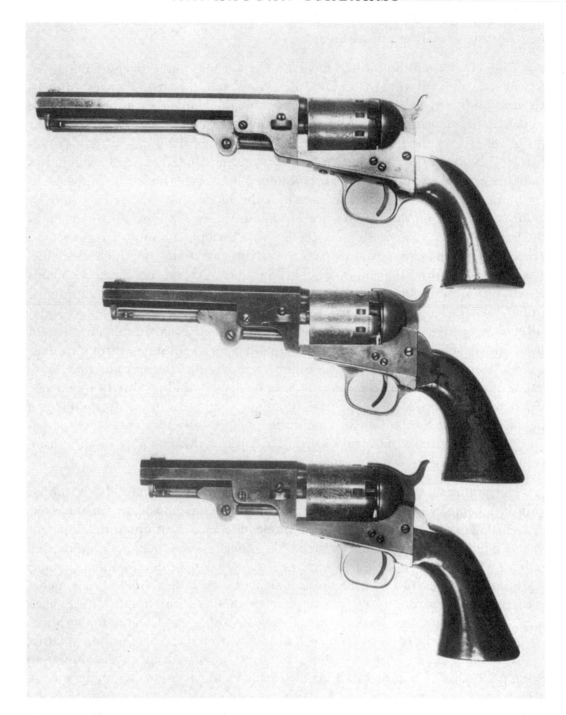

PLATE 44. SERIES III .36-CALIBER MANHATTAN REVOLVERS.

Figure 1. Five-Shot, Six-and-a-Half-Inch Barrel, Number 29,910.

Figure 2. Five-Shot, Five-Inch Barrel, Number 17,276.

Figure 3. Five-Shot, Four-Inch Barrel, Number 18,718.

The Series III revolvers were the most numerous of the .36 caliber model as about 30,000 (estimated range of serial numbers: 14,500 to 45,200) were made between the approximate dates of September 1, 1861 and April 1, 1864. It is probable that production of the .36 caliber model reached a peak of 1000 per month during the period mentioned. A new innovation, the spring plate, made its appearance on a limited quantity of Series III revolvers.

our present opinion that there was no lengthy period of initial development of Manhattan's .36-caliber model. In anticipation of the thoughts of our friends with a penchant for Colt's arms, it is probably appropriate to inquire: Indeed, why should there have been such a period of development? We agree; the original pattern was the best one obtainable. However, there were certain characteristics attached to the early .36-caliber revolvers which give clear evidence that Manhattan made an effort to produce an arm quite different from any model that Colt was then manufacturing.

A study of the early .36-caliber revolvers indicates that Manhattan established the basic standards of design for this model following production of the first 1000 revolvers. With the basic standards thus established, they were retained during the entire period of production of the model with only minor modifications. We have made an earlier reference to the quality of orderliness which is exhibited in the entire line of Manhattan arms. This quality of orderliness permits the classification of all of the production of the .36-caliber revolvers into five distinct categories. In most cases, the distinction is slight but nevertheless quite clear. These categories will be discussed and illustrated, separately, under the titles of Series I, Series II, Series III, Series IV and Series V.

SERIES I .36-CALIBER REVOLVERS

The distinguishing characteristics of the Series I .36-caliber revolvers are these:

1. Five-shot cylinder
2. Barrel signed with New York address
3. Absence of 1859 patent date on the cylinder
4. Estimated range of serial numbers: 1 to 4200.

A distinctive feature of all of the .36-caliber revolvers is found in the type of engraving which decorated the cylinders. While Manhattan probably rejected a five-panel motif of engraving for their .31-caliber revolvers, as mentioned in Chapter IV, a five-panel motif was developed for and applied to the cylinders of the .36-caliber model. The name of the original engraver is unknown but the quality of the design, in our opinion, was not excelled during that period of roller-die engraving. The engraving design for the cylinders of the .36-caliber model has been expertly described by C. Meade Patterson, as follows:

> The .36-caliber Manhattan percussion revolvers have five different scenes engraved in their cylinders. Each scene is enclosed in an oval frame which is adorned with floral and scroll designs. Identical flowers with six petals each join the decorative oval frames at their midpoints on each side. The background between the oval frames is filled with sprays of leaves.

Scene 1 is readily recognizable as containing "ships in full sail." This scene depicts three sailing ships and, in the foreground, a rowboat containing six men. By rotating the cylinder from left to right, beginning with Scene 1, the other scenes will be Scene 2 through 5, respectively.

Scene 2 shows three men with pistols firing at man with sword and at two soldiers with muskets and fixed bayonets.

Scene 3 shows a wounded soldier, seated on the ground, firing a pistol at a cavalryman charging with upraised saber. Two soldiers are in the back-ground. One is pointing a rifle with bayonet, the other points a pistol.

Scene 4 pictures two men standing in bow of rowboat approaching shore and being rowed by two other men. The men in the bow of the boat are shooting at a group of men standing on shore.

Scene 5 depicts a cavalry charge against infantry. One man on horse-back is shooting a pistol and another mounted soldier is swinging a saber. They are attacking infantry soldiers armed with rifles.

It would appear that Manhattan made an initial production-run of about 1000 .36-caliber revolvers in Series I with certain features which are not present in the guns produced in the latter part of this series.

The first of these features is represented by the cylinder-stops of unusual shape which are to be found on the cylinders of examples in the first few hundred guns manufactured. These stops are trapezoidal in shape, as differentiated from the rectangular stops of the later guns, and are shown on the cylinder in Plate 33. (See page 120.) According to our study of the earlier revolvers, this type of cylinder-stop was used on guns with serial numbers below 800. In searching for an explanation of the purpose of the trapezoidal slot, it is our view that Manhattan was endeavoring to accomplish the same result obtained by a lead-in shot milled into the leading edge of the rectangular stops as found on the cylinders of Colt's revolvers and covered by Colt's patent of September 10, 1850. The theory behind the trapezoidal shape may have been that the wider opening provided by the leading edge, coupled with the angular sides, would permit of improved engagement of the cylinder-bolt by the stop. Whatever the theory may have been, this innovation must have failed to function as expected and was discontinued after a relatively short period of application.

A second distinguishing feature is exemplified by the larger or "fat" grips of the revolvers with serial numbers below 1000. The "fat" grip is an interesting characteristic of the revolver pictured in Plate 34; the feature is more clearly set forth in the comparison of the butt of this gun with the butt of a later specimen, as shown in Plate 35. It may have been the intent to create the "feel" of a larger weapon, in the use of the larger grips on the early revolvers. Although this effect may not have been attained, the larger grips are certainly distinctive. One of our waggish collector-friends has suggested that the early revolvers with

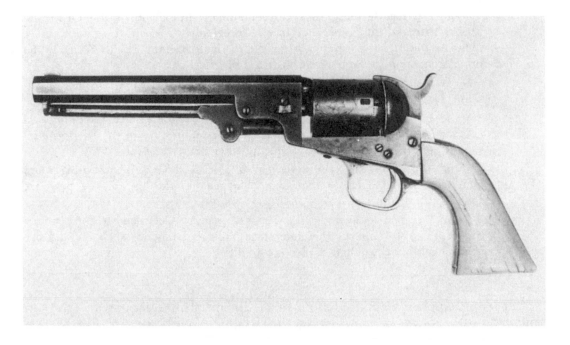

PLATE 45. SERIES III .36-CALIBER REVOLVER EQUIPPED WITH SPRING PLATE.

Five-Shot, Six-and-a-Half-Inch Barrel, Special Serial Number 23.

The above example bears the one-line Newark address and was manufactured early in the period of the Series III revolvers. It is believed that the gun was one of about one hundred similar revolvers which were produced on a pilot-model basis, given a special series of serial numbers beginning with #1 and issued to show the advantages of the operation of the spring plate.

the "fat" grips be designated as the "Miss America Model," because of the fully-rounded butt. The suggestion has considerable merit.

The third feature associated with the guns of early manufacture is found in the barrel length of 6″. The usual barrel lengths of Manhattan's .36-caliber revolvers were 4″, 5″ and 6½″. However, the 6″ barrel length is a peculiarity of the guns with serial numbers below 1000 and it is probable that less than half of this group had 6″ barrels. In our opinion, the .36-caliber revolvers with 6″ barrels occupy the same position in the Manhattan line of firearms as that attributed to the Colt 1851 Navy Model with square-back trigger-guard and must be regarded as very desirable rarities of the .36-caliber model. Two examples with 6″ barrels are shown in Plate 36 (see page 125); it is to be noted that the gun displayed as Fig. 1 has an extended barrel catch of unusual design. This feature is entirely original to the gun and has been observed on two other and similar specimens with 6″ barrels; the extended barrel catch appears to have been an improvement over the usual type, functionally as well as design-wise. The grips were made of an exceptionally good piece of walnut. The revolver shown as Fig. 2 in the above plate has the usual type of barrel catch, although it bears a serial only 19 numbers higher than that of the other gun, and is marked on both sides of the trigger-guard with the name of a former (and perhaps the original) owner, one "Lefty Yotz."

An additional feature which belongs to the revolvers in Series I is a type of rifling not used in guns of the later categories. In most of the revolvers manufactured in Series I the rifling of the barrels consisted of three lands and three grooves, of about equal widths and of right twist; thereafter, rifling of the barrels was five lands and five grooves, of right twist, with the grooves being somewhat narrower than the lands. The ratchets on the cylinders of the revolvers in Series I were of a smaller diameter (9/16″) than those noted in the later series which measure ⅝″. This change occurred during production of the Series II revolvers.

We consider the .36-caliber Manhattan bullet molds to have been directly connected with the .36-caliber revolvers manufactured in Series I. An earlier statement set forth the fact that development of the .36-caliber Manhattan revolver must have created the need for a paper cartridge of a size not then available. Thus, the manufacture of molds to cast bullets of appropriate size would have been a necessary consequence in providing a required accessory for the revolvers. It is probable that many of the early .36-caliber revolvers were sold in cardboard boxes which included the marked Manhattan molds. A group of four Manhattan .36-caliber molds is exhibited in Plate 37. (See page 128.) It is to be noted that the semi-circular signing used for marking the molds is the same signing used for marking the barrels of Manhattan's First Model .22-caliber revolvers. It is our view that the semicircular stamping die was developed initially for the .36-caliber molds and was used later for marking the barrels of

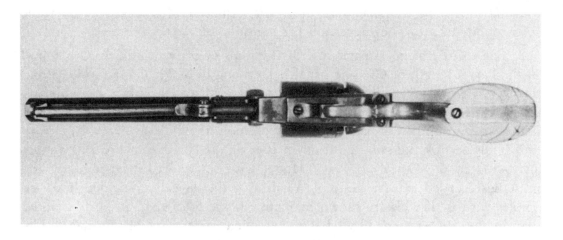

PLATE 46. SERIES III .36-CALIBER REVOLVER NUMBER 23, BOTTOM VIEW.

In addition to the spring plate and the special number designation, a distinctive feature of the pilot model revolver is the absence of any external serial numbers. Serial numbers on each of the major parts are found in unusual locations. The number on the cylinder is on the front face; barrel, on the rear face of the lug; frame, on the left rear face; triggerguard, left side of grip curve; back-strap, left side of strap.

the .22-caliber revolvers, although the application may have been concurrent during 1860.

The standard examples of the Series I .36-caliber Manhattan revolvers are represented by the guns pictured in Plate 38. (See page 130.) The revolvers in Series I were made in 4″, 5″, 6″ and 6½″ barrel lengths; as previously indicated, the 6″ barrel length represents a definite rarity and the 5″ barrel length was probably the most common. The 6½″ barrel length appears to have replaced the 6″ barrel length at a point between serial numbers 1000 and 1500 and was retained as a standard length for the ensuing production in all of the series. We are not inclined to designate the Manhattan revolvers with 6½″ barrels with the generally accepted title of "Manhattan Navy"; it is our view that the title of "Navy" belongs more properly to .36-caliber revolvers of larger dimensions. "Flat" grip, Fig. 1 in Plate 36a is a rarity.

The details of finish for the .36-caliber Manhattan revolvers in all of the series were: barrels and cylinders were blued; frames, hammers and loading levers were case-hardened in colors; brass trigger-guards and back-straps were silver plated; one-piece walnut grips were mahogany stained and given several coats of varnish to produce a high finish of excellent durability. Serial number locations on the various parts were: barrel, bottom of lug; frame, at junction of barrel lug; trigger-guard, forward of bow; back-strap, on butt near screw-hole (earlier models), horizontally along butt on guns with serials above four digits; loading lever, on right side adjacent to screw-hole; plunger, right side of flat portion on guns with low serials, not marked on guns of later manufacture; cylinder, at rear, on face of area between two nipples or cones; wedge, bottom side; cylinder pin, left side; grips, in pencil, underneath back-strap.

The estimated period of production of the .36-caliber revolvers in Series I was from the early part of 1859 until January 30, 1860.

We were able to find, in the New York City Hall of Records, the official Annual Report covering the results of Manhattan's operations for 1859. Although the report is not fully informative, it is considered to be worthy of reproduction.

> The Manhattan Fire Arms Manufacturing Company, in pursuance of the statute, in such case made and provided, do hereby report: That the total amount of the capital of the said company is twenty thousand dollars, divided in four hundred shares of fifty dollars each, the full amount of which has been paid in. That the amount of its existing debt is, Fifteen thousand two hundred, and sixty two dollars, and twenty-two cents. In witness whereof this report is signed by the subscribers, being the president and a majority of the Trustees of the said company this first day of January 1860.
>
> F. H. Smith President
>
> R. D. Baldwin)
> D. W. Bailey) Trustees
> S. T. Peters)

City and County of New York . . . Albert Beach being sworn says that he is the Secretary of the said Manhattan Fire Arms Manufacturing Company, that he has prepared and read the foregoing report, and knows the contents thereof, and that the same is true.

Albert Beach
Sworn to this seventh day of February 1860
Thos. S. Riveth
Notary Public
in the city and county of New York.

. . . .

SERIES II .36-CALIBER REVOLVERS

The distinguishing characteristics of the Series II .36-caliber revolvers are these:

1. Five-shot cylinder
2. Barrel signed with New York address
3. Cylinder stamped with 1859 patent date
4. Estimated range of serial numbers: 4200 to 14,500.

An example of the New York address, used in signing the barrels of the .36-caliber revolvers manufactured in Series I and in Series II, is displayed in Plate 39. (See page 133). Although very similar to the signing of the barrels of the Series II .31-caliber revolvers, the signing on the barrels of the .36-caliber revolvers involved a die with larger characters and other minor differences.

Beginning with the Series II .36-caliber revolvers, the stamping of the cylinders with the 1859 patent date became a standard feature of the model. The legend "PATENTED DEC 27, 1859" was stamped in very small characters on two projections between the cones at the extreme rear edge of the flat portion of the cylinder, between the cylinder stops and the curvature of the rear of the cylinder. The word "PATENTED" was stamped on one projection and "DEC 27, 1859" was stamped on the adjoining projection at the right. Thus, the stamping appeared on about 74,000 guns of the .36-caliber model.

We have previously mentioned the fact that Manhattan settled on the basic standards of their .36-caliber model in a relatively short time. Except for the increased diameter of the cylinder ratchet and the stamping of the patent date on the cylinder, we have found no variations of consequence in the Series II revolvers. This point is indicative of a sound plan for economical production of their arms.

The Manhattan in-plant inspection markings made their appearance on the .36-caliber revolvers somewhere between the later production in Series I and the early production in Series II. These markings were stamped on the bottom flats of the barrels of the Series I, Series II and Series III revolvers. The markings consisted of a "v," a single dot, two dots, the letter K, the letter E within a circle and, occasionally, *a miniature pair of spectacles;* the latter stamping is a prime example of American humor in industry. Beginning with the Series IV revolvers, the in-plant inspection markings appear on the rear face of the barrel lug, just below the breech end of the barrel.

A revolver produced within Series II and possessing considerable color and interest is pictured in Plates 40 and 41. (See pages 135 and 136.) The gun is considered noteworthy because of its connection with Naval Service during the War Between the States. Similar examples made by any manufacturer of the period can scarcely be regarded as common. In the case of a Manhattan, we regard it as a desirable rarity since it was a personal sidearm and not of service issue. The inscribed owner, Eugene Littell, was commissioned in the grade of Assistant Paymaster at New York on July 3, 1863; he served on U. S. S. *Racer,* U. S. S. *Dan Smith* and U. S. S. *Kansas* and was discharged on October 17, 1865.[1] We make the observation, for whatever it may be worth, that gun collectors generally have too little appreciation of the value of arms similar to the one just above. Relics with an historical attachment, whether the man's name was Robert E. Lee, U. S. Grant, or just plain Private Jones, are worthy of much more appreciation than is usually given to them.

The standard examples of the Series II .36-caliber Manhattan revolvers are represented by the guns shown in Plate 42. (See page 138.) As indicated, the revolvers in Series II were made in 4", 5", and 6½" barrel lengths.

The estimated period of production of the .36-caliber revolvers in Series II was from January 30, 1860, until September 1, 1861.

The official Annual Report covering the results of Manhattan's operations for 1860, as taken from the New York City Hall of Records, was substantially the same as for the preceding year.

The Manhattan Fire Arms Manufacturing Company, in pursuance of the statute, in such case made and provided, do hereby report: That the total amount of the capital of the said company is twenty thousand dollars, divided in four hundred shares of fifty dollars each, the full amount of which has been paid in. That the amount of its existing debt is, Eleven thousand eight hundred and seventy eight dollars and thirty cents. In witness whereof this report is signed by the subscribers, being the president and a majority of the Trustees of the said company this seventh day of February 1861.

F. H. Smith   President

R. D. Baldwin   )
D. W. Bailey   ) Trustees
S. T. Peters   )

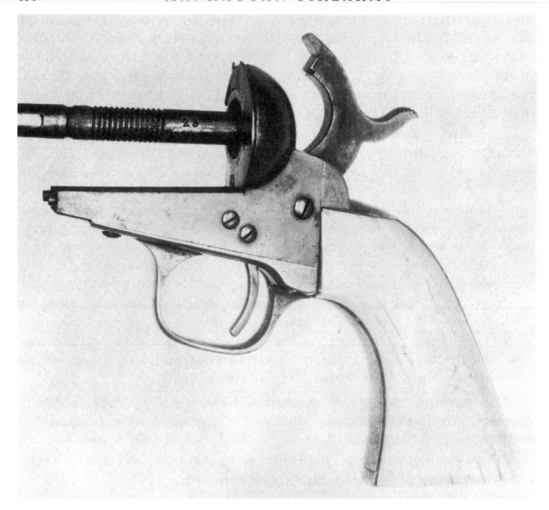

PLATE 47. METHOD OF ATTACHMENT OF SPRING PLATE, .36-CALIBER REVOLVERS.

The spring steel plate was attached to the recoil shield by means of a single small screw located at the bottom of the shield and in line with the centerline of the arbor or cylinder pin. As shown, the plate extended from the bottom edge of the capping aperture to a point about ⅛″ past the channel in the recoil shield for the hammer. The top of the plate was notched to a depth of 1/16″ to accommodate the hammer. Purpose of the plate was to deflect laterally the fire from the nipple, thus reducing the possibility of multiple discharge of other loaded chambers.

City and County of New York . . . Albert Beach being sworn says that he is the Secretary of the said Manhattan Fire Arms Manufacturing Company, that he has prepared and read the foregoing report, and knows the contents thereof, and that the same is true.

Albert Beach
(Sworn to and notarized, etc.)

The company's Annual Reports for 1859 and 1860 were the only reports discovered during the period of research. However, a Newark City Directory for 1861 shows the first such listing for the company, as follows: "*Manhattan Fire Arms Manufacturing Company,* corner of Spring and Bridge Streets." It is believed that this was the location of Manhattan's operations during 1859, 1860, 1861, and a part of 1862. The property at Spring and Bridge streets had been owned by Oba Meeker & Company (Meeker was to become a minor stockholder in American Standard Tool Company) and was occupied by the firm of Phillips & Hewes from 1847 through 1858. At the beginning of the War, Phillips & Hewes altered 8000 stands of arms from flintlock to percussion for the State of New Jersey, at their later location at Orange and Ogden streets, and subsequently altered 12,000 stands of arms for the U. S. Government.*

SERIES III .36-CALIBER REVOLVERS

The distinguishing characteristics of the Series III .36-caliber revolvers are these:

1. Five-shot cylinder
2. Barrel signed with one-line Newark address
3. Cylinder stamped with 1859 patent date
4. Estimated range of serial numbers: 14,500 to 45,200.

An example of the one-line Newark address, used in signing the barrels of the .36-caliber revolvers manufactured in Series III, is shown in Plate 43. (See page 144.) It is to be noted that the abbreviation for the word "Manufacturing" is no longer included as a part of the barrel signing. Until this time, an abbreviation of the word "Manufacturing" had appeared as a part of the signing on all of the products made by Manhattan which included the single-shot pistols, pepperboxes, .31-caliber percussion revolvers, .22-caliber revolvers, Series I and Series II of the .36-caliber percussion revolvers and the .36-caliber molds. It will be recalled that two direct references were made to the company in the testimony connected with the suit between *White et al v. Boker et al* and that the testimony was given in June of 1862. In each of these references, the company's name was stated as "Manhattan Fire Arms Company." Further, the

History of Essex and Hudson Counties by Shaw. (Everts and Peck) 1884.

PLATE 48. ENGRAVED .36-CALIBER MANHATTAN REVOLVERS.

Figure 1. Five-Shot, Five-Inch Barrel, Number 24,804, Series III.

Figure 2. Five-Shot, Five-Inch Barrel, Number 24,799, Series III.

Engraved specimens are fairly common in Manhattan's Series III and Series IV .36 caliber revolvers; similar examples appear to be more scarce in Series I, Series II and Series V. Grips of the engraved guns were in the "fancy" category and were made of burled walnut, plain ivory and carved ivory. The carved ivory grips carried a variety of designs including a wreath, the bust of Mars, Liberty and two or more Eagle designs.

Newark City Directory for 1862 appears to reflect a change in the style of the company's name, as follows: *"Manhattan Fire Arms Company, corner Spring and Bridge streets."* It is logical that the information in the directory would have been tabulated a few months prior to printing; thus, a change which occurred in 1861 would have been recorded in the directory for 1862.

The change in the style of the company's name, simple as it seems, became an intriguing point with us because it indicated one of two possible circumstances: (1) the company made the change in the latter part of 1861 and continued to operate under its New York charter or (2) that Manhattan abandoned its New York charter and was rechartered under the laws of New Jersey during the later months of 1861. It required considerable digging to determine that both of the above circumstances did prevail, with one following in sequence to the other. Following the change in the name of the company, Manhattan continued to operate under the New York charter until the end of 1863. Information made available to us through the courtesy of the office of the Secretary of State, State of New Jersey, shows that Articles of Incorporation for Manhattan Arms Company of Newark, New Jersey, were drawn up on August 19, 1863, and the new charter was issued by the State of New Jersey on January 9, 1864. A complete transcript of the records is available in an appendix, including an interesting comment on the reason for the delay in issuance of the charter, and we will discuss some of the pertinent details in a later part of this section.

As will be seen in the estimated range of serial numbers for Series III, a total of about 30,000 arms were manufactured within this series with the result that these are the most common of Manhattan's .36-caliber revolvers. The standard barrel lengths continue to be 4″, 5″, and 6½″, as represented by the guns displayed in Plate 44. (See page 146.) Although there were no marked innovations or model changes made within the Series III revolvers, the period of their manufacture must have been a high point of prosperity for the company with production of the .36-caliber revolvers reaching a peak of 1000 per month. The span of this period covered several interesting developments, including the purchase of a small quantity of Manhattan arms by the Ordnance Department of the U. S. Army.

One of the developments associated with the Series III .36-caliber revolvers is the appearance of spring plates on some of the early examples of this series. Although the spring plate is more closely identified with the Series IV revolvers and was to become the basic subject of the March 8, 1864, patent date, spring plates are to be found on guns in the 15,000 serial range of Series III. We date this initial application of the spring plates as about September or October of 1861, two and one-half years prior to the date of the covering patent grant. It is to be noted that specimens shown as Fig. 2 and Fig. 3 in Plate 44 are equipped with spring plates. It is our opinion that attachment of the spring plates to the revolvers in Series III was limited to the first few thousand in the series as we have observed none with serial numbers above 21,000 that were fitted with the device. The reason for discontinuing usage of the spring plate on revolvers with serial numbers between 21,000 and 45,000 is unknown and its existence on the guns in Series III must be regarded as somewhat experimental in nature. Two views of a revolver produced within Series III, and equipped with a spring plate, are shown in Plates 45 and 46. (See pages 150 and 152.) An enlarged view of the lock-frame and grip-assembly, showing the method of attachment of the plate to the recoil shield, is pictured in Plate 47. (See page 156.) In addition to being equipped with the spring plate, the revolver is noteworthy for several other reasons: (1) the absence of external serial numbers in their usual locations; (2) the absence of any inplant inspection markings and (3) the use, of an obviously "special" serial designation, #23. The combination of these characteristics leads us to the conclusion that it was one of a number of similar revolvers, possibly fewer than 100, which were made for a specific purpose. We are not inclined to classify the revolver as a "salesman's sample" although the absence of any in-plant inspection markings might indicate that it was not intended for sale in the usual manner. Because of its unusual features, the chief one of which is the spring plate, we believe the revolver should be placed in the category of a pilot-model which was manufactured for the purpose of exhibiting the advantages of the spring plate. These advantages were to confine the fire or detonation to a single chamber and to protect the cones from the effects of the impact of the hammer; these points will be discussed further under Patent No. 41,848 in the section on the Series IV .36-caliber revolvers.

In the prologue of this work, it was stated that the Manhattan company did not receive any sizeable contracts for small arms from the Ordnance Departments of the U. S. Army and/or Navy. However, the research of Lt. Col. R. C. Kuhn has established the fact that the Ordnance Department of the U. S. Army purchased a small quantity of arms and cartridges from the company during the latter part of 1861.[2] The record of the purchase was found in the files of the U. S. Army Ordnance Department, under "Statement of Contracts" as a "Purchase of Arms," viz:

Ordered 23 September 1861 (36 cylinder pistols
                           (5000 cartridges
                           from Manhattan Fire Arms Co. Newark, N. J.

No entry for the receipt of the pistols and cartridges is shown. However, the record of payment for the same shows the following:

Paid 26 March 1862 (36 pistols
                    (5000 cartridges $423.80 to
                    Manhattan Fire Arms Co. Newark, N. J.

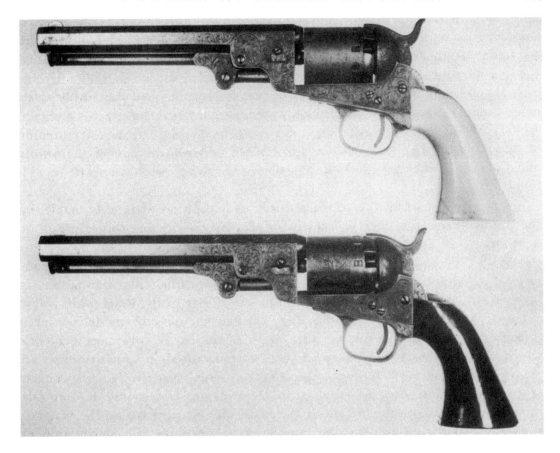

PLATE 49. ENGRAVED .36-CALIBER MANHATTAN REVOLVERS.

Figure 1. Five-Shot, Six-and-a-Half-Inch Barrel, Number 42,856, Series III.

Figure 2. Five-Shot, Six-and-a-Half-Inch Barrel, Number 47,387, Series IV.

The engraving on the pictured guns is representative of the work done in the shop of Wolfe, the noted engraver of the percussion period and known best for his embellishment of many fine Colt arms. A definite pattern of engraving appears to have been established for Manhattan's arms and only minor differences have been found on a number of observed specimens.

The absence of a formal contract covering the purchase plus the lack of a record showing the results of a trial or test of the pistols would indicate that the order originated outside the Ordnance Department. This circumstance was not an unusual one, especially during the early part of the War. Under certain conditions, any regimental or brigade commander had the authority to place orders for small arms and such a circumstance may have accounted for the origin of the order from the Manhattan company. Although the total amount of the purchase price, $423.80, was not divided between the cost of the pistols and the cost of the cartridges, it is probable that the pistols cost $10 to $11 each.

Since the record of the purchase gives no indication of type or model of the pistols, except that they were cylinder pistols, considerable conjecture must necessarily arise as to the type of arms which were involved. This conjecture should include consideration of that certain "will o' the wisp" model, the so-called "Big Manhattan." As we understand the story, the "Big Manhattan" is reputed to have been an exact copy of the .36-caliber Colt Model 1851 Navy, or Army, revolver. We do not take the position that no such model was ever produced by Manhattan but we have been unable to discover any evidence which would indicate that this model was manufactured in quantity or as an experimental model. We have done some very intensive searching for a specimen of this model, including advertising for information concerning it, but our efforts availed us nothing. On several occasions we felt we were on the verge of uncovering pertinent information, including the locating of a description of the wanted gun in a dealer's catalog issued in 1939. This description included a photograph of an engraved revolver, silver plated and ivory gripped, with a 7½" barrel and 6-shot cylinder—all of the attributes we were looking for, and described under the title of "Manhattan Army Model of .36-caliber." However, a closer reading of the description revealed that the cylinder was inscribed "New Orleans April 1862," which inscription clearly identified the revolver as a Metropolitan Navy. We would like to believe that Manhattan did make such a model. Manhattan could have such a model as the company had the facilities for manufacturing it and their organization certainly possessed the know-how. However, we can sum up the results of our personal search by stating that we failed to find an example of the model and we have never contacted another collector, either in conversation or by correspondence, who has actually seen a specimen of the so-called "Big Manhattan." For these reasons, we are inclined to the opinion that the arms purchased from Manhattan by the Ordnance Department were not comprised of a model different from the models known to have been in production by the company in September of 1861. While we express the hope that a subsequent discovery will prove us to have been in error, we believe that the arms covered by this purchase were the standard .36-caliber revolvers, as produced within Series III, with five-shot cylinders and 6½" barrels; the revolvers may have been equipped with spring plates and probably were stamped with U. S. Army inspection markings. We attach some importance to the cartridge portion of the purchase. It was not unusual for a manufacturer to furnish a quantity of ammunition with an initial order of small arms but it would seem that 160 rounds of ammunition per revolver was intended to cover more than the purpose of a trial. The standard .36-caliber Manhattan revolver required a cartridge which was not a standard item of Army ordnance, hence the order for a rather substantial quantity of ammunition to accompany the arms. To conclude our views on this interesting facet of Manhattan's history, we believe that this order of arms and ammunition may have been purchased for use by the officers of a single regimental or brigade command.

As previous chapters have noted, Manhattan made use of hand-engraving as a standard feature on the arms produced in each category with the exception of the .36-caliber revolvers. It may have been decided that the engraved panels on the cylinders constituted sufficient adornment for standard production in the .36-caliber category. However, Manhattan produced a relatively large number of fully engraved guns in the .36-caliber model and the engraving appears to have been done in the shop of Wolfe; the engraving has the characteristics of Wolfe's design and the hammers bear the noted wolfhead motif. Examples of .36-caliber revolvers engraved with these designs are shown in Plates 48 and 49. (See pages 158 and 161.) Peculiarly enough, we have not observed any engraved specimens, bearing Wolfe's design, in either the Series I or Series II revolvers although we are certain that engraved guns in these series are extant. Perhaps the most noteworthy of the engraved .36-caliber revolvers by Manhattan, and one of the most valuable in existence, is the General U. S. Grant Presentation displayed in Plate 50. (See page 164.) This historical arm, from the collection of William M. Locke, has been preserved within its original walnut case, together with the flask, mold and nipple wrench. The revolver was produced within Series III, was silver plated and bears serial #43; as in the case of gun #23 described previously, none of the serial number stampings is externally visible and the Grant revolver was equipped, originally, with a spring plate. The left side of the one-piece ivory grip is carved with an historical scene, commemorative of the Signing of the Declaration of Independence, which shows two men, dressed in colonial costume, standing with clasped hands beneath the motto: "UNITED WE STAND DIVIDED WE FALL." The presentation is reputed to have been made to General Grant, while he was confined to the hospital in New Orleans during September of 1863, on behalf of the officers and men of Company "B" of the 21st Regiment, Illinois Volunteers. The 21st Regiment of Illinois Volunteers was known as "Grant's Own"; this regiment was Grant's first command of the War, in which he served as Colonel. The circumstances leading to General Grant's confinement to the hospital in New Orleans, according to his memoirs, were these: "On the 7th of August (1863) I further de-

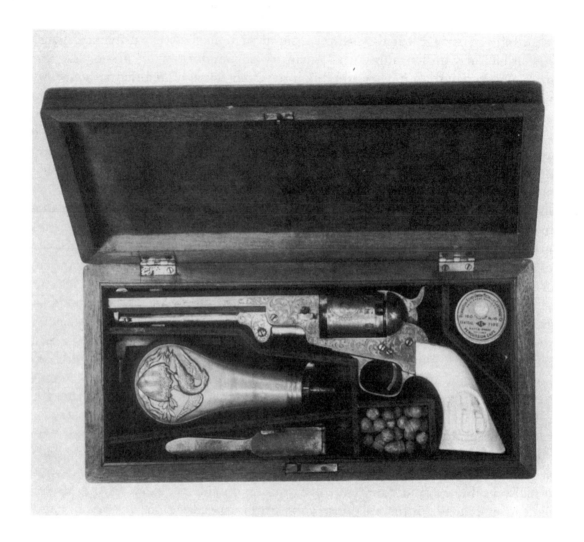

PLATE 50. GENERAL U. S. GRANT PRESENTATION .36-CALIBER MANHATTAN REVOLVER.

Five-Shot, Six-and-a-Half-Inch Barrel, Special Serial Number 43, Cased.

Illustrating one of the most valuable Manhattan revolvers of record. The gun bears serial number 43, of the special designation referred to in Plate 45, and was silver plated. The left side of the grip was carved with an unusually distinctive design commemorative of the signing of the Declaration of Independence and shows two men, dressed in Colonial costume, beneath the motto: "United we stand, divided we fall."

pleted my army by sending the 13th Corps, General Ord commanding, to (General) Banks. Besides this, I received orders to co-operate with the latter general in movements west of the Mississippi. Having received this order I went to New Orleans to confer with Banks about proposed movements. . . . During this visit I reviewed Bank's army a short distance above Carrolton. The horse I rode was vicious and but little used, and on my return to New Orleans ran away and, shying at a locomotive in the street, fell, probably on me. I was rendered insensible, and when I regained consciousness I found myself in a hotel near by with several doctors attending me."[3] It is probable that this gift had done a considerable amount of traveling before the presentation was made at New Orleans. It is our opinion that the revolver was manufactured 12 to 18 months before it was presented to General Grant.

Beginning with serial numbers in the 34,000 range, lead-in slots made their appearance on the cylinders of the .36-caliber Manhattan revolvers. The lead-in slots appear on only half the cylinder-stops, those stops which are effective when the revolver is cocked, and do not appear on the stops which operate to place the cylinder in a "safe" position. This innovation was to become a standard feature for the remainder of the production of the .36-caliber revolvers. We have previously stated that the Manhattan .36-caliber revolver was not an infringement of any of Colt's patents. However, the appearance of the lead-in slots on Manhattan's revolvers in the 34,000 serial number range, which numbers we would date about May or June of 1863, would have preceded the expiration of Colt's patent of September 10, 1850, by more than a year. Thus, it would appear that Manhattan's use of the lead-in slots on the cylinders of their .36-caliber revolvers was: (1) an infringement of Colt's patent of September 10, 1850, or (2) was had with the knowledge and consent of Colt or (3) the use of the lead-in slots was a matter of little significance. While we have no firm opinion regarding this point, we are inclined toward (3) as supplying the answer.

It is evident that Manhattan moved to a new address in 1862. Beginning with the directory for 1863, the company's address is shown as "523 Orange Street, corner of High" and the listing remains the same in the directories for 1864 through 1869.

Referring once again to the company's New Jersey charter of January 9, 1864, several points of interest appear to justify further comment. Previous chapters have noted that the company was capitalized for $40,000 in May of 1855 and that this amount was subsequently reduced to $20,000 in May of 1857. In the Articles of Incorporation drawn up in August of 1863, the amount of capital was established as $50,000 and consisted of 1000 shares of stock of $50 each. The increase in capital is indicative of an expansion of the company's operations with a corresponding requirement for additional capital. Alfred L. Dennis, James B. Pinneo and Jacob D. Vermilye, whose connections with and influence on the early affairs of the company has been mentioned previously, continued to hold a combined total of twenty percent of the stock. Albert Beach, not previously identified as a stockholder although he served in the dual capacities of Agent and Secretary of the company, owned 100 shares of stock in the newly formed corporation. The position of Andrew R. Arnold as General Superintendent of Manhattan's manufacturing operations is given considerable importance as he was also the owner of 100 shares of stock. It was the intent of the incorporators that the new company should commence its existence on August 19, 1863. However, as shown in the appendix, the original certificate of incorporation was mislaid in the Essex County Clerk's office and issuance of the New Jersey charter was delayed until January 9, 1864.

The estimated period of production of the .36-caliber revolvers in Series III was from September 1, 1861, until April 1, 1864.

SERIES IV .36-CALIBER REVOLVERS

The distinguishing characteristics of the Series IV .36-caliber revolvers are these:

1. Five-shot cylinder
2. Barrel signed with two-line Newark address
3. Cylinder stamped with 1859 patent date
4. Estimated range of serial numbers: 45,200 to 69,200.

After manufacturing approximately 41,000 .36-caliber revolvers with little change in the basic standards of the model, Manhattan introduced several changes during the period of manufacture of the Series IV revolvers in addition to a change in the signing of the barrels.

An example of the two-line Newark address, used in signing the barrels of the .36-caliber revolvers manufactured in Series IV and in Series V, is shown in Plate 52. (See page 170.) This change in barrel signing was occasioned by the granting of Patent No. 41,848 to Ben Kittredge of Cincinnati, Ohio; the patent became the fourth to be associated with the company and the second to be directly identified with the Manhattan arms. This patent enabled the feature of the spring plate to become an integral part of the .36-caliber revolvers manufactured by the company from about April 1, 1864, until production of the model ceased in 1868. Existence of the patent raises two points of interest which justify some consideration and discussion. As set forth in the section on the Series III revolvers, the spring plate made its appearance on guns manufactured during the latter part of 1861; further, Manhattan made a special production run of about 100 revolvers and the indicated purpose of these guns

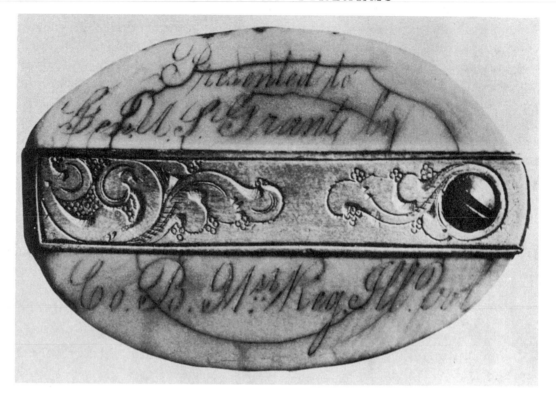

PLATE 51. PRESENTATION INSCRIPTION, GENERAL U. S. GRANT MANHATTAN
REVOLVER.

The Manhattan revolver was presented to General Grant by the officers and men of Company B, 21st Regiment of Illinois Volunteers. The regiment was Grant's first command of the War in which he served as Colonel. The presentation was allegedly made to Grant while he was confined to a hospital in New Orleans, during August or September of 1863, following a severe injury suffered in a fall from a runaway horse.

was to show the advantages of the operation of the spring plate. However, slightly more than two years appear to have elapsed before application for the patent was made and about two and one-half years elapsed between the time of the first usage of the feature and the granting of the patent. There must have been a reason for this rather long lapse of time although none is immediately apparent. The question of practicability would have been long since answered, and that of patentability could have been determined quite readily. This point represents an enigma for which we have no ready answer. The second point revolves around the absence of any record of assignment of the patent to Manhattan by Kittredge. An examination of the original patent file failed to disclose any such assignment nor is there any reference to an assignment in the patent specification. It is possible that the assignment was a part of a file which we were unable to locate. It is to be assumed that Manhattan held an exclusive right to the use of the patent and that Kittredge received a royalty for each gun produced that incorporated the spring plate feature. B. Kittredge & Co. of Cincinnati, Ohio, must have become agents for the sale of Manhattan arms not later than 1861. We have observed several .36-caliber Manhattan revolvers which were marked with the Kittredge name, and an example of the marking is depicted in Plate 53. On this specimen, the stamping is "B. Kittredge & Co." in one line on the left side of the barrel. We have observed other guns on which the stamping, similarly located, was a semi-circular design with "B. Kittredge & Co." forming a semi-circle over "Cin. O." We consider the Kittredge-marked Manhattan revolvers to be very desirable items and examples will be found which will antedate the Series IV revolvers.

Some of the details of the file for Patent No. 41,848 are considered to be of sufficient interest for reproduction at this point. The application for the patent was received at the Patent Office in Washington on December 14, 1863, along with the specification, drawings and model. On December 14, 1863, the Patent Office advised Kittredge that "a 5¢ Revenue Stamp, canceled, is required to complete the oath"; this requirement was met by Kittredge under date of December 19, 1863. The Patent Office then advised Kittredge as follows:

> U. S. Patent Office
> Washington, D. C.
> January 14, 1864

Sir:

Your specification for alleged improvement in fire arms has been examined, and it will be found the following examples, among others, anticipated your claim—viz; R. White Pat. April 3, 1855 (*sic.*)—August Spellors Pat. Oct. 2, 1860—Myron Moses Pat. Sept. 30, 1862. Your claim therefore, must be rejected,

> S. S. F.

Ben Kittredge
Cincinnati, Ohio

PLATE 52. BARREL SIGNING FOR .36-CALIBER REVOLVERS, SERIES IV AND SERIES V.

The above signing represents the third and last mode of identification applied to the barrels of Manhattan's .36 caliber revolvers and appeared on about 33,000 guns. In this signing, the one-line Newark address was supplemented with the legend "PATENTED MARCH 8, 1864" which referred to Patent #41,848, granted to Benj. Kittredge, and covered the usage of the spring plate.

The rejection by the Patent Office caused Kittredge to revise his claim, as follows:

Cincinnati, Ohio
January 30th, 1864

Hon. D. P. Holloway
Commissioner of Patents

Sir:

In the matter of my application for letters patent for Improvement in Fire Arms filed in December, 1863 and rejected. I desire to submit the following amendment:

Strike out the claim and insert in lieu thereof the following

I am aware that metal shields have been heretofore placed between the nipple and the hammer, but they have been so made as to surround the nipple at the sides and rear so as to prevent the fire from passing off laterally. While, therefore, I do not claim broadly the interposition of a shield between the cock and nipple, I do claim as my invention

A metal shield, constructed substantially as described, and placed between the cock and nipple to throw the fire laterally from the nipple.

Yours respectfully,
Ben. Kittredge

The foregoing amendment served to satisfy the patent examiner. The patent was cleared for issuance on February 17, 1864, and the patent was granted on March 8, 1864.

The drawing and specification for Patent No. 41,848 are reproduced herewith. (See pages 172 and 173.) As will be seen in the drawing, the revolver shown in Fig. 1 is obviously a Manhattan; the blade-type front sight and the additional cylinder-stops give sufficient evidence to justify this assumption. It will be noted that Fig. 2 shows the shield or spring plate attached to the recoil shield by means of two screws. We have observed no examples on which the plate was attached with two screws; in actual manufacture, the recoil shield was cut out to receive the plate flush with its surface and the plate could be held in place, without movement, by a single screw.

One of the changes which was instituted during the period of manufacture of the Series IV revolvers involved the introduction of another length to the lengths of 4″, 5″ and 6½″ which had been established as basic standards early in the production of the Series I revolvers. The newly-introduced barrel length was 4½″ and was accompanied by a change in the front sight. While the silver (or white brass) blade-type front sight was the standard on the 4″, 5″, 6″, and 6½″ lengths, the 4½″ barrel length was made with a brass post-type front sight. An example of the 4½″ barrel length is shown as Fig. 3 in Plate 54 (see page 178); this specimen is fully-engraved and is equipped with one-piece ivory grips. We regard the Series IV .36-caliber revolvers in the 4½″ barrel

B. KITTREDGE.

Revolver.

No. 41,848.   Patented Mar. 8, 1864.

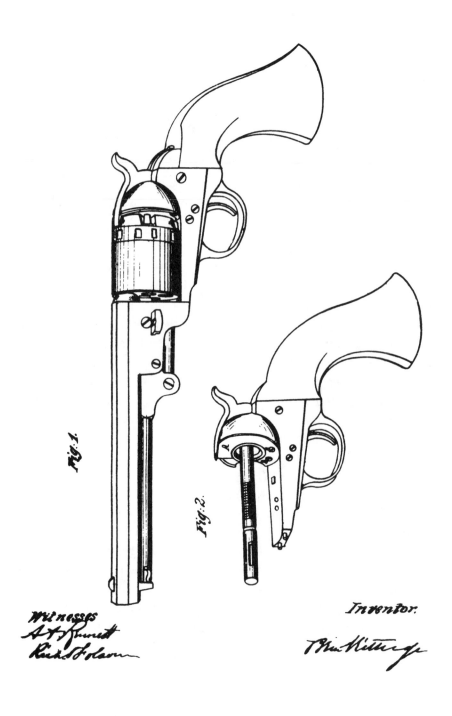

Fig. 1.

Fig. 2.

Witnesses

Inventor.

UNITED STATES PATENT OFFICE.

BEN. KITTREDGE, OF CINCINNATI, OHIO.

IMPROVEMENT IN REVOLVING FIRE-ARMS.

Specification forming part of Letters Patent No. **11,818,** dated March 8, 1861.

To all whom it may concern:

Be it known that I, BEN. KITTREDGE, of Cincinnati, in the county of Hamilton and State of Ohio, have invented a new and useful Improvement in Fire-Arms; and I do hereby declare that the following is a full and exact description thereof, reference being had to the accompanying drawings, and to the letters of reference marked thereon.

The nature of my invention consists of a metal shield or plate inserted between the nipple and face of the cock in such a manner that when the arm is discharged the shield or plate will throw the fire from the nipple off in lateral direction and prevent its being thrown back into the lock, and in such a manner also that, whether the cock be down or up, it will tend to hold the cap or caps in place upon the nipple or nipples and prevent them from clogging the cylinder as it revolves.

To enable others skilled in the art to make and use my invention, I will proceed to describe its construction and operation.

I construct the shield or plate A (seen in Figure 2 of the drawings that accompany this specification) of steel or other metal, and insert it between the cylinder and recoil-plate in such a manner that the cock as it descends will press it against the nipple that is in front of the cock. This will allow the cap to be exploded the same as if the shield were not there, and will serve to compel the fire from the nipple to pass off laterally, instead of being thrown back and injected into the lock. It will also serve to keep cap in place upon the nipple, and to prevent the caps from working back so as to clog the cylinder as it revolves. The shield or plate may be fastened to the recoil-plate by screws, as at B, or in any other manner.

I am aware that metal shields have been heretofore placed between the nipple and hammer; but they have been so made as to surround the nipple at the sides and rear, so as to prevent the fire from passing off laterally. While therefore I do not claim broadly the interposition of a shield between the cock and nipple,

I do claim as my invention—

A metal shield constructed substantially as described and placed between the cock and nipple to throw the fire laterally from the nipple.

BEN. KITTREDGE.

Witnesses:
RICHD. FOLSOM,
A. A. BENNETT.

length as definite rarities and, therefore, as very desirable. Plate 54 shows each of the barrel lengths to be found in Series IV revolvers, these lengths being 4", 4½", 5", and 6½".

Two other changes which occurred during the period of manufacture of the Series IV revolvers were: (1) a change in the design of the loading lever and (2) a definite slimming of the grips into a "Slim Jim" shape. These two changes appear to have been made coincidentally and in the range of serial numbers close to #50,000. It is our opinion that the change from a round loading lever to one with a tapered design was made to strengthen the lever as well as to improve the appearance of the revolver in the 6½" barrel length. An example of the tapered lever, as applied to the 6½" barrel length, is shown as Fig. 1 in Plate 54; the loading levers of the other barrel lengths were not changed in the Series IV revolvers. We consider the Series IV revolvers with the tapered levers to be the handsomest of all of the Manhattan revolvers.

The fourth change which was instituted during the period of manufacture of the Series IV revolvers apparently occurred quite late in this period and involved the shapes of the heads of the frame screws, the wedge screw and the screws for the loading lever and the plunger. For the most part, the change was constituted by reducing the radii of the screw-heads, making them more flat, and, in the case of the loading lever and plunger screws, counter-boring the affected parts. In our opinion, these changes were long overdue because we have always felt that the design of the loading lever and plunger screws was very poor. It is to be noted that the wedge screws of the later design will not fit in the barrels of earlier revolvers.

We feel that no work such as this would be complete without a "gun collector's yarn." We have such a story and it concerns the specimen displayed as Fig. 4 in Plate 54. (See page 178) In 1952 we purchased the two Series V revolvers which are pictured in Plate 57. (See page 190.) These guns had been imported from England by Robert Abels and were excellent pieces except that one had the grips and back-strap from a Series IV revolver with serial #68,822. Despite this discrepancy, the quality of the revolver justified its retention in our collection. In 1956 we were seeking a specimen in Series IV with a 4" barrel. We located the example on the lists of another dealer and upon being advised that the serial number of the back-strap did not match the serial number of the gun, it was ordered on approval. The rest of the story is obvious: the serial number of the revolver ordered was found to be #68,822. We wish that it could be reported that the odd back-strap from #68,822 matched the number of the Series V revolver; however, such was not the case. We hope that, somewhere, some collector has a Series V .36-caliber Manhattan revolver, serial #2904 but with a back-strap #2165. We will be glad to exchange a back-strap and set of grips with this collector and thus correct an error committed in England which involved at least three Manhattan revolvers. It will be noted that the revolver shown as Fig. 4 in Plate 54 (See page 178) bears the London proof marks.

An excellent pair of fully-engraved Series IV revolvers with carved ivory grips, and bearing consecutive serial numbers, are shown in Plate 55. (See page 182) Judging from their serial numbers, these revolvers were manufactured after the conclusion of the War Between the States; the wreath design on the grips of Fig. 2 may have been intended to portray the victor's symbol.

The estimated period of production of the .36-caliber revolvers in Series IV was from April 1, 1864, until June 30, 1867.

SERIES V .36-CALIBER REVOLVERS

The distinguishing characteristics of the Series V .36-caliber revolvers are these:

1. Six-shot cylinder
2. Barrel signed with two-line Newark address
3. Cylinder stamped with 1859 patent date
4. Estimated range of serial numbers: 1 to 9000.

The Series V .36-caliber revolvers have been designated occasionally by other sources as the 1864 Model Manhattan revolvers. We are certain that this designation is a misnomer. It will have been seen that the estimated period of manufacture of the Series IV revolvers extended well into 1867. The Series V revolvers did incorporate several changes which serve to differentiate them from guns of the preceding series but these changes did not occur until much later than 1864. However, it is apparent that Manhattan must have regarded the Series V .36-caliber revolver as a new model as evidenced by the assignment of a new range of serial numbers to the series, beginning with serial #1.

The principal and distinct change effected in the Series V revolvers was the change from a five-shot cylinder to a six-shot cylinder. The change is all the more noteworthy because it was made without increasing the diameter of the cylinder and, thereby, making possible the continued use of the five-panel engraving die. The centers of the chambers of the five-shot cylinders were located within the 1⅜" diameter of the cylinder in such a manner as to provide a considerable thickness of metal between the walls of the individual chambers. The additional chamber of the six-shot cylinder was supplied by utilizing a portion of the excess metal which was available between the chambers of the five-shot cylinder. The feature of two cylinder-stops per chamber continued in use on the six-shot cylinders, with the locking stops having the lead-in slots and the safety stops having no slots. The change from a five-shot cylinder to

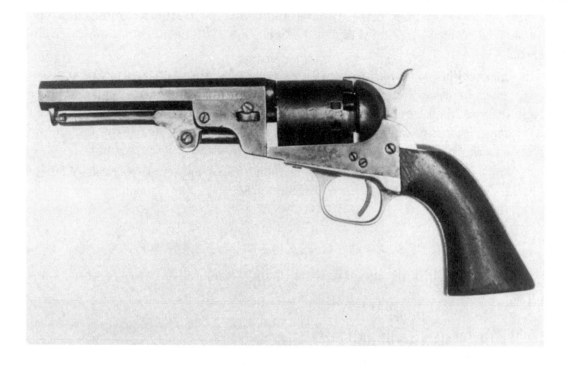

PLATE 53. .36-CALIBER MANHATTAN REVOLVER MARKED "B. KITTREDGE & CO."

Five-Shot, Five-Inch Barrel, Number 44,370, Series III.

     B. Kittredge & Company of Cincinnati, Ohio became agents for the sale of Manhattan's arms not later than 1861 and the two firms may have been associated earlier than that time. The above marking, "B. KITTREDGE & CO." is the plainest and perhaps the rarest of the Kittredge-marked Manhattans. In another style of marking, B. KITTREDGE & CO. forms a semi-circle above "CIN. O."

a six-shot cylinder was a very desirable improvement and one may reasonably question why it was not made much earlier.

The Series V revolvers were further distinguished by a change in the design of the loading levers. The length of the taper was reduced and all four sides of the tapered portion were beveled to produce a graceful appearance. As differentiated from the Series IV revolvers, in which only the 6½″ barrel length was made with a tapered lever, it appears that the tapered loading lever was applied to each barrel length above 4″ in the Series V revolvers. Examples of Series V revolvers in 4″, 4½″, and 6½″ barrel lengths are displayed in Plate 56. (See page 186) A specimen with a 5″ barrel is conspicuous by its absence from this group. This does not mean that the 5″ barrel length was not produced within the Series V revolvers but that we have been unable to locate this variation. Since the 5″ barrel length appears to have been produced in substantial quantities in each of the preceding four series, it would seem to be illogical that this barrel length would be discontinued in Series V. Although the Series V revolvers were the last of the .36-caliber revolvers produced by Manhattan, with a resultant higher probability of survival, and although 4500 to 5000 more arms were produced in Series V than were made in Series I, we experienced considerably more difficulty in locating examples in Series V than was found in Series I, with the exception of the 4″ barrel length. Therefore, it is our opinion that the major portion of the arms produced in Series V had 4″ barrels. It will be noted that the 4½″ barrel length, with the brass post-type front sight, continued to be produced in Series V and application of the tapered loading lever served to improve the appearance of this scarce variation. The revolver with 6½″ barrel, shown as Fig. 1 in Plate 56 (See page 186), was nickle-plated and this appears to have been the original finish because of the sharpness of the barrel flats and the clarity of the cylinder engraving. We have observed very few .36-caliber Manhattan revolvers with nickle-plated finish.

Although the guns displayed as Fig. 1 and Fig. 2 in Plate 56 (See page 186) were equipped with spring plates, this feature is not to be found on all of the Series V. revolvers. Our examination of specimens in this series would indicate that less than half were machined for use of the spring plate, especially those with serials below 3000. Application of the spring plate appears to have been more common on the arms produced in the later period of the series.

A peculiarity of the Series V .36-caliber revolvers is the apparent total absence of in-plant inspection markings. We have handled no examples in this series which were marked with any of the in-plant inspection symbols that have been mentioned previously. In our opinion, no conclusion may be drawn that Manhattan's in-plant inspection processes were discontinued but rather that the stamping of the inspectors' symbols were no longer considered as a necessary part of the inspection operations. Another peculiarity of the series is the re-

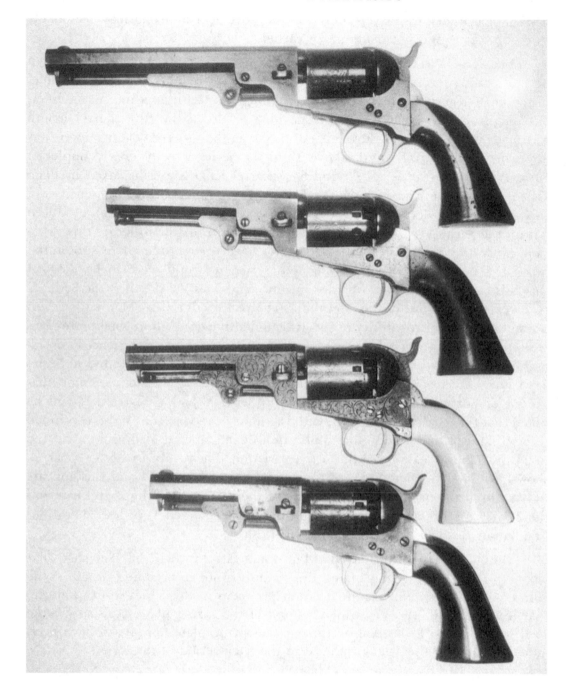

PLATE 54. SERIES IV. .36-CALIBER MANHATTAN REVOLVERS.

Figure 1. Five-Shot, Six-and-a-Half-Inch Barrel, Number 56,180.
(From the collection of Miles W. Standish)

Figure 2. Five-Shot, Five-Inch Barrel, Number 48,321.

Figure 3. Five-Shot, Four-and-a-Half-Inch Barrel, Number 46,414.

Figure 4. Five-Shot, Four-Inch Barrel, Number 68,822.

Several minor modifications were made during the period of production of the Series IV revolvers. The design of the loading levers on the 6½″ barrel length was changed at about serial number 50,000, coincidental with a change to the "Slim Jim" grips. A new barrel length of 4½″ was introduced during this series. A change in several of the screws was made in the later part of this period. Examples with British proof marks are to be found in the Series IV revolvers. Approximately 24,000 guns were produced in Series IV (numbered from 45,200 to 69,200) between April 1, 1864 and June 30, 1867.

appearance of serial numbers on the plungers. The plungers of the early revolvers in Series I were serially marked on the right side of the flat part of the plunger; the plungers of the Series V revolvers were serially marked on the top surface of the rounded part, or body, of the plunger.

It is apparant that Manhattan attempted to find a market for their .36-caliber revolvers in England, during the last two years of the company's existence. Reference has been made to a revolver with London proof marks and produced late in the period of Series IV which would indicate that the export phase had been explored not later than 1867. Two examples of Series V revolvers, bearing London proof marks, are shown in Plate 57. (See page 190) While we have observed a number of Manhattan revolvers with London proof marks, we have observed none with barrels longer than 4″. The London-proofed guns are usually found in excellent condition, indicating that our British cousins have done a better job of preserving relics than we have done here in the States or that the sale of Manhattan's arms in England was something less than a resounding success.

The Series V .36-caliber Manhattan revolvers may have been the best arms produced in the several series. In our opinion, the company performed a very creditable and commendable task in producing and selling percussion revolvers into the very end of the period of percussion revolvers. In this performance, Manhattan was probably exceeded in its length of tenure by Colt, but few if any of the other arms manufacturers produced percussion arms as late as the end of 1868.

The estimated period of production of the .36-caliber revolvers in Series V was from June 30, 1867, until December 1, 1868.

REFERENCE NOTES

CHAPTER VII: 1. N. Y. State Civil War Records (Albany) Office of the Adjutant General.

2. National Archives (Washington, D. C.).

3. *Personal Memoirs of U. S. Grant*
New York: Chas. L. Webster & Co., 1885, vol. 1, p. 581.

CHAPTER VIII

~~~~~~

TRANSITION:
AMERICAN STANDARD
TOOL COMPANY

HE EMERGENCE of American Standard Tool
Company as the successor to Manhattan Fire Arms Company was an ambitious
and challenging venture. The ambitiousness of the incorporators is clearly
expressed in the amount of capital, $120,000, which was subscribed for the
operations of the new company. Although no details of the financial success
of the parent company have been made available, it would appear that the
expanded capitalization of the successor company furnishes the best kind of
evidence that Manhattan Fire Arms Company must have been a very profitable operation. The expanded scope of operations contemplated for American
Standard Tool Company, into several fields of endeavor not previously identified
with the Manhattan company, represents the aspect of challenge in the new
enterprise. However, one needs only to recall that the original incorporators
of Manhattan were comparative tyros in the firearms field in order to understand the indicated hardihood of the planning behind the founding of American Standard Tool Company.

The existence of two models of firearms supplies the material evidence of

PLATE 55. ENGRAVED .36-CALIBER MANHATTAN REVOLVERS, SERIES IV.

Figure 1. Five-Shot, Six-and-a-Half-Inch Barrel, Number 58,490.

Figure 2. Five-Shot, Six-and-a-Half-Inch Barrel, Number 58,491.

Choice specimens with consecutive serial numbers, to form a "pair" as exemplified by the guns pictured above, are considered to be the acme of an arms collection by many collectors. Manhattan produced a sizeable quantity of engraved guns immediately following the end of the War and the intended market may have been for presentations or remembrances in connection with military service.

the connection between the two companies; factual proof of the relationship is present in the appendix which sets forth the details of the formation of American Standard Tool Company. Several factors may have been responsible for the transition to the new undertaking: (1) the period of manufacture of percussion firearms had come to its closing days; (2) the Manhattan company had prospered and the owners were seeking a means of extending its operations until production of cartridge arms could be resumed and (3) the desire to engage in activities not previously within the company's sphere. From the statement of purpose set forth in the Certificate of Organization, it would appear that manufacture of firearms was not considered as being the most important phase of the company's operations. Instead, it would seem that operations relating to Tools and Machinery were to occupy the primary positions and this intent was reflected in the name of the new company.

As set forth in the appendix, American Standard Tool Company was incorporated for $120,000 on November 23, 1868. The stockholders were substantially the same as those comprising the ownership of Manhattan Fire Arms Company in 1863. Two of the stockholders of the Manhattan company, Matthias W. Day and William H. Talcott, dropped out and were replaced by Oba Meeker and Frederick H. Smith, Jr., both of Newark, and by Henry J. Stevenson of New York City; Stevenson was a major stockholder with 440 shares of stock. However, the most significant development in stock ownership was the marked increase in the holdings of Albert Beach. Beach owned 10% of Manhattan Fire Arms Company, as noted, but his ownership of 562 shares in American Standard Tool Company amounted to 23% of the total shares and accounted for the largest single block of stock. This holding was equivalent to $28,000 and besides indicating a condition of affluence for Beach, amounted to 40% more than the total capitalization of Manhattan Firearms Manufacturing Company in 1857.

The Newark City Directories for 1870, 1871, and 1872 listed the address of American Standard Tool Company as follows: "218 High Street, corner of Orange." It would appear that the company's office was moved from its previous location at 523 Orange Street to a new location at 218 High Street, or, just around the corner. In addition to the address listings, the following advertisement appeared in each of the directories:

AMERICAN STANDARD TOOL COMPANY
OFFICE, 218 HIGH STREET

President Frederick H. Smith   *Sec'y* Stephen C. Morehouse

The Fourth Annual Report of the Newark Board of Trade, dated December 31, 1871, showed the following information, as taken from the Census of 1870:

"FIREARMS"
No. of Establishments: (1); Capital Invested, $40,000
No. of Hands Employed: 50; wages: $35,000; Products: 50,000.

This listing is believed to have referred to American Standard Tool Company, despite the apparent discrepancy in the amount of capital. Information regarding other phases of the company's business was not found in the above reference.

The two models of firearms which constituted the connecting link between Manhattan Fire Arms Company and American Standard Tool Company were Manhattan's single-shot percussion "Hero" pistol and the revival of Manhattan's Second Model .22-caliber revolver with the barrel marking of "American Standard Tool Co."

The "Hero" pistol was a poor man's derringer. It was the last model of firearm manufactured by Manhattan and was probably brought out in the latter part of 1868. The pistol was undoubtedly one of the cheapest percussion firearms ever produced and, representing competitive conditions in low-priced firearms, sold for a very moderate price. The "Hero" pistol was well made and the design was simple but sufficient for the intended use of the arm; at point-blank range, the pistol was as deadly as a weapon of higher price. The basic design may have been originated by Manhattan although similar single-shot pistols were produced by other makers. Two examples of Manhattan "Hero" pistols are shown in Plate 58. (See page 191) As will be seen, the pistols were made in two barrel lengths, 2″ and 3″, of .34-caliber, and the screw-off barrels were not rifled. The forged brass frames were stamped "Hero" above "M. F. A. Co." Details of original finish of the pistols are believed to have been these: barrel and trigger were blued; hammer was case-hardened; frame was polished but not plated; walnut grips were varnished. It is to be noted that the two-piece grips were held in place on the grip-frame by means of a simple wood-screw, without the use of metal escutcheon plates. None of the MFA "Hero" pistols that we have examined were serially marked and this characteristic would preclude any estimate of the quantity produced. The outstanding feature of the pistol is the extreme economy evidenced in its design and manufacture. Although it is our view that relatively few "Hero" pistols with the MFA markings were produced, the survival rate has been unusually low because of the lack of desirability of the pistols and their initial cost which, as noted, must have been quite small.

The American Standard Tool Company's "Hero" pistols were similar to the counterparts by Manhattan except for the stamping on the frames. The American Standard Tool Company pistols were stamped "A. S. T. Co." above "Hero." Additionally, the AST "Hero" pistols were serially marked; we have

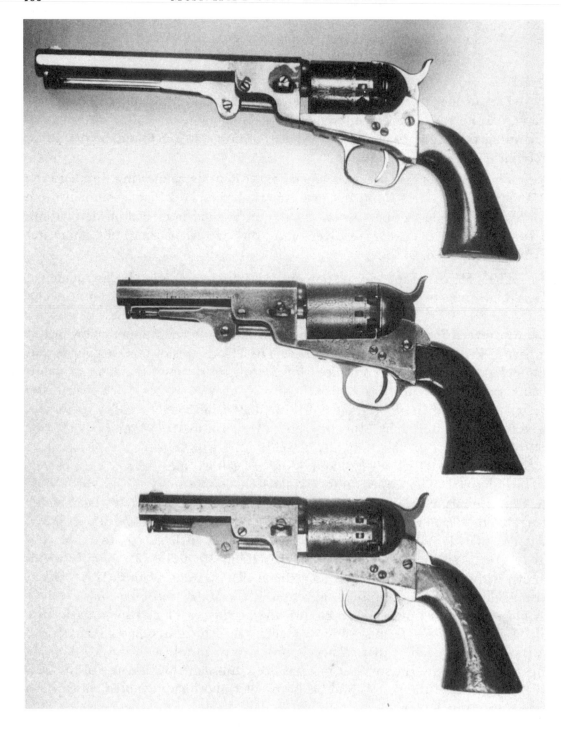

PLATE 56. SERIES V .36-CALIBER MANHATTAN REVOLVERS.

Figure 1. Six-Shot, Six-and-a-Half-Inch Barrel, Number 5197.

Figure 2. Six-Shot, Four-and-a-Half-Inch Barrel, Number 5302.

Figure 3. Six-Shot, Four-Inch Barrel, Number 842.
(From the collection of John Stapleton)

A significant change marked the introduction of the Series V revolvers with the six-shot cylinder replacing the five-shot cylinder of the preceding four series. Manhattan apparently regarded Series V as a new model and assigned a new run of serial numbers. A change in the design of the loading levers was likewise made for barrel lengths above 4″. It is estimated that about 9000 were produced between June 30, 1867 and December 1, 1868. The Series V revolvers may have been the best arms produced by Manhattan.

observed no specimens with serial numbers that were higher than the numbers of the pistols shown in Plate 59 (See page 193), but it is our opinion that the quantity manufactured was in excess of 30,000. The details of finish of the AST "Hero" pistols were the same as have been described for the MFA pistols in this category. Plates 58 and 59 depict examples in 2″ and 3″ barrel lengths but it is possible that pistols will be found with 2½″ barrels. In view of the accomplishments of the Manhattan company in the manufacture of arms during the years of 1855 through 1868, production of the "Hero" pistols was anything but complimentary to the company's prior achievements. However, the formation of American Standard Tool Company represented a complete takeover of the operations of Manhattan Fire Arms Company. American Standard Tool Company lacked the color and interest of the parent company, from the collector's viewpoint, but it continued to operate during four difficult business years that terminated in the beginnings of the Panic of 1873. It would seem that some substantial part of the company's ability to remain in business must be attributed to the acceptance of their .22-caliber revolvers in a market that was not only competitive but almost chaotic due to the large numbers of poorly made cartridge revolvers.

Rollin White's patent covering the bored-through cylinder expired on April 3, 1869. It is evident that either Manhattan Fire Arms Company or American Standard Tool Company anticipated the date of this cessation by producing a few hundred unsigned .22-caliber revolvers. These may have been made by either of the two companies but we are inclined to credit their manufacture to the parent company. Two examples are shown on Plates 60 and 61 and only a cursory examination is required to establish their origin as they possess all of the usual attributes of Manhattan's Second Model .22-caliber revolver. It is not known whether a separate series of serial numbers was used on the unmarked revolvers. As will be seen, the highest serial number of the displayed specimens is #311; likewise, the lowest serial number observed for the marked American Standard Tool Company .22-caliber revolvers has been #429. If there was no separate series of numbers for the unmarked .22-caliber revolvers, and the series extended into the products of American Standard Tool Company, it is likely that less than 400 of the unmarked revolvers were manufactured.

American Standard Tool Company's .22-caliber revolvers resembled Manhattan's Second Model .22-caliber revolver in all details, apart from the barrel signing, with these exceptions: (1) hand engraving of the barrels was discontinued; (2) the 1859 patent date stamping (found on the bottom flats of the barrels of Manhattan's Second Model .22's) was not applied to the barrels of American Standard Tool Company's revolvers and (3) the location of the serial number on the barrel was changed from the breech, or rear face, of the barrel to the bottom flat of the same, near the muzzle end. Elimination of hand engraving was, of course, done for the purpose of reducing the cost of the product but the change detracted considerably from the appearance of the guns. However, American Standard Tool Company continued to use full application of hand engraving on a substantial quantity of their revolvers and two such examples are depicted on Plate 62. (See page 196) The revolver shown as Fig. 1 is decorated with an overall design reminiscent of Wolfe's motifs, as found on the Manhattan percussion revolvers, and is considerably more elaborate than that applied to the gun displayed as Fig. 2; the latter example of engraving may have been the better of the two, due to its appealing simplicity. The usual or standard specimen of an American Standard Tool Company .22-caliber revolver is shown as Fig. 3 in Plate 62, although the illustration is limited to general appearance and details of finish such as blued barrel, plated frame, roller-die engraved cylinder, case-hardened hammer, wood grips, etc. The revolver has one characteristic which is worth noting: the serial number of the barrel was stamped on the rear face or breech of the barrel, the same as on both models of Manhattan's .22's, and this example has influenced our opinion that the unsigned revolvers mentioned earlier were manufactured by Manhattan. In addition, gun #429 was altered in the following points: the front sight is a well-made replacement and a small plate was attached to the top portion of the recoil shield by means of two brass screws extending rearward through the recoil shield. The purpose of the plate may have been to seat the cartridges more securely in the chambers of the cylinder as they approached the firing position. We are not inclined to consider the alterations on this specimen as having been of factory origin, although the workmanship was of very good quality.

The .22-caliber revolvers manufactured by American Standard Tool Company are occasionally referred to as being taken from an "obsolete" pattern. It is true that the pattern was nearly eight years old when production of the model was resumed, possibly in 1868; however, the "obsolete" pattern provided a marketable product since, based upon our survey of serial numbers, more than 40,000 of this model were produced during the four years of the company's existence. We have never been especially impressed with the appearance or utility values of the bird-head style of grips which came into wide usage on the cartridge arms of the period and, citing once again the obvious merits of the .22-caliber long cartridge, we are inclined to the opinion that the model developed by Manhattan in 1861 and subsequently perpetuated by American Standard Tool Company was scarcely excelled by any competitive models.

It is not known whether American Standard Tool Company attempted to develop any new models of cartridge revolvers, although it may be assumed that efforts were directed along this line, and the need for other models must

PLATE 57. SERIES V. .36-CALIBER REVOLVERS WITH BRITISH PROOF MARKS.

Figure 1. Six-Shot, Four-Inch Barrel, Number 2165.

Figure 2. Six-Shot, Four-Inch Barrel, Number 2928.

Due largely to the active importation of antique arms from England during recent years, Manhattan revolvers with British proof marks have appeared in increasing numbers. It is evident that the company exported arms to England as early as 1867 since British proof marks are to be found on a few Series IV revolvers. The British-proofed guns are usually found in excellent condition.

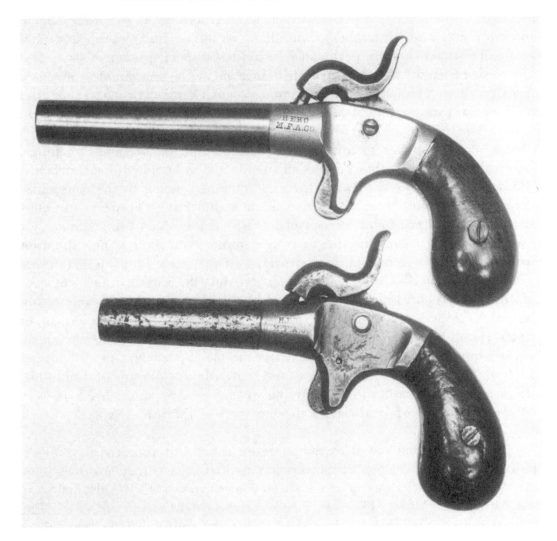

PLATE 58. "HERO" SINGLE-SHOT PISTOLS BY MANHATTAN FIRE ARMS COMPANY.

Figure 1. Three-Inch Round Barrel, Caliber .34; No Serial Number.

Figure 2. Two-Inch Round Barrel, Caliber .34; No. Serial Number.

The "Hero" single-shot pistol was the last model of percussion firearm produced by Manhattan and is believed to have been brought out about the end of the company's existence in 1868. The model represented the extremely competitive condition of the arms market and was manufactured in the most economical manner from a very simple but effective design. The "Hero" pistol was the poor man's derringer.

have been apparent to Messers Smith, Beach, Arnold, *et al.* We were able to find two models which might be considered as falling into this category and, because no better or more pertinent location has thus far presented itself, they will be discussed at this point. The first such model, a very simple conversion of a .31-caliber Manhattan revolver from percussion to cartridge, is pictured on Plate 63 (See page 202.) and is the only one of the type that we have observed. The conversion was made by turning down the rear end or nipple portion of the cylinder to form a long neck for the ratchet and attaching a spacer plate of proper size to the recoil shield. It is to be noted that a defective cylinder was used, as one chamber had been rendered useless by the penetration of the milling cutter through the slot of the cylinder stop. However, the most interesting characteristic of the conversion is that the nose of the hammer was evidently formed to fire centerfire cartridges, rather than rimfire. The alteration may or may not have been of factory origin (it may have been the handiwork of an employe and had no such commection) but the workmanship was good and the gun was used, to some extent, with cartridge ammunition. The second example is found in the Moss & Johnson patent model revolver shown on Plates 64 and 65. (See pages 203 and 204.) The covering patent, for which the pictured revolver is believed to have been the model, was No. 116,078, issued on June 20, 1871, to John L. Moss and Edward W. Johnson of Columbus, Mississippi. The patent attorneys for the inventors were Munn & Co. of New York and Washington, and one of the members of the firm was A. E. Beach.

This information was of extreme interest to us as it appeared that Albert Beach might have changed his profession to that of a patent attorney; however, such was not the case as investigation showed that A. E. Beach's first name was Alfred, not Albert. The specification of the patent stated, in part: "This invention has for its object to facilitate the loading and shell-extracting process in revolving rifles and pistols; and consists, principally, in the use of a rotary breech-plate, which is hung upon the base-pin, so that it wall revolve but not slide thereon, while the cylinder can freely slide, being, by keys, connected with the barrel. The breech-plate has grooved supports for the cartridge-head, and will retain the shells when the cylinder is carried forward, extracting them from the latter." Summed up, the invention provided for a very quick method of extracting the empty shells, albeit the mechanism was a bit complicated. The apparent connection of the Moss & Johnson patent model revolver with our story is this: the major parts of the revolver (barrel, frame, back-strap, trigger-guard, grips, hammer, etc.) were obviously the corresponding parts of a .36-caliber Manhattan revolver. The patent model revolver has no external markings or numbers of identification, as required by Patent Office procedures. The only number on any part of the gun is a serial number on the grips, underneath the back-strap; the number is in the 30,000 range, dating about

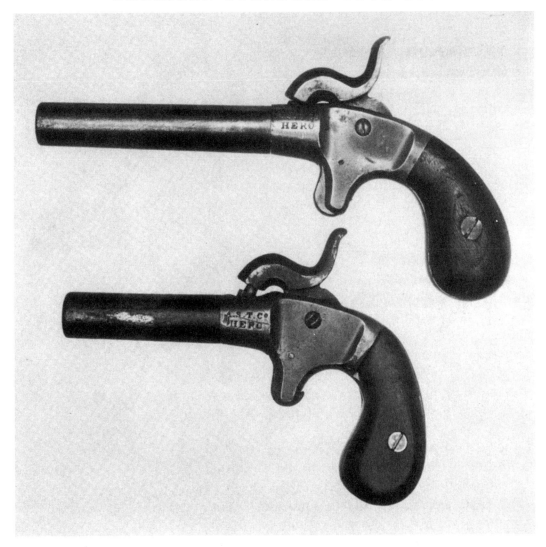

PLATE 59. "HERO" SINGLE-SHOT PISTOLS OF AMERICAN STANDARD TOOL COMPANY.

Figure 1. Three-Inch Round Barrel, Caliber .34, Number 26,116.

Figure 2. Two-Inch Round Barrel, Caliber .34, Number 24,884.

The AST "Hero" pistols were identical in all details to the MFA "Hero" pistols except for the marking on the side of the frame. The MFA "Hero" pistols were not serially marked and the quantity manufactured is unknown. The AST "Hero" pistols were serially marked; it is estimated that upwards of 30,000 were manufactured. Examples with 2½" barrels may be found in addition to the 2" and 3" barrel lengths shown.

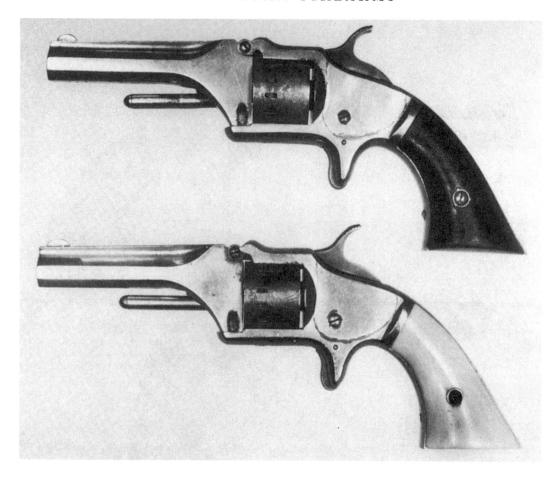

PLATE 60. UNSIGNED MANHATTAN SECOND MODEL .22-CALIBER REVOLVERS.

Figure 1. Left Side View, Number 287.

Figure 2. Left Side View, Number 311.

The above examples are believed to be among the rarest of the .22 caliber revolvers manufactured by Manhattan or its successor, American Standard Tool Company. Possessing all of the principal features of Manhattan's Second Model .22 caliber revolvers, the barrels are unsigned as to manufacturer or patent date and lack the engraving usually found on Manhattan's products.

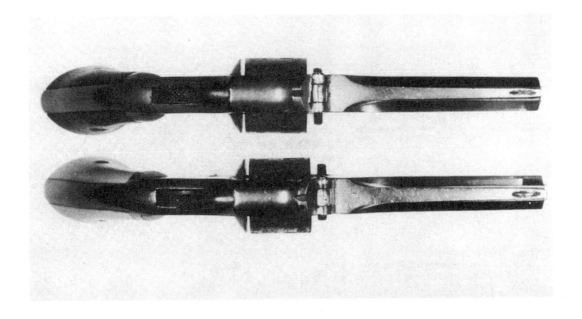

PLATE 61. UNSIGNED MANHATTAN SECOND MODEL .22-CALIBER REVOLVERS.

Figure 1. Top View, Number 87.

Figure 2. Top View, Number 311.

The expiration of Rollin White's patent of April 3, 1855 on April 3, 1869 was probably responsible for the absence of the barrel signing on the pictured revolvers. Thus, it would seem logical that these examples were manufactured prior to April 3, 1869 and during the period of transition of operations from Manhattan to its successor company. These revolvers were the forerunners of the numerous products of American Standard Tool Company.

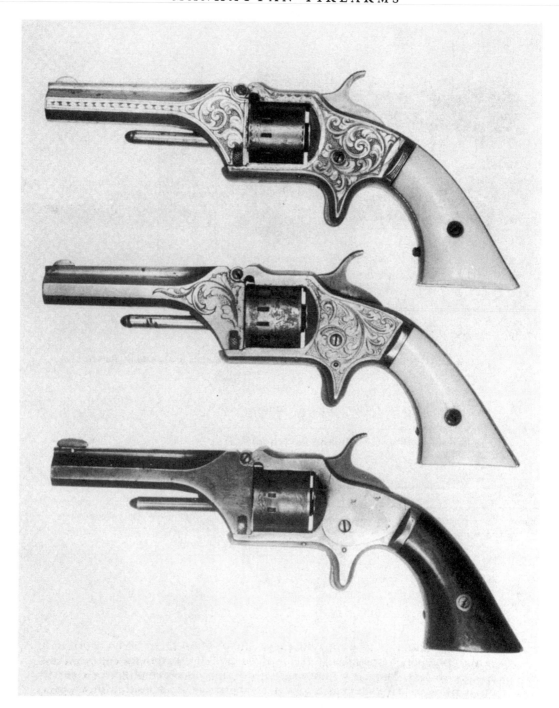

PLATE 62. AMERICAN STANDARD TOOL COMPANY .22-CALIBER REVOLVERS.

Figure 1. Fully Engraved, Number 21,872.

Figure 2. Fully Engraved, Number 32,749.

Figure 3. Plain Frame and Barrel, Number 429.

Continuing with substantially the same model developed by the Manhattan Company in 1861, American Standard Tool Company's .22 caliber revolver was the mainstay of its arms production between April of 1869 and February of 1873; upwards of 40,000 guns were manufactured during this period. The engraved specimens reflect, to some degree, the garish decoration of the low-priced arms of the 70's.

1863. It is our view that the model revolver was made up in the plant of American Standard Tool Company from unused or reclaimed Manhattan parts; we are confident on this point: the workmanship exhibited is of the highest order and much beyond the capabilities of an ordinary mechanic. It is to be noted that a complete gun, capable of performing the intended functions, was somewhat unusual in patent models of the period. We have no information to indicate that the Moss & Johnson revolver was produced in quantity by American Standard Tool Company or by any other American maker. However, revolvers employing the same or a similar principle of shell loading and extraction were manufactured in France and examples of this revolver are occasionally seen.

As has been noted, American Standard Tool Company managed to sustain and justify its existence throughout four difficult business years which included the infamous "Black Friday" of September 24, 1869. Nonetheless, it would appear that after reviewing the company's accomplishments for 1872 and, perhaps, foreseeing with remarkable acuity the coming events of the latter part of 1873 (it will be recalled that the list of stockholders included a number of successful men, plus two bankers of eminent position), the Board of Directors decided that it was "advisable and most for the benefit of the Company that the same should be dissolved," as noted in the appendix which deals with the dissolution of the company. The decision for dissolution was made at a meeting of the Directors on January 11, 1873, and the concurrence and consent to the action was given by the stockholders on February 20, 1873. It may be assumed that if the operations of the company had not ceased by this date, they were probably closed out immediately thereafter. The reasons for the action are unknown but were probably found in the generally worsening conditions of business and, perhaps, the lack of success in certain of the company's endeavors, especially those in the fields of merchandising of articles other than firearms. One wonders if the rise and fall of American Standard Tool Company may not have been a case of the shoemaker moving too far away from his last.

Not all of the stockholders were present at the last meeting, although 2284 of the 2400 shares were represented. Oba Meeker, the probable landlord of Manhattan's first location in Newark, presided as chairman of the meeting. Frederick H. Smith, together with his son Frederick H. Smith, Jr., accounted for 765 shares or 31% of the soon-to-be-ended enterprise. Andrew R. Arnold's holdings of 120 shares at the time of incorporation had risen to 230 shares at the termination. But what of Albert Beach's holdings, he who had been the owner of the largest block of stock, 562 shares, at the inception of the company? At the end, Beach owned but 71 shares or less than 3%. Albert Beach was the last stockholder to sign the document consenting to dissolution and the signature, unquestionably of Beach's penning, was distinctive, unusual and unlike his signatures on a dozen or more letters and other papers, the copies of which we have in our files. Beach's signature was embellished with flourishes which are not to be found on any one of his other signatures and it is our view that the embellishment was meaningful. Albert Beach was the man in charge when the young Manhattan venture took its first faltering footsteps in Norwich in 1855 and he reported "present" on the days and years that were to follow; days and years of hope and despair, of winning and losing, of pleasure and unpleasantness, of fat and lean, of failure and of success. These thoughts must have passed through Beach's mind as he prepared to affix his signature to the stockholders' Consent to Dissolution of American Standard Tool Company on that twentieth day of February, 1873. To us, the flourishes appended to his signature held the essence of finality. Beach knew, as we now know, that as he signed, he wrote "finis" to the story of Manhattan Firearms.

*   *   *   *

EPILOGUE

W̶e have come to the bottom of the hill with
this work, to that point where the author usually unties the tie, or unhasps
the girdle, relaxes and indulges in a privilege that is peculiar to authors.
This privilege is sometimes found under the title of "Conclusions." Actually,
as a device unto itself, "Conclusions" are unnecessary if the author has done his
job well; besides, the device is nothing if not anti-climactic. We shall have no
"Conclusions" but not because we feel that the task has been well done or even
passably done. We did the best we could with the material at hand and, in
the doing, we had the help of a large number of good, knowledgeful and oblig-
ing people. Instead of concluding conclusions, we will, in these last few lines
allotted to us, express an opinion, as likewise a hope and a wish.

The opinion: we think it significant that the holders of the two most valuable patents on handguns of the percussion and early cartridge periods, Colt and
Smith & Wesson, still dominate that market after the passage of more than one
hundred years. This fact detracts nothing from the success story of Manhattan
but, rather, adds emphasis to the company's achievements; Manhattan owned

PLATE 63. MANHATTAN .31-CALIBER REVOLVER CONVERTED TO CARTRIDGE.

Six-Shot, Four-Inch Barrel, Number 2940, Caliber .32 Centerfire.

An unusual revolver in Manhattan's line of firearms, in which conversions
are notably absent, the oddity of the above example is heightened by the
fact that the intended use was for centerfire cartridges rather than rimfire.
A rather incomplete conversion with no loading gate and no means of shell
extraction, the changeover probably was not of "factory" origin.

PLATE 64. PATENT MODEL OF MOSS & JOHNSON REVOLVER: CLOSED VIEW.

Five-Shot, Four-Inch Barrel, Caliber .41, Rimfire.

The major parts of the above model are obviously the similar parts of a Manhattan .36 caliber revolver, including the barrel, frame with internal parts, grips, back-strap and trigger-guard. Bore of the barrel was enlarged to .41 caliber and barrel signing was removed. It is believed that the model was made in the plant of American Standard Tool Company from Manhattan parts.

PLATE 65. PATENT MODEL OF MOSS & JOHNSON REVOLVER: OPENED VIEW.

Five-Shot, Four-Inch Barrel, Caliber .41, Rimfire.

As will be seen, the principal purpose of the invention was to provide for a very rapid means of shell extraction. As far as is known, the model was not produced in quantity in this country although a revolver of similar characteristics was manufactured in France.

one good patent and had the use of a second, but this was not enough. Eighteen years is not a long life for a corporation, although longer than the average, and the amazing facet of the Manhattan story is that the company did so well without the immeasurable help of an outstanding inventor. The feats performed by the inexperienced management in wresting a toehold in a competitive market, riding the market in its ascendancy during the years of the War, and thereafter, and thence into the shoals and shallows of the Panic of 1873 will be marked by all who know, understand and appreciate the principles of good management.

The hope: the source material which we were able to find and use has not been, by any means, complete or fully informative. True, we were able to find both ends of the thread—the beginning and the end—but there was little to be found between these points. Therefore, we are certain that errors of omission and commision exist in the tale as we have set it down. It is our sincerest hope that copies of the book will find their way into the hands of those who can add to our scanty knowledge of Manhattan and the men who were a part of the story. Letters to the author, in care of the publisher, will be gratefully received and acknowledged.

The wish: we wish that we knew more about the men who were a part of the Manhattan company. We are aware that the company was not a large one and that it probably employed scarcely more than one hundred "hands" during the peak period of 1863 to 1865. In our professional life, we have served a number of companies of relative size, and many that are larger, and we like the people who own, operate and manage and work for and in the smaller companies. We would have liked the Manhattan Company and Frederick H. Smith, the president who guided its destinies during those eighteen years; and Albert Beach, the General Manager who, like Mr. Smith, helped in the founding and was still around at the finish; and Andy Arnold, the competent mechanic and General Superintendent who contributed much to the quality and excellence of Manhattan's guns; and Joe Gruler and Gus Rebetey and Tom Bacon, who made the early arms. Most of all, we wish we could have known the unnamed mechanic who made the in-plant inspection punch that left the mark of a miniature pair of spectacles. There, indeed, was a fellow after our own heart.

*   *   *   *

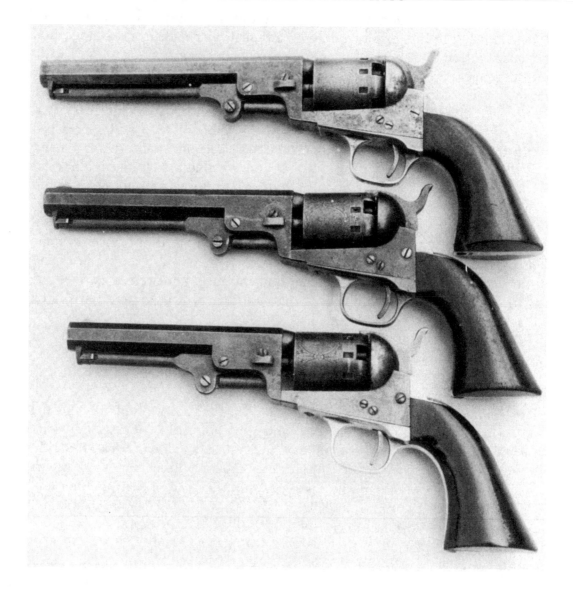

PLATE 66. "SERIES I .36 CAL. MANHATTAN REVOLVERS WITH "MISS AMERICA" GRIPS."

Figure 1. 5 shot, 6½″ bbl. #586
    (from the collection of Henry M. Stewart)

Figure 2. 5 shot, 6″ bbl. #681
    (from the collection of Mrs. Geraldine Briefer)

Figure 3. 5 shot, 5″ bbl. #551
    (from the collection of Mrs. Geraldine Briefer)

155212A

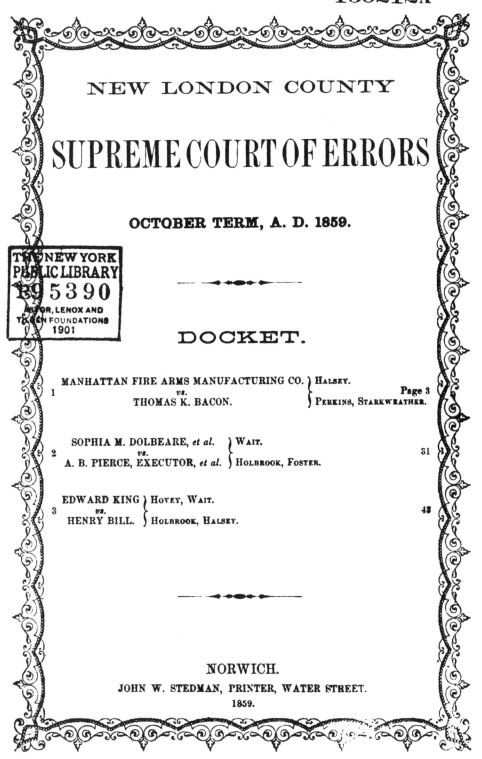

NEW LONDON COUNTY

SUPREME COURT OF ERRORS

OCTOBER TERM, A. D. 1859.

DOCKET.

NORWICH.

JOHN W. STEDMAN, PRINTER, WATER STREET.
1859.

NOTE. Pages 207 to 234 are photographic reproductions of photostated Court records of the trial of the Manhattan Fire Arms Manufacturing Company vs. Thomas K. Bacon.

THE MANHATTAN FIRE ARMS MANUFACTURING COMPANY

vs.

THOMAS K. BACON.

To the Honorable Superior Court to be holden at Norwich, within and for the county of New London, on the third Tuesday of November, A. D. 1858.

The petition of " The Manhattan Fire Arms Manufacturing Company," a joint stock corporation, duly and legally formed and organized under the laws of the state of New York, having an office in the city, county and state of New York, and having also their manufactory and doing business at Norwich aforesaid, respectfully represents, that the business of said company is the manufacture and sale of fire arms, and that they have full power and authority as such corporation to transact said business and all other powers incidental' thereto, and to make all contracts proper and convenient thereto; that on the 1st day of September, 1857, and for some time prior thereto, they had been engaged in the manufacture of fire arms of various kinds, particularly pistols, at said Norwich; that prior to said first day of September, 1857, one Thomas K. Bacon, of said Norwich, had been making arrangements to engage in the same line of business, and had contracted sundry liabilities in relation thereto, and that, wishing to extricate himself from said liabilities, and to engage in business in the employ of the petitioners, on said first day of September, 1857, he entered into an agreement with the petitioners, which agreement was in writing, and as follows, to wit:

4

"Norwich, Sept. 1st, 1857.

"In consideration of payment to me by the **Manhattan Fire Arms Manufacturing Company** of fifty dollars, the receipt whereof is hereby acknowledged, with which fifty dollars I am to pay Charles A. Converse, to obtain a release from further payment to him for rent of part of his factory, which I had hired, and also in consideration of said company agreeing to pay, and thereby releasing me from all responsibility for bills which I had contracted with the following, namely :

John G. Huntington,	$ 2	56
Backus & Barstow,	3	04
J. M. Huntington & Co.	9	26
John Breed & Co.	23	46
C. N. Farnam,	24	36
Phenix Foundery,		
George H. Brown,		
Charles A. Converse,	39	44
Wood, Light & Co.		
Union Machine Co.		

I hereby covenant and agree to and with said company, that I will not engage, or be in any way concerned, in the manufacture or sale, or in any other way connected with dealing in fire arms of any kind whatever, during twenty years from this date, provided said company allows me, as another consideration, to make for them, at the prices annexed, all that they use of the following parts of pistols :

Barrels for 2 inch single pistols,	5	cents each.
do. 3 do. do. do.	6 1-2	do.
do. 4 do. do. do.	8 1-2	do.
do. 5 do. do. do.	10 1-2	do.
do. 6 do. do. do.	12 1-2	do.
do. 3 barrel revolvers	17	do.
do. 5 do. do. do.	23	do.
do. 3 inch 6 barrel do.	25	do.
Barrels for 4 inch 6 barrel revolvers	30	do.
do. 5 inch 6 do. do.	40	do.

5

If at any time I relinquish the making of the parts of pistols at the prices annexed, as heretofore mentioned, then the Manhattan Fire Arms Manufacturing Company may employ any others to make such parts without being liable to me in any damages therefor, but in such case I shall then and thereafter be prohibited, as heretofore mentioned, from engaging in making or selling fire arms. It is understood that if the company can not supply me with work sufficient to employ my time and that of three boys, in making the kinds of barrels mentioned, then I shall have the preference, over any one else, at same price, in making barrels or cylinders for any other kinds of pistols the company may then require.

It is understood that the foregoing obligations are binding upon T. K. Bacon only so long as the Manhattan Fire Arms Manufacturing Company, or its successor, remains in business.

(Signed)   T. K. BACON.

The petitioners further represent, that in consideration of the agreement aforesaid, they paid to said Bacon said sum of fifty dollars, with which to obtain a release from said Converse, and that they also paid to said several persons all bills which said Bacon had contracted with them for the purposes aforesaid, and that said Bacon was thereby released from all liability for the same, and that they have, from said 1st day of September until the time hereafter mentioned, when said Bacon voluntarily quitted their employ, and refused to make for them any more of the parts of pistols hereinbefore specified, allowed said Bacon to make for them, at the prices before named in said agreement, all that they use or have used of said parts of pistols, and have paid him, from time to time, for the same, and have in all respects executed, performed and fulfilled all the considerations upon which said agreement was made, and have been at all times willing and desirous of allowing him to continue to make for them all that they use of said parts of pistols, at said prices, according to said agreement, but that said Bacon, on or about the 11th day of September, 1858, voluntarily quitted said manufacture, and

6

informed the petitioners that he should no longer continue the same.

The petitioners further represent, that after thus ceasing to manufacture said parts of pistols for the petitioners, the said Bacon, in violation of said agreement, has threatened to engage in the manufacture and sale of fire arms, and has been actively engaged in organizing a joint stock corporation under the laws of this state, called the Bacon Manufacturing Company, and that he is a large stockholder in said company, the business of which corporation, as specified in their articles of association, is the manufacture and sale of fire arms, with other powers incident thereto, having their office and place of business at said Norwich.

The petitioners further represent, that said Bacon, as agent for said company, and a stockholder therein, and in other ways, is preparing to, and threatens that he will engage in the manufacture and sale of fire arms, particularly pistols, in violation of his agreement with the petitioners.

And the petitioners aver, that said violation of said agreement by said Bacon, is contrary to equity and good conscience, and tends to their great and irreparable loss and damage, and that they are without adequate remedy at law, and must lose their just rights in the premises unless relieved by this Court, as a Court of equity.

The petitioners therefore pray this Court to inquire into the truth of the foregoing allegations, and to order and enjoin the said Thomas K. Bacon, under a suitable penalty, not to engage, or be in any way concerned in the manufacture or sale, or in any way connected with dealing in fire arms, during the remainder of said term of twenty years, in violation of said agreement, or in some other or different way to grant the petitioners relief in the premises, and they, as in duty bound, will ever pray.

Dated at Norwich this 4th day of November, A. D. 1858.

The Manhattan Fire Arms Manufacturing Company,

By J. HALSEY, *their Attorney.*

7

To the sheriff of the county of New London, his deputy, or either constable of the town of Norwich, in said county, GREETING :

By authority of the state of Connecticut, you are hereby commanded to summon Thomas K. Bacon, of said Norwich, to appear before the Superior Court to be holden at Norwich, within and for the county of New London, on the third Tuesday of November, A. D. 1858, then and there to show reasons, if any he has, why the prayer of the foregoing petition should not be granted. Hereof fail not, and make due and legal service and return. Nathan C. Chapell recognized $50 for prosecution.

Dated at Norwich, the 4th day of November, A. D. 1858.

Certified and signed by

JEREMIAH HALSEY, *Justice of the Peace.*

New London county, ss.

NORWICH, November 4, 1858.

Then and there, by virtue hereof, I made service of this petition and citation by placing in the hands of Thomas K. Bacon a true and attested copy of the same.

Attest,   N. C. CHAPELL, *Sheriff's Deputy.*

FEES—Travel	.	.	.	$ 25
Copy	.	.	.	2 50
Service	.	.	.	12
2 indorsements	.	.		24
				$3 11

The respondent denies the truth and sufficiency of the allegations in the petition contained.

By EDMUND PERKINS and H. H. STARKWEATHER,
                              his Attorneys.

8

New London county, ss.

SUPERIOR COURT, January term, 1859.

THE MANHATTAN FIRE ARMS CO. }
        vs.   } *Petition for Injunction.*
THOMAS K. BACON. }

Upon the trial of this case upon the issue formed by the pleadings as on file, the following facts are found by the Court:

The petitioners are a joint stock corporation, organized under the laws of the state of New York. The rights, powers and duties of said corporation are contained in the original certificate of the formation of "The Manhattan Fire Arms Manufacturing Company," a copy of which is hereto annexed, marked A; the certificate of the reduction of the capital stock of said corporation, a copy of which is hereto annexed, marked B; the articles of association and by-laws of said corporation, a copy of which is hereto annexed, marked C; and a certain statute law of the state of New York, entitled "An act to authorize the formation of corporations for manufacturing, mining, mechanical and chemical purposes," passed February 17, 1848, which said statute is made a part of this finding for the purpose of reference.

Said corporation was organized in May, 1855, and commenced business in New York city, and continued their business operations in said city five or six months. They then removed to Norwich, in said county of New London, and commenced the manufacture of pistols in said Norwich about the first of January, 1856, and have ever since continued said manufacture in said Norwich; have rented rooms, employed workmen, and have purchased and constructed machinery and materials for said manufacture. But said corporation has had, and still has, an office in the city of New York, where the business meetings of said corporation are held, and where many of their manufactured articles are sold.

Albert Beach, the secretary of said corporation, has acted as its general agent since its organization, has taken

9

the general charge and management of its business at said Norwich, and made all the necessary contracts therefor, but there is no vote of said corporation or of its trustees, appointing said Beach general agent, nor any vote authorizing him to act in that capacity.   But he has so acted with the knowledge and consent of said corporation and its trustees, to whom he has annually, and oftener when required, rendered an account of his said transactions.

On the first day of September, 1857, the respondent, Thomas K. Bacon, was, and for some time previous had been, making arrangements to engage in the business of manufacturing and selling fire arms, in said Norwich, and had contracted certain liabilities for the rent of a building in which to carry on said business, and for certain machinery and material to be used in said business.   On said day the said Beach, acting for the said Manhattan Fire Arms Manufacturing Company, and the said Thomas K. Bacon, made an agreement respecting the said liabilities of said Bacon, and his giving up his said contemplated business, which was reduced to writing, and is correctly recited in said petition, except so far as the same may be modified by the following facts, to wit : It was understood and agreed that the said agreement between said Beach and Bacon should be reduced to writing in duplicates to be signed by both parties, one of which duplicates was to be kept by one of the parties and the other duplicate by the other party ; and thereupon an agreement, a copy of which is set out in said petition, was made by the said Beach, and a duplicate thereof, except the prices affixed to the articles named therein, which said Bacon was to make for said corporation ; and the said Bacon signed said agreement, which said Beach took, but said Beach refused to sign said duplicate, and never did sign the same, though requested so to do by said Bacon.

Upon the execution of said contract, as aforesaid, Bacon relinquished the idea of commencing said business on his own account ; and commenced to work for the petitioners under said contract, making the parts of pistols therein mentioned, and continued so to work until the 11th day of

10

September, 1858. The petitioners paid the said Charles A. Converse said sum of fifty dollars for rent, and assumed the other liabilities named in said contract, and paid said Bacon for doing said work the said sums affixed to the different articles, and in various settlements made between said parties for work between said first day of September, 1857, and the 11th day of September, 1858, the said written contract was referred to by both parties as the rule by which said settlement was to be made. There is no vote of said corporation, or of its trustees, authorizing Beach to make any such contract, nor does it appear that he ever consulted them about it before it was made. He informed them of the existence of said contract with the respondent, but they took no action concerning it, and it does not appear that the corporation or its trustees ever approved or disapproved of the contract, except what may be inferred from their said inaction.

The respondent voluntarily left the employment of the petitioners on the 11th day of September, 1858. Since that time he has been instrumental in organizing a joint stock corporation under the laws of the state of Connecticut, under the name of the Bacon Manufacturing Company, for the manufacture and sale of fire arms. The respondent is a stockholder in this corporation, is the agent thereof and its principal manager. This corporation, before the 4th day of November, 1858, commenced the manufacture of the same kind of pistols, in said town of Norwich, that the petitioners were making at the time the respondent was in their employment, and continue to manufacture and sell said pistols. The respondent has not been, and is not in any other way concerned in the manufacture and sale of fire arms than as a member and agent of said corporation.

The said Manhattan Fire Arms Manufacturing Company are about to remove their said business to the state of New Jersey.

Upon the foregoing facts the question as to what decree shall be rendered is reserved for the advice of the Supreme Court of Errors, to be holden at New London, within and for the county of New London, on the second Tuesday of March, 1859.   By WALDO, *Judge.*

11

[A.]

CERTIFICATE OF THE FORMATION OF THE "MANHATTAN FIRE
ARMS MANUFACTURING COMPANY."

We, Montagnie Ward, Jacob F. Wyckoff, and David W.
Bailey, all of the city, county and state of New York, and
Alfred L. Dennis, Reuben D. Baldwin, Jeptha C. Groshong,
James B. Pinneo, Mathias W. Day, Thomas L. Miller,
Charles P. Hall, Charles W. Badger, Linn Adams, William
McMurty, Alfred Lyon, Charles T. Day, jr., Daniel Dodd,
jr., David C. Berry, and Frederick H. Smith, all of Newark,
county of Essex, and state of New Jersey, have formed
and do hereby form a company for the purpose and object
of manufacturing and dealing in fire arms, ammunition and
other articles pertaining to fire arms business; also to secure improvements in fire arms and machinery for manufacturing the same. The corporate name of said company
is " The Manhattan Fire Arms Manufacturing Company."
The capital stock thereof is forty thousand dollars, and
consists of four hundred shares of one hundred dollars
each. The term of its existence is twenty years. The
number of trustees are five, and their names are as follows:
Montagnie Ward, Jacob F. Wyckoff, and David W Bailey,
all of the city of New York, in the county and state of
New York, Frederick H. Smith, of Newark, in the county
of Essex and state of New Jersey, and Reuben D. Baldwin, also of the city of Newark, county of Essex and state
of New Jersey, and that said trustees are all citizens of the
United States of America, and that the operations of said
company are to be carried on in the city, county and state
of New York.

Montagnie Ward, fifteen (15) shares.
Jacob F. Wyckoff, ten (10) shares.
D. W. Bailey, ten (10) shares.

State of New York, city and county of New York, ss.

On this twenty-sixth day of May, A. D. 1855, personally
came before me, Montagnie Ward, Jacob F. Wyckoff, and

2

12

David W. Bailey, known to me to be the persons described in, and who executed the foregoing instrument, and severally acknowledged to me that they executed the same for the purposes therein mentioned.

THOMAS A. RICHMOND, *Commissioner of Deeds.*

A. L. Dennis, forty (40) shares.
Reuben D. Baldwin, fifty (50) shares.
Jeptha C. Groshong, twenty (20) shares.
James B. Pinneo, fifty (50) shares.
Matthias W. Day, twenty (20) shares.
T. L. Miller, five (5) shares.
C. P. Hall, twenty (20) shares.
Charles W. Badger, ten (10) shares.
Linn Adams, fifteen (15) shares.
Wm. McMurtry, ten (10) shares.
Alfred Lyon, five (5) shares.
Charles T. Day, jr., ten (10) shares.
Daniel Dodd, jr., twenty (20) shares.
David C. Berry, ten (10) shares.
Frederick H. Smith, eighty (80) shares.

State of New Jersey, Essex county, ss.

On this thirtieth day of May, A. D. 1855, personally came before me Alfred L. Dennis, Reuben D. Baldwin, Jeptha C. Groshong, James B. Pinneo, Matthias W. Day, Thomas L. Miller, Charles P. Hall, Charles W. Badger, Linn Adams, William McMurtry, Alfred Lyon, Charles T. Day, jr., Daniel Dodd, jr., David C. Berry and Frederick H. Smith, known to me to be the persons described in and who executed the foregoing instrument, and severally acknowledged to me that they executed the same for the purposes therein mentioned.

JAMES F. BOND, *Commissioner of Deeds.*

State of New Jersey, Essex county, ss.

I, James J. Terhune, clerk of the said county of Essex, and also clerk of the Court of Common Pleas, in and for

13

said county, do hereby certify that James F. Bond, who purports to have made and signed the foregoing certificate of acknowledgment, was, at the time of making and signing the same, a commissioner of deeds in and for said county, and that full faith and credit may and ought to be given to his official acts, and that the signature set to the foot of said certificate is in the proper hand-writing of the said James F. Bond.

In testimony whereof I have hereunto set my hand
L. S.   and official seal this thirty-first day of May, A. D. eighteen hundred and fifty-five.

J. J. TERHUNE, *Clerk.*

Endorsed—Certificate of the formation of The Manhattan Fire Arms Manufacturing Company. Filed 2d June, 1855.

State of New York, city and county of New York, ss.

I, John Clancy, clerk of the said city and county, do certify that I have compared the preceding with the original certificate of incorporation, on file in my office, and that the same is a correct transcript therefrom, and of the whole of such original.

In witness whereof, I have hereunto subscribed my
L. S.   name, and affixed my official seal, this 14th day of February, 1859.

JOHN CLANCY, *County Clerk.*

[B.]

CERTIFICATE OF REDUCTION OF CAPITAL.

Whereas, The Manhattan Fire Arms Manufacturing Company heretofore duly organized and commenced business under and by virtue of the statute in such case made and provided, as appears by the certificate of such organization, filed on second day of June, 1855, in the office of the clerk of the city and county of New York.

14

And *whereas*, the capital of said company was originally fixed at the sum of forty thousand dollars, divided in four hundred shares of one hundred dollars each.

And *whereas*, it has been proposed, under and by virtue of the provisions of said statute, to diminish said capital to twenty thousand dollars, divided in four hundred shares of fifty dollars each.

And *whereas*, the sum of twenty thousand dollars, being fifty dollars on each share of said original capital stock was, within one year from the original incorporation of said company, actually and in good faith paid in in cash.

Now it is hereby certified that the trustees of said company have published a notice signed by a majority of them in a newspaper published in the city, county and state of New York, called the New York Evening Post, for three successive weeks, specifying that a meeting of the stockholders of said company would be held at the office of said Manhattan Fire Arms Manufacturing Company, No. 163 Fulton street, in said city of New York, on the 29th day of April, 1857, at 11 o'clock in the forenoon, for the purpose of diminishing the capital stock of said company from forty thousand dollars to twenty thousand dollars, and the amount of its shares from one hundred dollars to fifty dollars each, and said trustees also deposited a copy of said notice in the post office in the city of New York, addressed to each stockholder at his usual place of residence at least three days previous to said 29th day of April, 1857.

And it is further certified that at the meeting, of which notice was so published, three hundred and thirty-five shares of stock were represented, either in person by parties owning same, or by proxy, and said meeting was organized by choosing Reuben D. Baldwin, one of the trustees of said company, chairman of the meeting, and Albert Beach, the secretary of said company, secretary of said meeting, and upon calling the roll the number of shares represented, as above stated, was found to be 335, and thereupon the following resolution was proposed:

Resolved, That the capital stock of this company be diminished from forty thousand dollars, its present amount, to twenty thousand dollars, and the amount of the shares

15

from one hundred dollars each, their present amount, to fifty dollars each.

Which resolution was unanimously adopted, the following persons owning the number of shares opposite their respective names having voted in person or by proxy in favor thereof.

Reuben D. Baldwin,	fifty-eight,	58,	shares in person.
David C. Berry,	thirty-seven,	37,	" " "
Charles T. Day, jr.,	ten,	10,	" " "
Alfred L. Dennis,	forty,	40,	" " "
Wm. McMurtry,	ten,	10,	" " "
Jacob F. Remer,	sixty,	60,	" " "
Frederick H. Smith,	forty,	40,	" " "
Jacob D. Vermilye,	ten	10,	" " "
		265	
David W. Bailey,	ten,	10,	shares by proxy.
Mathias W. Day,	twenty,	20,	" " "
James B. Pinneo,	forty,	40,	" " "
		335	shares.

And it is hereby further certified that the amount of capital actually paid in is the sum of twenty thousand dollars, that the business of the company is not extended or charged, and that the whole amount of debts and liabilities of the company is the sum of fourteen thousand five hundred and fifty-six dollars and eighteen cents.

In witness whereof, this certificate is signed and verified by the said chairman, countersigned by the secretary, and acknowledged by the said chairman this twenty-first day of May, 1857.

REUBEN D. BALDWIN, *Chairman.*

ALBERT BEACH, *Secretary.*

Witness—JAMES F. BOND.

16

State of New Jersey, Essex county, city of Newark.

Reuben D. Baldwin being duly sworn, says he was the chairman of the meeting in the foregoing certificate mentioned, and that the facts stated in the said certificate are correct and true.

REUBEN D. BALDWIN.

Sworn before me this — day of May, 1857.

JAMES F. BOND.

State of New Jersey, Essex county, ss.

I, James F. Bond, a commissioner for the state of New York, residing in the city of Newark, county and state aforesaid, do certify that on the twenty-first day of May, one thousand eight hundred and fifty-seven, the above named Reuben D. Baldwin subscribed the foregoing affidavit in my presence in the city of Newark, county and state aforesaid, and did depose and swear that the matters therein set forth were true.

In witness whereof, I have hereunto set my hand and affixed my official seal this twenty-first day of May, [L. S.] in the year one thousand eight hundred and fifty-seven, in the city of Newark, county and state aforesaid.

JAMES F. BOND,

A Commissioner for the state of New York in New Jersey.
Endorsed—Filed 23d May, 1857.

State of New York, city and county of New York, ss.

I, Richard B. Connolly, clerk of said city and county of New York, do hereby certify that I have compared the preceding with the original of a " certificate of diminution of capital," on file in my office, and that the same is a correct transcript therefrom and of the whole of said original.

In witness whereof, I have hereunto set my hand and [L. S.] affixed my official seal this 27th day of July, 1857.

RICHARD B. CONNOLLY , *Clerk.*

17

[C.]

ARTICLES OF ASSOCIATION AND BY-LAWS OF THE MANHATTAN FIRE ARMS MANUFACTURING COMPANY.

ARTICLE I. The association shall be known by the name of "The Manhattan Fire Arms Manufacturing Company," and shall continue in existence for the term of twenty years.

ART. II. The capital stock of said company shall be forty thousand dollars, divided into four hundred shares of one hundred dollars each.

ART. III. The object and purpose of the company is to manufacture and deal in fire arms, ammunition, and other articles pertaining to the fire arms business; also to secure improvements in fire arms and machinery for manufacturing the same.

ART. IV. The office of said company shall be located in the city, county and state of New York.

ART. V. All matters pertaining to the business of this company, not specified in the foregoing articles, shall be conducted in conformity with the by-laws of the company.

BY-LAWS.

SECTION 1. The business of this company shall be managed by a board of five trustees, who shall be chosen annually by ballot, on the third Tuesday in June, at the company's office, in the city of New York, and each share shall entitle the holder thereof to one vote, which may be given in person or by proxy. Two inspectors of election, (stockholders, but not candidates for office,) shall be appointed to preside, who shall declare the five persons having the greatest number of votes to be duly elected for one year, to serve as trustees of the company, and until others shall be elected in their stead.

SEC. 2. No person shall be or remain a trustee, unless he holds at least ten shares of the capital stock of the company.

18

Sec. 3. The trustees shall, at their first meeting after the annual meeting of the stockholders, choose one of their number president, who shall hold his office for one year, and until another shall be appointed in his stead. They shall also fill vacancies which may occur in their own body. They shall also from time to time elect a secretary, treasurer, and such other agents as they may deem necessary, who shall respectively occupy said positions during the pleasure of the trustees.

Sec. 4. The president shall exercise a general supervision over the affairs of the company, and shall perform all other duties usually devolving upon such officer.

Sec. 5. A stated meeting of the trustees shall be held at the office of the company, on the second Tuesday in every month, at 12 o'clock M., (which meeting may be adjourned at the pleasure of the trustees,) when the following order of business shall be observed:

1st. Reading the minutes of the previous meeting.

2d. Communications from the president and other officers.

3d. Reports of standing and other committees.

4th. Miscellaneous business.

Sec. 6. The president, or a majority of the trustees, may call a special meeting of the trustees, at such time and place as he or they may deem necessary for the interest of the company, by giving a written notice through the post office, or otherwise, to each trustee, previous to the time of meeting.

Sec. 7. At all meetings of the trustees, a majority shall be required to constitute a quorum, and the concurrence of a majority of the whole number of trustees shall be requisite to transact any business.

Sec. 8. The secretary shall furnish satisfactory security for the faithful performance of his duty, in the sum of twenty-five hundred dollars. It shall be his duty to take charge of and keep the common seal of the company; to keep all the records of the company, and also of the trustees, in suitable books provided for such purpose; to keep regular stock books and transfer books, issue certificates of stock,

19

to be signed by the president and secretary, to the holders thereof, to which the seal of the company shall be attached; to attend to the correspondence of the company, and keep a copy of such correspondence; to see that all necessary records are made in the secretary of state's office, and county clerk's office, according to law; to make an annual statement in writing of the situation and standing of the company, so far as he has the means of knowing the same; to keep a regular account with the treasurer and agents; to keep a correct account of all moneys received and paid out; at all suitable times to keep an office open, and at all times during usual business hours, the books of the company shall be subject to the inspection of the stockholders, or other persons authorized to inspect the same; he shall also keep a book for the transfer of the capital stock of the company; and perform all other duties usually devolving upon a secretary.

SEC. 9. The treasurer shall furnish satisfactory security for the faithful performance of his trust, in the sum of five thousand dollars. It shall be his duty to take charge of the funds of the company, give receipts for the same, which shall be filed in the secretary's office; pay out such sums as may be drawn for by the secretary, countersigned by the president; keep an account of receipts and disbursements, and make a report in writing of the state of the treasury, annually, or oftener, if requested by the trustees.

SEC. 10. The transfer book of the company shall be closed the last three week days previous to, and on the day of, the annual meeting of the stockholders.

SEC. 11. The by-laws of the company may be altered or amended at any meeting of the stockholders, by a vote of a majority in interest, of said stockholders.

SEC. 12. The trustees may call a meeting of the stockholders at such time and place as they may deem necessary, by giving a written notice to each of the said stockholders, either personally or by leaving the same at his residence or at the post office, previous to said meeting, and the concurrence of a majority in interest of said stockholders shall be requisite to transact any business.

20

[D.]

AN ACT TO AUTHORIZE THE FORMATION OF CORPORATIONS FOR MANUFACTURING, MINING, MECHANICAL, OR CHEMICAL PURPOSES. PASSED FEBRUARY 17, 1848.

The people of the state of New York, represented in senate and assembly, do enact as follows:

SECTION 1. At any time hereafter, any three or more persons, who may desire to form a company for the purpose of carrying on any kind of manufacturing mining, mechanical or chemical business, may make, sign and acknowledge, before some officer competent to take the acknowledgment of deeds, and file in the office of the clerk of the county in which the business of the company shall be carried on, and a duplicate thereof in the office of the secretary of state, a certificate in writing, in which shall be stated the corporate name of the said company, and the objects for which the company shall be formed, the amount of capital stock of the said company, the term of its existence, not to exceed fifty years, the number of shares of which the said stock shall consist, the number of trustees and their names, who shall manage the affairs of said company for the first year, and the names of the town and county in which the operations of the said company are to be carried on.

SEC. 2. When the certificate shall have been filed as aforesaid, the persons who shall have signed and acknowledged the same, and their successors, shall be a body politic and corporate, in fact and in name, by the name stated in such certificate; and by that name have succession, and shall be capable of suing or being sued in any court of law or equity in this state, and they and their successors may have a common seal, and may make and alter the same at pleasure; and they shall, by their corporate name, be capable in law of purchasing, holding and conveying any real and personal estate whatever which may be necessary to enable the said company to carry on their operations named in such certificate, but shall not mortgage the same or give any lien thereon.

21

Sec. 3. The stock, property and concerns of such company shall be managed by not less than three nor more than nine trustees, who shall respectively be stockholders in such company and citizens of the United States, and a majority of whom shall be citizens of this state, who shall, except the first year, be annually elected by the stockholders, at such time and place as shall be directed by the by-laws of the company; and public notice of the time and place of holding such election shall be published not less than ten days previous thereto, in the newspaper printed nearest to the place where the operations of the said company shall be carried on; and the election shall be made by such of the stockholders as shall attend for that purpose, either in person or by proxy.   All elections shall be by ballot, and each stockholder shall be entitled to as many votes as he owns shares of stock in the said company, and the persons receiving the greatest number of votes shall be trustees; and when any vacancy shall happen among the trustees, by death, resignation or otherwise, it shall be filled for the remainder of the year in such manner as may be provided for by the by-laws of the said company.

Sec. 4. In case it shall happen at any time, that an election of trustees shall not be made on the day designated by the by-laws of said company, when it ought to have been made, the company for that reason shall not be dissolved, but it shall be lawful on any other day, to hold an election for trustees, in such manner as shall be provided for by the said by-laws, and all acts of trustees shall be valid and binding as against such company, until their successors shall be elected.

Sec. 5. There shall be a president of the company, who shall be designated from the number of trustees, and also such subordinate officers as the company by its by-laws may designate, who may be elected or appointed, and required to give such security for the faithful performance of the duties of their office as the company by its by-laws may require.

Sec. 6. It shall be lawful for the trustees to call in and demand from the stockholders respectively, all such sums of money by them subscribed, at such times and in such

22

payments or installments as the trustees shall deem proper, under the penalty of forfeiting the shares of stock subscribed for, and all previous payments made thereon, if payment shall not be made by the stockholders within sixty days after a personal demand or notice requiring such payment shall have been published for six successive weeks in the newspaper nearest to the place where the business of the company shall be carried on as aforesaid.

SEC. 7. The trustees of such company shall have power to make such prudential by-laws as they shall deem proper for the management and disposition of the stock and business affairs of such company, not inconsistent with the laws of this state, and prescribing the duties of officers, artificers, and servants that may be employed; for the appointment of all officers, and for carrying on all kinds of business within the objects and purposes of such company.

SEC. 8. The stock of such company shall be deemed personal estate, and shall be transferable in such manner as shall be prescribed by the by-laws of the company; but no shares shall be transferable until all previous calls thereon shall have been fully paid in, or shall have been declared forfeited for the non-payment of calls thereon. And it shall not be lawful for such company to use any of their funds in the purchase of any stock in any other corporation.

SEC. 9. The copy of any certificate of incorporation, filed in pursuance of this act, certified by the county clerk or his deputy, to be a true copy, and of the whole of such certificate, shall be received in all courts and places, as presumptive legal evidence of the facts therein stated.

SEC. 10. All the stockholders of every company incorporated under this act, shall be severally individually liable to the creditors of the company in which they are stockholders to an amount equal to the amount of stock held by them respectively for all debts and contracts made by such company, and the whole amount of capital stock fixed and limited by such company shall have been paid in, and a certificate thereof shall have been made and recorded as prescribed in the following section; and the capital stock, so fixed and limited, shall all be paid in, one half thereof with-

23

in one year, and the other half thereof within two years from the incorporation of said company, or such corporation shall be dissolved.

SEC. 11. The president and a majority of the trustees, within thirty days after the payment of the last installment of the capital stock, so fixed and limited by the company, shall make a certificate stating the amount of the capital so fixed and paid in; which certificate shall be signed and sworn to by the president and a majority of the trustees; and they shall, within the said thirty days, record the same in the office of the county clerk of the county wherein the business of the said company is carried on.

SEC. 12. Every such company shall annually, within twenty days from the first day of January, make a report which shall be published in some newspaper, published in the town, city or village, or if there be no newspaper published in said town, city or village, then in some newspaper published nearest the place where the business of said company is carried on, which shall state the amount of capital, and of the proportion actually paid in, and the amount of its existing debts, which report shall be signed by the president and a majority of the trustees; and shall be verified by the oath of the president or secretary of said company and filed in the office of the clerk of the county where the business of the company shall be carried on; and if any of said companies shall fail so to do, all the trustees of the company shall be jointly and severally liable for all the debts of the company, then existing, and for all that shall be contracted before such report shall be made.

SEC. 13. If the trustees of any such company shall declare and pay any dividend when the company is insolvent, or any dividend, the payment of which would render it insolvent, or which would diminish the amount of its capital stock, they shall be jointly and severally liable for all the debts of the company then existing, and for all that shall be thereafter contracted, while they shall respectively continue in office.

Provided, That if any of the trustees shall object to the declaring of such dividend or to the payment of the same, and shall at any time before the time fixed for the payment

24

thereof, file a certificate of their objection in **writing with the clerk of the company** and with the clerk of the county, they shall be exempt from the said liability.

Sec. 14. Nothing but money shall be considered **as payment** of any part of the capital stock, and no loan of **money** shall be made by any such company to any stockholder therein; and if any such loan shall be made to **a stock-holder, the officers** who shall make it, or who shall assent thereto, shall be jointly and severally liable to the extent of such loan and interest, for all the debts of the company contracted before the repayment of the sum so loaned.

Sec. 15. If any certificate or report made, or public notice given, by the officers of any such company, in pursuance of the provisions of this act, shall be false in any material representation, all the officers who shall have signed the same, knowing it to be false, shall be jointly and severally liable for all the debts of the company, contracted while they are stockholders or officers thereof.

Sec. 16. No person holding stock in any such company, as executor, administrator, guardian or trustee, and no person holding such stock as collateral security shall be personally subject to any liability as stockholder of such company; but the person pledging such stock shall be considered as holding the same, and shall be liable as a stockholder accordingly, and the estates and funds in the hands of such executor, administrator, guardian or trustee, shall be liable in like manner and to the same extent as the testator or intestate, or the ward or person interested in such trust fund would have been, if he had been living and competent to act, and held the same stock in his own name.

Sec. 17. Every such executor, administrator, guardian or trustee shall represent the share of stock in his hands at all meetings of the company, and may vote accordingly as a stockholder; and every person who shall pledge his stock as aforesaid, may nevertheless represent the same at all such meetings, and may vote accordingly as a stockholder.

Sec. 18. The stockholders of any company organized under the provisions of this act shall be jointly and severally individually liable for all debts that may be due and owing to all their laborers, servants and apprentices, for services performed for such corporation.

25

SEC. 19. The legislature may at any time alter, amend
or repeal this act, or may annul or repeal any incorporation
formed or created under this act; but such amendment or
repeal shall not, nor shall the dissolution of any such company take away or impair any remedy given against any
such corporation, its stockholders or officers, for any liability which shall have been previously incurred.

SEC. 20. Any corporation or company heretofore formed,
either by special act or under the general law, and now
existing for any manufacturing, mining, mechanical or
chemical purposes, or any company which may be formed
under this act, may increase or diminish its capital stock by
complying with the provisions of this act, to any amount
which may be deemed sufficient and proper for the purposes of the corporation, and may also extend its business
to any other manufacturing, mining, mechanical or chemical
business, subject to the provisions and liabilities of this act.
But before any corporation shall be entitled to diminish
the amount of its capital stock, if the amount of its debts
and liabilities shall exceed the amount of capital to which
it is proposed to be reduced, such amount of debts and liabilities shall be satisfied and reduced so as not to exceed
such diminished amount of capital; and any existing company, heretofore formed under the general law, or any
special act, may come under and avail itself of the privileges and provisions of this act, by complying with the
following provisions, and thereupon such company, its officers and stockholders, shall be subject to all the restrictions,
duties and liabilities of this act.

SEC. 21. Whenever any company shall desire to call a
meeting of the stockholders, for the purpose of availing itself of the privileges and provisions of this act, for increasing or diminishing the amount of its capital stock, or for
extending or changing its business, it shall be the duty of
the trustees to publish a notice signed by at least a majority
of them, in a newspaper in the county, if any shall be published therein, at least three successive weeks, and to de-
posit a written or printed copy thereof in the post office,
addressed to each stockholder at his usual place of residence,
at least three weeks previous to the day fixed upon for

26

holding such meeting ; specifying the object of the meeting, the time and place when and where such meeting shall be held, and the amount to which it shall be proposed to increase or diminish the capital, and the business to which the company would be extended or changed, and a vote of at least two-thirds of all the shares of stock shall be necessary to an increase or diminution of the amount of its capital stock, or the extension or change of its business as aforesaid, or to enable a company to avail itself of the provisions of this act.

Sec. 22. If at any time and place specified in the notice provided for in the preceding section of this act, stockholders shall appear in person or by proxy, in number representing not less than two-thirds of all the shares of stock of the corporation, they shall organize by choosing one of the trustees chairman of the meeting, and also a suitable person for secretary, and proceed to a vote of those present, in person or by proxy, and if on canvassing the votes it shall appear that a sufficient number of votes has been given in favor of increasing or diminishing the amount of capital, or of extending or changing its business as aforesaid, or for availing itself of the privileges and provisions of this act, a certificate of the proceedings, showing a compliance with the provisions of this act, the amount of capital actually paid in, the business to which it is extended or changed, the whole amount of debts or liabilities of the company, and the amount to which the capital stock shall be increased or diminished, shall be made out, signed and verified by the affidavit of the chairman, and be countersigned by the secretary ; and such certificate shall be acknowledged by the chairman, and filed as required by the first section of this act, and when so filed, the capital stock of such corporation shall be increased or diminished, to the amount specified in such certificate, and the business extended or changed as aforesaid, and the company shall be entitled to the privileges and provisions, and be subject to the liabilities of this act, as the case may be.

Sec. 23. If the indebtedness of any such company shall at any time exceed the amount of its capital stock, the trustees of such company assenting thereto shall be per-

27

sonally and individually liable for such excess to the creditors of such company.

SEC. 24. No stockholder shall be personally liable for the payment of any debt contracted by any company formed under this act, which is not to be paid within one year from the time the debt is contracted, nor unless a suit for the collection of such debt shall be brought against such company within one year after the debt shall become due; and no suit shall be brought against any stockholder who shall cease to be a stockholder in any such company, for any debt so contracted, unless the same shall be commenced within two years from the time he shall have ceased to be a stockholder in such company, nor until an execution against the company shall have been returned unsatisfied in whole or in part.

SEC. 25. It shall be the duty of the trustees of every such corporation or company to cause a book to be kept by the treasurer or clerk thereof, containing the names of all persons, alphabetically arranged, who are, or shall, within six years, have been stockholders of such company, and showing their places of residence, the number of shares of stock held by them respectively, and the time when they respectively became the owners of such shares, and the amount of stock actually paid in; which book shall, during the usual business hours of the day, on every day except Sunday and the fourth day of July, be open for the inspection of stockholders and creditors of the company, and their personal representatives, at the office or principal place of business of such company, in the county where its business operations shall be located; and any and every such stockholder, creditor or representative, shall have a right to make extracts from such book; and no transfer of stock shall be valid for any purpose whatever, except to render the person to whom it shall be transferred liable for the debts of the company, according to the provisions of this act, until it shall have been entered therein as required by this section, by an entry showing to and from whom transferred. Such book shall be presumptive evidence of the facts therein stated, in favor of the plaintiff, in any suit or proceeding against such company, or against any one or more stock-

28

holders. Every officer or agent of any such company, who shall neglect to make any proper entry in such book, or shall refuse or neglect to exhibit the same, or allow the same to be inspected, and extracts to be taken therefrom, as provided by this section, shall be deemed guilty of a misdemeanor, and the company shall forfeit and pay to the party injured a penalty of fifty dollars for every such neglect or refusal, and all the damages resulting therefrom : And every company that shall neglect to keep such book open for inspection as aforesaid, shall forfeit to the people the sum of fifty dollars for every day it shall so neglect, to be sued for and recovered in the name of the people, by the district attorney of the county in which the business of such corporation shall be located ; and when so recovered, the amount shall be paid into the treasury of such county for the use thereof.

SEC. 26. Every corporation created under this act shall possess the general powers and privileges and be subject to the liabilities and restrictions contained in title third of chapter eighteen of the first part of the Revised Statutes.

SEC. 27. This act shall take effect immediately.

State of New York, Secretary's Office.

I have compared the preceding with the original law on file in this office, and do certify that the same is a correct transcript therefrom and of the whole of said original.

C. MORGAN, *Secretary of State.*

29

At a Superior Court held at New London, within and for the county of New London, on the 3d Tuesday of January, A. D. 1859.

Present, Hon. LOREN P. WALDO, *Judge.*
WM. L. BREWER, *Clerk.*
N. P. PAYNE, *Sheriff.*

The Manhattan Fire Arms Manufacturing Company, a joint stock corporation, duly and legally formed and organized under the laws of the state of New York, having an office in the city, county and state of New York, and having also their manufactory, and doing business at Norwich, in New London county, petitioners, *vs.* Thomas K. Bacon, of said town of Norwich, respondent.

This was a bill in equity, bearing date the 4th day of November, A. D. 1858, and praying that the said respondent be restrained under a suitable penalty from manufacturing or sale of fire arms, &c., as stated in said petition.

The case came to the November term of this Court, A. D. 1858, when the parties appeared, and thence, by continuance, to the present term, when the parties appeared, and were heard.

After such hearing and due consideration, the Court finds the facts as on file, and reserves the questions of law arising theron for the advice of the Supreme Court of Errors, at its term next to be holden at New London, within and for the county of New London, on the second Tuesday of March, A. D. 1859.

A true copy of record.

Attest,   WM. L. BREWER, *Clerk.*

APPENDIX "B":

CERTIFICATE OF INCORPORATION MANHATTAN FIRE ARMS COMPANY

We whose names are hereto subscribed do hereby certify that we have associated ourselves into a Company, by the name of the

"Manhattan Fire Arms Company"

for the purpose of carrying on a Manufacturing business in this State, under the following Articles of Association.

(1) The name of said Company shall be the Manhattan Fire Arms Company.

(2) The Business of said Company shall be conducted in the City of Newark and State of New Jersey and the object and purpose of the Company is to manufacture and deal in Fire Arms, ammunition and other articles pertaining to Fire Arms business and to manufacture machinery also to secure improvements in Fire Arms and Machinery for Manufacturing the same.

(3) The Capital Stock of said Company shall be the sum of Fifty thousand Dollars which shall be divided into One thousand shares of Fifty dollars each.

(4) The following are the names and residences of the Stockholders in said Company and the number of shares held by each, viz:

Jay L. Adams of Bloomfield, N. J., 30 shares
Charles W. Badger of Newark, N. J., 20 shares
Reuben D. Baldwin of Newark, N. J., 140 shares
David C. Berry of Newark, N. J., 74 shares
Alfred L. Dennis of Newark, N. J., 80 shares
Charles T. Day of Newark, N. J., 20 shares
Matthias W. Day of Toledo, Ohio, 40 shares
James B. Pinneo of Newark, N. J., 104 shares
Jacob F. Remer of Newark, N. J., 120 shares
Frederick H. Smith of Newark, N. J., 142 shares
William H. Talcott of Jersey City, N. J., 10 shares
Jacob D. Vermilye of Newark, N. J., 20 shares
Andrew R. Arnold of Newark, N. J., 100 shares
Albert Beach of Newark, N. J., 100 shares

(5) The said Company shall commence its existence on the nineteenth day of August, Eighteen hundred and Sixty three and terminate it on the Nineteenth day of August, Eighteen hundred and eighty eight.

In Witness whereof we have hereto set our hands and seals at the City of Newark in the County of Essex and State of New Jersey this Nineteenth day of August eighteen hundred and sixty three.

Sealed and delivered
in presence of   }

s/   Jay L. Adams
Jas. B. Pinneo
Charles T. Day
Reuben D. Baldwin
A. L. Dennis
J. F. Remer
David C. Berry
F. H. Smith
Chas. W. Badger
Jacob D. Vermilye
Matthias W. Day
W. H. Talcott
Andrew R. Arnold
Albert Beach

New Jersey   }
           ss
Essex County }

Be it remembered that on the Nineteenth day of August eighteen hundred and sixty three before me, the subscriber, a Master in Chancery of New Jersey, personally appeared Jay L. Adams, James B. Pinneo, Charles T. Day, Reuben D. Baldwin, Alfred L. Dennis, Jacob F. Remer, David C. Berry, Frederick H. Smith and Charles W. Badger, on the twentieth day of the same month also appeared before me Jacob D. Vermilye, on the twenty first day of the said month also appeared before me Matthias W. Day, on the ninth day of September in the year aforesaid also appeared before me William H. Talcott and on the tenth day of September aforesaid appeared before me Andrew R. Arnold and Albert Beach known to me to be the persons named in the foregoing instrument and to whom I made known the contents thereof who thereupon severally executed the same as their voluntary act and deed for the uses and purposes therein expressed.

Daniel Dodd M. C. C.

Received in the Office and Recorded
15th September 1863

John McChesney, Clerk

State of New Jersey ⎤
                    ⎬ ss
Essex County   ⎦

I, John McChesney, Clerk of the County of Essex, do hereby certify that the above is a true copy of the Certificate duly recorded in this office on the 15th day of September 1863 and that the original Certificate of which the above is a true copy has been mislaid in this office and after diligent search cannot be found.

seal

In testimony whereof I have hereunto set my hand and official seal this 16th of December A. D. 1863.

John McChesney
Clerk

State of New Jersey

Department of State.

I, the Secretary of State of the State of New Jersey, do hereby Certify that the foregoing is a true copy of the Certificate of Incorporation of MANHATTAN FIRE ARMS COMPANY _____ and the endorsements thereon, as the same is taken from and compared with the original filed in my office on the Ninth day of January A.D. 1864, and now remaining on file and of record therein.

In Testimony Whereof, I have hereunto set my hand and affixed my Official Seal at Trenton, this Twelfth day of March A.D. 1958.

Edward J. Patten

Secretary of State.

APPENDIX "C":

CERTIFICATE OF ORGANIZATION
AMERICAN STANDARD TOOL COMPANY

We whose names are hereto subscribed do hereby certify that we have associated ourselves into a Company, by the name of:

"American Standard Tool Company"

for the purpose of transacting a Manufacturing business and the needful trading operations connected therewith. in the State of New Jersey, under the following

"Articles of Association"

The name of such Company shall be

"American Standard Tool Company"

The principal business of the said Company shall be conducted at its factory and office in the City of Newark, and State of New Jersey, but offices for the sale of the Company's products and for the transaction of general business, thereto pertaining, may be located in the City of New York, and elsewhere, as may hereafter appear to be expedient.

The object and purpose of the Company is to manufacture and deal in Tools, Machinery, Hard Ware, Fire Arms, Ammunition, Silver Ware, Plated Ware, German Silver Ware, Britania Ware and other articles pertaining to such several products, as well as to conduct a general repairs and jobbing and foundry business in the several departments mentioned, besides to secure by Patent, or otherwise, improvements in the same and in tools and processes incident to their production.

A further object and purpose of the Company is purchasing and selling manufactured articles, also acquiring and disposing of rights to make and use the same.

The Capital Stock of said Company shall be the sum of One Hundred and Twenty Thousand Dollars, which shall be divided into Twenty Four hundred shares of Fifty Dollars each, with which the Company shall commence business.

The following are the names, with the residence, of the Stockholders in said Company and the number of Shares held by each, viz:

Frederick H. Smith of Newark, N. J., 310 shares
Reuben D. Baldwin of Newark, N. J., 480 shares
David C. Berry of Newark, N. J., 8 shares
Jacob F. Remer of Newark, N. J., 120 shares
Charles T. Day of Newark, N. J., 40 shares
Charles W. Badger of Newark, N. J., 40 shares
Jacob D. Vermilye of New York City, N. Y., 12 shares
Henry J. Stevenson of New York City, 440 shares
Alfred L. Dennis of Newark, N. J., 46 shares
James B. Pinneo of Newark, N. J., 98 shares
Oba Meeker of Newark, N. J., 30 shares
Jay L. Adams of Bloomfield, N. J., 30 shares
Andrew R. Arnold of Newark, N. J., 140 shares
Frederick H. Smith, Jr. of Newark, N. J., 44 shares
Albert Beach of Newark, N. J., 562 shares

The said Company shall commence its business and its existence on the Twenty-third day of November, Eighteen hundred and Sixty Eight and terminate it on the Twenty-third day of November, Eighteen hundred and Eighty Eight.

In Witness Whereof, we have hereto set our hands and seals at the City of Newark, in the County of Essex and State of New Jersey, this Twenty-third day of November, Eighteen hundred and Sixty Eight.

s/   F. H. Smith
R. D. Baldwin
David C. Berry
J. F. Remer
Charles T. Day
Chas. W. Badger
Jacob D. Vermilye
H. J. Stevenson
A. L. Dennis
Jas. B. Pinneo
Oba Meeker
Jay L. Adams
Andrew R. Arnold
F. H. Smith, Jr.
Albert Beach

New Jersey
Essex County ss:

Be it remembered that on the.twenty third day of November, Eighteen hundred and Sixty Eight, before me, the Subscriber, a Master in Chancery of New Jersey, personnally appeared Frederick H. Smith, Charles W. Badger, Alfred L. Dennis, James B. Pinneo, Oba Meeker, Andrew R. Arnold and Frederick H. Smith, Jr. On the twenty fourth day of the same month also personally appeared before me Jacob F. Remer, and Charles T. Day, and on the twenty seventh day of said month also personally appeared before me David C. Berry, Reuben D. Baldwin and Albert Beach. Known to me to be the persons named in the foregoing instrument, and to whom I made known the contents thereof, who thereupon severally acknowledged that they executed the same as their voluntary act and deed for the uses and purposes therein expressed.

s/ Gilbert W. Cumming
Master in Chancery
of New Jersey

State of New York
City and County of New York ss:

Be it remembered that on the twenty fifth day of November in the year of our Lord Eighteen hundred and Sixty Eight before me, Aaron Pennington Whitehead, a Commissioner for the State of New Jersey, to take proofs and acknowledgements of Deeds and other Instruments in the State of New York, personally appeared Jacob D. Vermilye and on the twenty seventh day of the same month personally appeared Henry J. Stevenson which said Vermilye and Stevenson I am satisfied are two of the persons named in and who executed the foregoing instrument and I having first made known to them the contents thereof they thereupon severally acknowledge to me that they signed, sealed and delivered the same as their voluntary act and deed for the uses and purposes therein mentioned and expressed.

s/ A. P. Whitehead
Commissioner.

State of New Jersey

Department of State.

I, the Secretary of State of the State of New Jersey **Do hereby Certify** *that the foregoing is a true copy of* Certificate of Incorporation and Dissolution thereto of AMERICAN STANDARD TOOL COMPANY

_____

_____

_____

_____

as the same is taken from and compared with the original filed in this office on the dates set forth on each instrument *and now remaining on file and of record in my office*

In Testimony Whereof, *I have hereunto set my hand and affixed my Official Seal at Trenton, this*   Twelfth

day of   March   *A.D. 19* 58.

Edward J. Patten

Secretary of State.

APPENDIX "D":

CONSENT OF STOCKHOLDERS TO DISSOLUTION OF AMERICAN STANDARD TOOL COMPANY

Newark, N. J. Feb'y 20th 1873

At a meeting of the Stockholders of the American Standard Tool Company, held this day pursuant to call of the Directors, to act upon their proposition "to dissolve the Company before the expiration of the time limited in its certificate of incorporation," Oba Meeker was appointed Chairman and Stephen C. Morehouse Secretary.

The following action was taken:

Whereas the Directors, at a meeting held on the Eleventh day of January, ultimo, adopted the following resolution: "Resolved, that the Board deem it advisable and most for the benefit of the Company that the same should be dissolved before the expiration of the time limited in its Certificate of Incorporation, and that a meeting of the stockholders of the Company be called, to be held at No. 35 Clinton St., Newark, N. J., on Thursday, the 20th day of February, 1873, at ten o'clock, AM., to act upon such proposition, and that the Secretary be directed to give notice of such meeting to each Stockholder and to publish the same according to the requirements of law."

Now, therefore, we, the subscribers, owners of the number of shares of the Capital Stock of the American Standard Tool Company written opposite to our respective names, do hereby consent that such dissolution shall take place.

s/ Estate of Reuben D. Baldwin .... 460 shares
    by Edward F. Baldwin, Ex'r
Jas. B. Pinneo .... 98 shares
J. F. Remer .... 120 shares
Oba Meeker .... 30 shares
Chas. W. Badger .... 40 shares
Charles T. Day .... 40 shares
Andrew R. Arnold .... 230 shares
F. H. Smith, Jr. .... 127 shares
F. H. Smith .... 638 shares

Joseph Slagg .... 440 shares
Att'y W. O. Woodford
Jay L. Adams .... 30 shares
by F. H. Smith, Att'y
Albert Beach .... 71 shares

Adjourned:

Oba Meeker, Chairman

S. C. Morehouse, Secretary

State of New Jersey ⎫
⎬ ss
Essex County ⎭

Personally appeared before me, William Frame, a Commissioner of Deeds . . . Stephen C. Morehouse, who deposeth and saith that he is the Secretary of the American Standard Tool Company; that the whole number of shares of the Capital Stock of the said Company is twenty-four hundred; that the persons subscribing to the foregoing paper are the owners of the number of shares set opposite to their respective names; and that they signed the same in his presence.

s/ Stephen C. Morehouse

Sworn and Subscribed
before me this 20th day
of February, 1873.

s/ William Frame
Commissioner of Deeds

BIBLIOGRAPHY

BRUCE, ROBERT V. *Lincoln and the Tools of War*. New York: The Bobbs-Merrill Co., Inc., 1956.

CAREY, A. MERWYN *American Firearms Makers*. New York: T. Y. Crowell Co., 1953.

Encyclopaedia Britannica. Vol. XVII. Article, "Patents." 1946.

GARDNER, ROBERT C. *American Arms and Arms Makers*. Columbus, O.: College Book Co., 1944.

GLUCKMAN, ARCADI AND SATTERLEE, L. D. *American Gun Makers*. Harrisburg, Pa.: The Stackpole Co., 1953.

GRANT, U. S. *Personal Memoirs of U. S. Grant*. New York: Chas. L. Webster & Co., 1885.

MOATS, FRED A. "The Smith & Wesson Revolvers, No's. 1, 2 & 3." *The Gun Report*, Vol. 1 (Dec. 1939).

PARSONS, JOHN E. *Smith & Wesson, Revolvers*. New York: William Morrow & Co., 1957.

RILING, RAY *Guns and Shooting*. New York: Greenberg, 1952.

SERVEN, JAMES E. *Colt Percussion Pistols*. Dallas, Tex.: Carl Metzger, 1947.

SMITH, SAM E. "The American London Pistol Company," *The Gun Collectors Letter*, (Dec. 25, 1946).

. . . . "Evolution of the Plant Revolver," *The American Arms Collector*, Vol. 1, (April, 1957).

WINANT, LEWIS *Pepperbox Firearms*. New York: Greenberg, 1952.

INDEX